Refrigeration for Pleasureboats

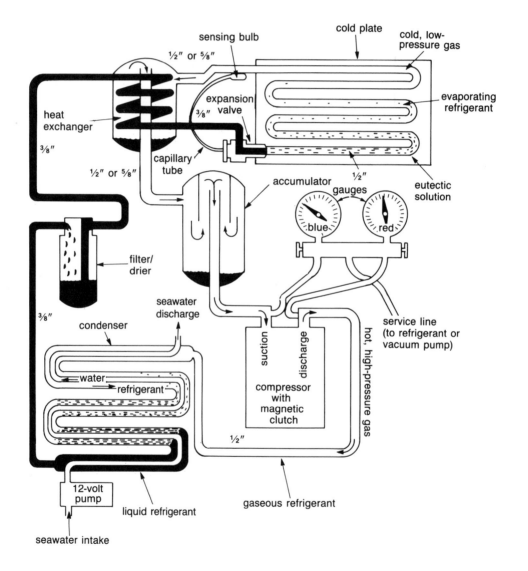

An engine-driven cold plate refrigeration system (shown with gauge set attached).

Refrigeration for Pleasureboats

Installation, Maintenance, and Repair

Nigel Calder

International Marine
Camden, Maine

Other Books by Nigel Calder
Repairs at Sea
Marine Diesel Engines, Second Edition
The Cruising Guide to the Northwest Caribbean
Boatowner's Mechanical and Electrical Manual

Questions regarding the content of this book should be addressed to:

International Marine
P.O. Box 220
Camden, ME 04843

Typeset by TAB BOOKS, Blue Ridge Summit, PA
Printed by Fairfield Graphics, Fairfield, PA

Library of Congress Cataloging-in-Publication Data

Calder, Nigel.
    Refrigeration for pleasureboats : installation, maintenance, and
repair / Nigel Calder.
        p. cm.
    Includes bibliographical references and index.
    ISBN 0-87742-286-9
    1. Marine refrigeration. 2. Yachts and yachting—Furniture.
equipment, etc. 3. Boats and boating—Equipment and supplies.
4. Cold storage on shipboard. I. Title.
VM485.C35 1991
623.8'535—dc20   90-45029
                                                                           CIP

Published by International Marine

10 9 8 7 6 5 4 3 2

Contents

Preface

I wrote the first edition of this book to enable an amateur to design and build a refrigeration system that could be run from a boat's engine with the minimum possible amount of engine running time. In that edition, the refrigeration unit, particularly the compressor, was driven hard and to the limits of what is practical.

Since the first edition, my ideas have broadened and I have matured somewhat. The current edition offers advice and help to anyone refrigerating a pleasureboat and enables just about any kind of a system to be worked out and put together. It is far more detailed and extensive than the first edition, and yet more clearly thought out and presented. I have greatly expanded the chapter on troubleshooting, added a completely new chapter on overhauling compressors, and doubled the number of illustrations.

When I was almost finished, someone asked if the principles outlined could be adapted to wilderness cabins without a power company hookup, using as power source a standby generator, a wind generator, solar panels, DC batteries, or a lawnmower engine in place of a boat engine. The answer is a resounding, "Yes!" Just substitute *wilderness cabin* for *boat* throughout the book.

Sections of this text and some of the illustrations have appeared in two of my other books—*Marine Diesel Engines* and *Boatowner's Mechanical and Electrical Manual*. I am grateful to International Marine for permission to use this material.

I would also like to thank the following for assistance:

Michael Adler and Eric Risch of Adler Barbour; Bob Williams of Grunert; George Harrison of the Dole Refrigeration Company; V.V. Solomon of ALCO Controls, and the ALCO Controls Division of the Emerson Electric Company for permission to quote from their Catalog #23; Roger Sherburn of Sanden; Bob Brown of the Tecumseh Products Company; Robert Kocher of the University of Maryland Sea Grant College; Jed Weldon and Paul Landry.

The following companies have also provided information and illustrations: Climate Controls, Inc.; Danfoss; Four Seasons; ITT/Jabsco; Standard Refrigeration Company; Ample Power Company; The Battery Council International; Rolls and Rae; and Surrette. Dennis Caprio performed an incredibly detailed edit on the entire text. Molly Mulhern and the production crew at International Marine never once complained (at least in my hearing) about all the formulas and tables (which are a typesetter's nightmare). The book has benefited greatly from their input. Any mistakes remaining are solely mine.

I have gone to considerable trouble to ensure the accuracy of the information contained in this book, and every care has been taken in putting it together. The information is thus given in good faith, but nevertheless, because of the current legal climate in this country, and because I have no control over the use of this information, I must disclaim any responsibility as regards its accuracy or the consequences of using it.

Nigel Calder
Hammond, Louisiana
August 1990

Introduction

You want a refrigerator or freezer for your house? Essentially the only decisions to be made are what size, and can you afford it. If only boat refrigeration were this simple! Unfortunately, it is not.

Once the shore-power cord to a boat is unplugged, energy sources are strictly limited and frequently intermittent. What is more, unlike houses, which are connected to a public utility company, no two boats have exactly the same power resources. *Refrigeration systems must be custom-tailored to individual boats and to specific patterns of boat use.*

Whereas there are hundreds of millions of household refrigeration units in use, the number of boat refrigeration units can be measured in tens of thousands. Production costs are higher, and installations are far more complex. These two factors together make boat refrigeration phenomenally expensive. It is not uncommon for a modest refrigerator/freezer system, professionally built and installed, to cost more than $4,000.

In spite of these high costs, many boat refrigeration units still fail to perform satisfactorily, or have unexpected and unwanted side effects, such as regularly killing the boat's batteries. This arises from a failure to properly match a unit to a boat's energy resources and usage. The cost of failure can be high—in fact, the cost of installing a refrigeration unit that is not matched to a boat is equal to the cost of installing a properly matched unit.

This book, therefore, has three objectives:

1. To enable boat owners to select an appropriate refrigeration unit for their boat and for a specific type of boat usage (e.g., offshore cruising);
2. To impart an adequate understanding of practical refrigeration so that those who already have refrigeration can come to terms with it and troubleshoot it;
3. To provide the adventurous with all the information necessary for an amateur to design and build a boat refrigeration unit without recourse to any other books or outside help. In many cases, a home-built unit will cost considerably less than half the cost of a commercial unit, and may well out perform it.

The primary focus of this book is the needs of cruising sailors because anyone who intends to sail offshore with refrigeration should have a good understanding of the system. What is more, the refrigeration demands of cruising sailors tend to be the hardest to satisfy. They want the highest capacity possible with the least possible energy consumption! In trying to come to terms with these extreme demands, it is necessary to cover all the information required to understand the less demanding refrigeration needs of weekend and coastal sailors.

When dealing with refrigeration, some theory just cannot be avoided. It is probably a reflection of my

Puritan, Anglo-Saxon background that when I have something unpleasant to face, I like to get it over with. Accordingly, I start the book with refrigeration theory, and I would advise at least reading through it before you advance into the rest of the book. Do not be discouraged if at first it makes little sense.

Thereafter the book is structured around the construction and refrigeration of a 6-cubic-foot icebox, which is an average size for most boats of 35 to 40 feet in length. This is the easiest way to introduce all the concepts you will need to understand boat refrigeration. The latter part of the book deals with system analysis, adjustment, and troubleshooting, drawing on all the previous material.

There is nothing quite like sitting under an awning, anchored off a palm-fringed beach, sipping an ice-cold drink as you watch the tropical sun sink over the horizon in a blaze of glory. Just about any boat can have effective refrigeration, allowing its crew to enjoy such pleasures. What is more, given a little maintenance, there is no reason why a refrigeration unit should not give years of trouble-free service. It is my fond hope that this book will help to make such dreams come true for many boat owners.

Ozone Alert and Update, 1993

Extensive atmospheric tests conducted over the Arctic during the winter of 1991–92 by the National Aeronautics and Space Administration produced some alarming results. In late January 1992, the space agency announced that an ozone "hole" similar to one that has formed over the Antarctic was not only probable but imminent. Given a certain set of atmospheric conditions, ozone loss over the Arctic could occur at a rate of one to two percent a day, with the "hole" extending as far south as 50°N latitude. While those conditions did not occur and the hole did not materialize, the situation is no longer a question of "if" but of "when." It will take up to 100 years for CFCs in the atmosphere—the primary culprits in the ozone layer's destruction—to dissipate. Even if all production were to cease today, the damage would continue to increase for the next two decades.

In the wake of the NASA announcement, the U.S. has greatly accelerated the phase-out of CFCs. By the end of 1995, and perhaps sooner, CFCs will no longer be manufactured in the industrialized world. This includes R-12 (Freon-12), the refrigerant now used in all marine refrigeration systems, and the one on which this entire book is based. R-12 will not only be difficult if not impossible to obtain, but it will also be illegal to use it without specialized recovery equipment that prevents leaks into the atmosphere. There will be heavy fines for those releasing CFCs, and rewards for informers who turn in offenders. Those of us with refrigeration systems using R-12 must limit the damage done by keeping leaks to a minimum, and by seeing that the refrigerant in our systems is disposed of properly when the units are finally taken out of service.

An ozone-safe replacement for R-12 is just now coming onto the market. Its generic name is 134a; DuPont calls its product SUVA 134a, while the other major producer, ICA, calls its KLEA 134a. The new refrigerant is expensive and hard to find, but in the next year or two it will become cheaper and more plentiful as R-12 is phased out. However, 134a will never be available to the general public in the way that R-12 was. Given the terrible unforeseen damage caused by CFCs, governments are going to regulate the use of the new refrigerants to licensed personnel with proper recovery equipment.

These developments are causing a tremendous upheaval in the marine refrigeration world. And that begs the immediate question: How do these changes affect this book?

1. The book is obviously applicable in its entirety to all existing and currently produced R-12 refrigeration systems. I must however, reiterate the critical importance, on both moral and legal grounds, of not releasing R-12 into the atmosphere.

2. Inasmuch as a 134a system will have all the same basic components and operating characteristics as an R-12 system, the book still provides a perfectly adequate basis on which to size an icebox, select a system, and understand how that system functions.

3. Troubleshooting a 134a system, and compressor overhauls, are likewise virtually unchanged, with the exception of some relatively minor differences in likely operating pressures (see the accompanying table).

4. The difficulties arise if trying to design and build a system using 134a. Certain subtle modifications are essential. 134a has similar operating characteristics to R-12 (see the accompanying table and contrast this to the table on page 7), but it is not a "drop-in" replacement. *Whenever one of my tables assumes R-12 use (it will say so in the small print at the bottom of the table) it will be necessary to rework the numbers using the formulas and procedures outlined in the body of the text, but substituting the figures for 134a given in the accompanying table.* Aside from this the system remains the same. There are then a number of practical problems that must be addressed:

❑The only belt-driven compressor currently warranted for 134a marine use in the U.S. is the York from Climate Controls. Other automotive compressor manufacturers soon will be geared up for the new refrigerant, but given the likely lower suction pressures in the system I would not use a rotary or swash-plate compressor.

❑No hermetic compressor is now available in the U.S. for 134a use, but Danfoss is well on the way with both AC and DC models. In the meantime, for AC or DC refrigeration, an AC or DC motor can be used to drive a York compressor, gearing the compressor up or down to suit the size of the motor (e.g. ¼ horsepower or ½ horsepower).

❑The mineral oil used in R-12 systems is not compatible with 134a. The automotive industry will in the future be using PAG oils, but these are highly hygroscopic and not suited to the marine environment. A new class of oil—polyolester ("ester" for short)—is recommened on water-cooled units.(At the higher operating temperatures found in these units it is possible for copper to be dissolved from tubing and deposited on the compressor valves—a condition known as copper plating.)

❑134a has a smaller molecular structure than R-12 and will leak through current refrigeration hoses. If a compressor cannot be rigidly plumbed in, nylon-lined hoses or special flexible bronze pipe will be needed.

❑A 134a compatible dryer and expansion valve will be needed.

I believe current legislation has put the amateur out of the refrigeration business. But, ironically, more than ever the boatowner needs to understand marine refrigeration, including such obscure technicalities as cold-plate tubing sizes and coil lengths, and the differences between PAG and ester oils. With the radical changes about to take place, if such an understanding is lacking, it will be impossible to ensure that even a professionally manufactured and installed system is properly built, sized, and matched to the boat and to the owner's lifestyle.

Nigel Calder
January 1993

PROPERTIES OF 134A

1 Temp. (F)	2 Pressure (psig)	3 Vapor Volume (cu. ft./lb)	4 Heat Content Btus/lb. liquid	5 Heat Content Btus/lb. vapor	1 Temp. (F)	2 Pressure (psig)	3 Vapor Volume (cu. ft./lb)	4 Heat Content Btus/lb. liquid	5 Heat Content Btus/lb. vapor
-30	9.8*	2.54	2.87	98.06	120	171.9	0.14	52.08	118.06
-20	3.8*	1.98	5.81	99.57	130	199.8	0.12	55.83	118.91
-10	1.8	1.56	8.82	101.07	140	230.5	0.11	59.68	119.62
0	6.3	1.24	11.87	102.56	150	264.4	0.09	63.65	120.17
10	11.6	1.00	14.97	104.04	160	301.5	0.08	67.76	120.53
20	18.0	0.81	18.11	105.51	170	342.0	0.07	72.05	120.62
30	25.6	0.67	21.29	106.96	180	385.9	0.06	76.57	120.36
40	34.5	0.55	24.51	108.38	*inches of mercury below zero				
50	44.9	0.46	27.77	109.77					
60	56.9	0.38	31.08	111.13					
70	70.7	0.32	34.43	112.44					
80	86.4	0.27	37.83	113.70					
90	104.2	0.23	41.29	114.91					
100	124.3	0.20	44.82	116.04					
110	146.8	0.17	48.41	117.10					

Chapter 1

The Refrigeration Cycle: How It Works

Refrigeration is all about removing heat. All solids, liquids, and gases (bodies for short) contain heat to a greater or lesser degree.

British Thermal Units

In order to remove all heat from a body, you would have to cool it to minus 460° Fahrenheit ($-460°F$), a temperature known as absolute zero. This is a purely theoretical calculation, and it has never been achieved in practice. The higher the temperature of a body above $-460°F$, the more heat it contains. This quantity of heat is measurable. The unit of measurement is not, as many people think, degrees Fahrenheit or Celsius (Centigrade), but something called a British thermal unit (Btu for short).

One Btu is defined as the quantity of heat required to raise one pound of water by one degree Fahrenheit. Raising one pound of water from its freezing point (32°F) to its boiling point (212°F) requires 180 Btus ($212 - 32 = 180$).

(Note: The International Standard Unit for the measurement of heat is now a *Joule*. One Joule is defined as the quantity of heat required to raise one kilogram of water by one degree Kelvin. Since most people in the United States are not familiar with Joules, kilograms, or degrees Kelvin, I shall stick with Btus.)

Specific Heat

Different substances absorb different amounts of heat in undergoing a change in temperature. One pound of iron, for example, only absorbs 0.13 Btu per 1°F rise in temperature. This is known as its *specific heat*. Water, by definition, has a specific heat of 1.00 (since a Btu is defined in relation to water). Ice has a specific heat of 0.5; i.e., it absorbs 0.5 Btu per pound per 1°F temperature rise. One pound of ice cooled to 0°F will only absorb 16 Btus in coming up to its melting point of 32°F.

Sensible Heat

The Btu is used to measure *quantities* of heat. The thermometer, on the other hand, measures the *intensity* of the heat of a body, otherwise known as its sensible heat. Forty degrees F feels cold, 200°F feels scorching hot. We should note that the temperature of a body tells us very little about how much heat (how many Btus) it contains. Two examples should help to make this clear:

1. A pint of water and a gallon of water at the same temperature feel the same, but the gallon contains eight times more heat energy than the pint.
2. A pound of water at the same temperature as a pound of iron feels the same, but the pound of water contains many times the heat energy of the pound of iron.

Heat Transfer

Heat always seeks an equilibrium. If two objects of dissimilar temperatures are placed together, heat flows from one to the other until the temperature difference is eliminated. But note that what equalizes is the temperature (sensible heat), not the heat content of the two bodies. One may still contain many more Btus than the other because it either has a greater mass or a higher specific heat.

Basic Heat Calculations

In refrigeration work, you frequently must know the amount of heat being added to, or taken from, a body undergoing a change in temperature. To calculate this, take the specific heat of the body (SH) and multiply it by the weight of the body in pounds (W). This gives the Btus gained or lost by this body for every 1°F change in its temperature. Next multiply the Btus gained or lost by the actual change in temperature that the body undergoes. The result is the total number of Btus gained or lost. The formula looks like this:

$$\text{Btus (gained or lost)} = \text{SH} \times \text{W}(t_1 - t_2)$$

where:

SH is the specific heat
W is the weight of the body in pounds
$(t_1 - t_2)$ is the temperature change in °F

Two examples:

1. Thirty pounds of water heated from 65°F to 170°F will absorb $1.00 \times 30(170 - 65)$ which equals 3,150 Btus.
2. Thirty pounds of iron cooled from 170°F to 65°F will give up $0.13 \times 30(170 - 65)$ which equals 409.50 Btus.

Latent Heat

Latent heat is the heat absorbed or liberated during a change of state at a constant temperature and pressure. The concept of latent heat is at the very heart of the refrigeration cycle. Water can commonly take three forms: solid (ice), liquid (water), and vapor or gas (steam). At normal pressures (atmospheric pressure) water changes state from solid to liquid at 32°F, and from liquid to vapor at 212°F. The simple addition or removal of heat is all that is required to bring about these changes of state.

A change of state is the result of a change in the molecular structure of a substance, and this change takes a considerable amount of energy. In order to freeze a pound of water you must remove 144 Btus; to melt the ice you must add 144 Btus. In order to vaporize (evaporate, boil) a pound of water, you must add 970 Btus and you have to remove that amount of heat to condense the vapor back into liquid.

The significant point in refrigeration theory is that *this energy is absorbed or given up in the process of changing states and does not in any way raise or lower the temperature (sensible heat) of the substance.*

This is one of the hardest ideas to grasp in refrigeration. Take the example of water once again. Suppose that instead of starting with water at 32°F, we start with one pound of ice at 32°F. Rather than heating it to its boiling point at 212°F, we continue to add heat until it has all boiled away. That pound of water is still going through the same temperature change (180°F) but it also is going through two changes of state (ice to water and water to steam). The first change of state absorbs 144 Btus, the second 970 Btus. Although raising one pound of water from 32°F to 212°F takes only 180 Btus, turning one pound of ice at 32°F into steam takes 144 + 180 + 970, or 1,294 Btus, even though the temperature change is exactly the same. This example gives some idea of the tremendous amount of energy locked up in changes of state.

The absence of a temperature change during changes of state is why this form of energy is called *latent heat*—it is not apparent to the sensible touch and cannot be measured with a thermometer.

The term *latent heat of fusion or melting* is used to describe the energy liberated or absorbed when a

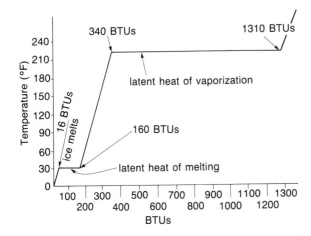

Figure 1-1. *Latent heat graph for water. Graph shows the amount of heat required to turn one pound of ice at 0°F into steam at 212°F.*

Pressure Measurement

The observant reader will have noticed that I slipped the notion of *constant pressure* into my definition of latent heat. This is the next subject that must be tackled.

Pressure is commonly measured in pounds per square inch absolute (psia) and pounds per square inch gauge (psig). Any measurement in pounds per square inch gauge (psig) is 14.7 pounds lower than the same measurement in pounds per square inch absolute (psia). In other words psig = psia − 14.7. Let's see how we arrive at that number.

Atmospheric Pressure. The earth is surrounded by an envelope of gases. Although we have no sensation of weight, these gases do have weight. Imagine stacking a pile of books one on top of another. The top two or three might weigh only a pound or so, but far-

ther down the stack the accumulated weight from that point up is greater. In other words, the lower down the stack, the more the downward pressure of the books increases.

In the atmosphere, the outer layers bordering on space weigh almost nothing and exert very little downward pressure. The closer one moves to the surface of the earth, the greater the accumulated mass of the atmosphere above, and the greater the downward pressure exerted. At sea level, the weight of the atmosphere exerts a pressure of 14.7 pounds per square inch on the surface of the earth. This pressure decreases by approximately 1/2 psi for every 1,000 feet above sea level.

Gauge and Absolute Pressure. Because atmospheric pressure is the norm—the *ambient* pressure—for most purposes, pressure gauges are calibrated to read zero at atmospheric pressure. The gauge will then register any deviation from this ambient pressure. This is known as pressure per square inch *gauge* (psig—commonly abbreviated to psi). On the other hand, a gauge that is calibrated to measure the real, or actual, pressure will have to register 14.7 pounds per square inch at atmospheric pressure. Such a gauge measures pressure per square inch *absolute* (psia).

Vacuum. Now let us imagine that we take our two gauges on a trip into space. As we rise ever higher into the earth's atmosphere, the pressure steadily decreases. When we finally enter deep space, the gauge calibrated in pounds per square inch absolute reads zero—a perfect vacuum. What about the other gauge? It has been calibrated to read zero when the pressure is actually 14.7 pounds per square inch. As we reach true zero, this gauge will have to read −14.7 psi. Refrigeration work, however, uses another scale to indicate readings below atmospheric pressure. This is *inches of mercury* (abbreviated Hg). A perfect vacuum (−14.7 psi) corresponds to minus 29.2 inches of mercury (−29.2″ Hg), and this is what the gauge will read in deep space. In other words, 30″ Hg is roughly equivalent to 15 psi; therefore a pressure that is one pound below atmospheric pressure will show −2″ Hg; 5 pounds below atmospheric pressure −10″ Hg, and so on.

Refrigeration work almost exclusively uses gauges indicating psig. Since parts of a refrigeration

---

liquid changes state into a solid, or vice versa. The term *latent heat of evaporation or condensation* is used to describe the energy absorbed or liberated when a liquid changes state into a vapor (or gas), or vice versa. The graph in Figure 1-1 illustrates these concepts with respect to water. Just as different substances have different specific heats, so too they have different latent heats of fusion and evaporation.

system commonly fall below atmospheric pressure, we will have to get used to dealing with inches of mercury of vacuum.

Evaporation/Condensation Curves

Changes in pressure alter the boiling point of liquids and, conversely, the condensation point of gases. This is easily demonstrated. Many people know that food takes longer to cook at high altitudes (e.g., when camping in mountains). This is because the higher we go, the lower the atmospheric pressure. The lower the pressure, the lower the boiling point of water and, as a consequence, the lower the temperature in our pot. At this lower temperature the food takes longer to cook. A pressure cooker operates in the opposite way. The pot is sealed; then, as the water boils, the steam given off raises the pressure in the pot. Raising pressure has the effect of raising the boiling point of water. This in turn creates higher than normal temperatures in the pressure cooker and that cooks food more quickly.

This relationship between evaporation (boiling) temperatures and pressure has important applications in refrigeration. Figure 1-2 illustrates the relationship between pressure and the boiling point of water.

Just as all liquids boil (evaporate) at some temperature and pressure, so too all gases (vapors) liquefy

(condense) at some temperature and pressure. A graph similar to Figure 1-2 showing the evaporation/condensation temperature at different pressures can be drawn for all liquids and gases (vapors).

Pressure and Temperature

When dealing with a gas or vapor, a change in pressure not only has a direct impact on its condensation temperature, but also bears a direct relationship to the temperature of the gas or vapor itself. If a gas or vapor is compressed into a smaller space, its temperature rises. This rise in temperature is caused, not by the addition of any heat, but by squeezing the heat already in the gas or vapor into a smaller space.

Imagine a closed cylinder with a complete vacuum. We fill it with a gas at a certain temperature. This gas contains a certain number of Btus of heat energy per pound. We now drive a piston up one end of the cylinder, compressing the gas. When we do this, the temperature will rise and the cylinder will rapidly become hotter than the surrounding atmosphere. It will give off heat. The pressurized gas will cool steadily. If this cooling process brings the gas below its condensation temperature at the current pressure in the cylinder, some of the gas will condense (liquefy). The difference in volume between a gas and the liquid into which it condenses is quite dramatic: 1,646 cubic feet of steam at atmospheric pressure condenses into just one cubic foot of water. So, as some of the gas in the cylinder liquefies, the pressure in the cylinder rapidly falls. Eventually the temperature of the gas equalizes with the ambient temperature outside the cylinder, and enough of the gas will have liquefied to reduce the pressure in the cylinder to the evaporation/condensation pressure corresponding to this temperature for this gas.

An example: If we have a cylinder of pressurized steam in an ambient temperature of 272°F, steam will condense into water until the pressure drops to 30 psi. At this point the temperature and pressure will be in equilibrium as shown by Figure 1-2. Now let us assume that the temperature falls to 212°F. More steam will condense into water until the pressure drops to atmospheric pressure, when stability will be restored. Finally the ambient temperature declines to 142°F. Yet more steam condenses, dragging the pressure in the cylinder into a vacuum of −24" Hg.

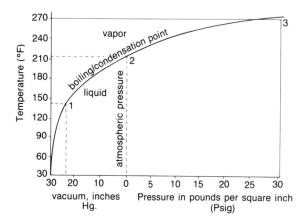

Figure 1-2. *The relationship between pressure and the boiling point of water. At 1 (24" Hg vacuum), water boils at 142°F. At 2 (atmospheric pressure), water boils at 212°F. At 3 (30 psig), water boils at 272°F.*

We now have some liquid and some gas in our cylinder. If we drive up our piston some more, the temperature and pressure will rise once again, but as the cylinder cools down to the ambient temperature, more of the gas will liquefy until the pressure has fallen to the same evaporation/condensation pressure corresponding to this ambient temperature. All that has happened is that now more liquefied gas is in the cylinder, but the temperature and pressure are the same. Further compression and cooling of the gas will merely increase the volume of liquid in the cylinder until it is finally filled with liquid. Only at this point will the pressure begin to rise rapidly until the cylinder bursts, since fluids are incompressible.

If a gas is held at a fixed temperature, until the point of total liquefaction is reached, the additional compression of the gas will not increase the pressure in the cylinder above that corresponding to the condensation point of this gas at this temperature. It will merely increase the volume of liquid.

This relationship between pressure and temperature, liquid and gas, only applies to a gas *in a closed system*. It enables us to hook a pressure gauge into certain points of a refrigeration system and then read the temperature of the system at that point (assuming we know which gas the unit uses and what its evaporation/condensation curve is).

The Refrigeration Cycle

We have finally assembled all the concepts needed to understand the refrigeration cycle. Figure 1-3 illustrates schematically a typical refrigeration system. Here is how it works:

1. A gas (normally, in boat refrigeration, a substance known as R-12) is compressed. This raises both the temperature of the gas and its condensation temperature. (See Figure 1-2.)
2. The hot compressed gas now passes through a

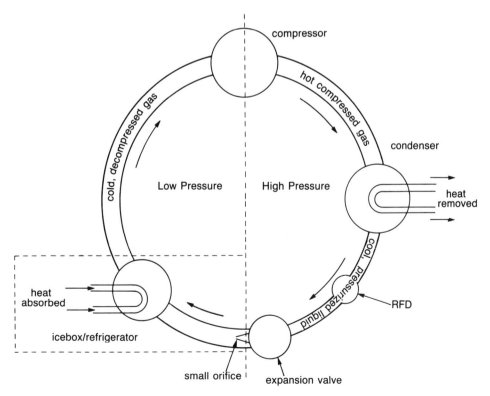

Figure 1-3. *The refrigeration cycle.*

cooler (condenser), which pulls its temperature below its condensation point at its present pressure.

3. The gas liquefies, and in the process gives up considerable quantities of latent heat of condensation. The condenser absorbs this heat and dissipates it to the surrounding environment. *This is the first key step.* In a refrigeration system, liquefaction does not lead to a loss of pressure, as it did in our example, because the constantly running compressor maintains pressure in the system.

4. The pressurized liquid now passes through an *expansion valve* (explained in more detail later), which allows it to decompress sharply. Decompressing the liquid drops its evaporation point to below its existing temperature and causes it to boil off into a gas again. For example, we can maintain water at a temperature as high as 272°F without its boiling into steam as long as we keep the pressure on the system at 30 psi or more. (See Figure 1-2.) If we suddenly drop the pressure in a cylinder of water at 272°F from 30 psi to atmospheric pressure, the boiling point will fall to 212°F. The water will now be 272 − 212, or 60°F, above its boiling point at this new pressure and will boil (vaporize) violently. (This is why you should never remove a car's radiator cap when the engine is hot—the release of pressure is likely to cause the radiator to boil violently, spewing out steam and boiling water, which can cause serious burns.)

5. As the liquid boils off (evaporates), it absorbs large amounts of latent heat of evaporation from its surrounding environment, causing the temperature to drop sharply. This is how a refrigerator or freezer is cooled. *This is the second key step.*

6. The decompressed gas passes back to the compressor, is recompressed, and the cycle starts again.

This refrigeration cycle is analogous to bailing a dinghy with a sponge. (I found this in *Modern Refrigeration and Air Conditioning* by Althouse, Turnquist, and Bracciano—an excellent textbook for anyone who wants to get heavily into this subject). The sponge is squeezed (compressed), wringing the water out of it

just as heat is wrung out of refrigerant vapor by compressing it and passing it through a condenser. The sponge is then allowed to expand in the dinghy, absorbing water in the same way that liquid refrigerant is expanded back into a vapor in an evaporator, absorbing heat. The sponge (refrigerant) is then removed from the dinghy (evaporator) and wrung out again (recompressed and condensed).

The keys to grasp are the changes of state of the refrigeration gas—first to a liquid in the condenser, giving off latent heat to the environment, and then back to a gas in the evaporator, absorbing latent heat from the refrigerator. Latent heat is what it is all about—without it refrigeration would be completely ineffective.

Refrigeration gases are specially formulated to undergo the necessary changes of state at temperatures and pressures readily obtainable during the refrigeration cycle.

Refrigeration Gases

In the systems dealt with in this book, the refrigeration gas employed is called R-12—dichlorodifluoromethane. It is also commonly referred to as Freon 12, which is the trade name of the Du Pont company for this gas. Other companies make the same gas under different names (e.g., Isotron 12). Other common refrigeration gases are R-22 and R-502.

At atmospheric pressure, R-12 condenses into a liquid only if its temperature falls to −21.6°F. At higher pressures it condenses at higher temperatures: At 11.8 psi it condenses at 5°F; at 93.3 psi it condenses at 86°F; at 169 psi it condenses at 125°F, and at 234.6 psi it condenses at 150°F.

In an adequately charged system (explained later), any compressor capable of raising the pressure of R-12 gas to 169 psi is going to bring its temperature to at least 125°F. This is well above the ambient temperature in most locations, which will cause the gas to lose heat to the environment and cool off. As it cools, it will fall below its condensation point (125°F) at this pressure (169 psi), and it will liquefy.

In a refrigeration system, the condenser's function is to cool the compressed gas and carry off its latent heat of condensation so that this liquefaction can occur.

Let us say the condenser has pulled down the temperature of the (now liquefied) R-12 to 100°F, while the compressor has maintained the pressure on the system at 169 psi. The liquid R-12 is now 25°F below

its condensation temperature at this pressure. This is known as *sub-cooling* of the liquid. Now let us drop the pressure in the system to 11.8 psi (this is done by the expansion valve). At 11.8 psi, liquid R-12 evaporates at 5°F. The liquid is now 95°F (100 − 5) above its evaporation temperature at this new pressure. In an attempt to restore equilibrium, the liquid will evaporate back into a gas very rapidly, but to do so it must absorb large amounts of latent heat of evaporation from its environment—in this case, the interior of a refrigeration unit.

We can see right away why R-12 is such an excellent refrigeration medium. It liquefies at relatively low temperatures and pressures—90 psi to 235 psi will enable condensation to take place at ambient temperatures from 85°F to 150°F. It then readily re-evaporates with easily attained changes in pressure. In other words, there is a minimum difference between the pressures that must be attained to achieve condensation and those required for evaporation.

Table 1-1 gives the evaporation/condensation pressure for R-12 at a variety of temperatures (columns 1 and 2). Columns 3 to 5 provide further information about the gas, which will be referred to later on. If the temperatures and pressures in columns 1 and 2 are put into graphical form we arrive at the curve shown in Figure 1-4.

Table 1-1. *Properties of R-12*

1	2	3	4	5
		Vapor	Heat content	
		volume	(Btus/lb)	
Temperature	Pressure	volume		
(°F)	(psig)	(cu.ft./lb.)	liquid	vapor
−50	15.4 *	4.97	−2.1	71.8
−40	11.0 *	3.88	0	72.9
−35	8.4 *	3.44	1.1	73.5
−30	5.5 *	3.06	2.1	74.0
−25	2.3 *	2.73	3.2	74.5
−20	0.6 *	2.44	4.2	75.1
−15	2.5	2.19	5.3	75.7
−10	4.5	1.97	6.4	76.2
−5	6.7	1.78	7.4	76.7
0	9.2	1.60	8.5	77.3
5	11.8	1.46	9.6	77.8
10	14.6	1.32	10.7	78.4
15	17.7	1.21	11.8	78.9
20	21.0	1.10	12.9	79.4
25	24.6	1.00	14.0	79.9
30	28.5	0.92	15.1	80.4
35	32.6	0.84	16.2	80.9
40	37.0	0.77	17.3	81.4
50	46.7	0.66	19.5	82.4
75	77.0	0.44	25.2	84.8
85	91.8	0.38	27.5	85.7
86	93.3	0.38	27.7	85.8
90	99.8	0.36	28.7	86.2
95	108.3	0.33	29.9	86.6
100	117.2	0.31	31.1	87.0
105	126.6	0.29	32.3	87.4
110	136.4	0.27	33.5	87.8
115	146.8	0.25	34.8	88.2
120	157.7	0.23	36.0	88.6
125	169.1	0.22	37.3	89.0
130	181.0	0.20	38.6	89.3
135	193.5	0.19	39.9	89.7
150	234.6	0.16	43.9	90.5
175	315.9	0.11	51.0	91.3
200	415.4	0.08	59.2	91.5

*=inches Hg below atmospheric pressure

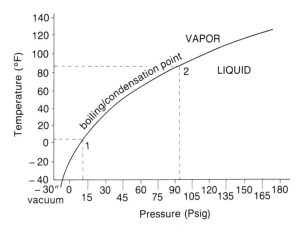

Figure 1-4. *Temperature/pressure curve for R-12 refrigerant. Example: For R-12, the vaporization/ condensation point at 5°F is 11.79 psig (1); at 86°F, it is 93.34 psig (2).*

Besides being easily condensed and then readily re-evaporated, R-12's other advantages include:

1. It is nonexplosive, inflammable, and nontoxic.
2. It is noncorrosive to metal, which means it will not eat out the insides of a refrigeration unit.
3. It mixes well with oil, which is important for lubricating the moving parts of a system.

Nevertheless, R-12 does have certain drawbacks compared to some other refrigerants. First and foremost, R-12 vented into the atmosphere significantly contributes to the destruction of the earth's ozone layer.

Within the refrigeration process, the only point at which the refrigerant absorbs heat from a refrigerator or freezer is during its evaporation. Therefore the refrigerant should have the highest possible latent heat of evaporation so that it absorbs the maximum possible number of Btus per pound from the refrigerator or freezer as it evaporates.

The latent heat of a refrigerant at any temperature and pressure is calculated by subtracting the heat content of the liquid at this temperature and pressure (which is shown in column 4 of Table 1-1) from the heat content of the vapor at the same temperature and pressure (column 5 of Table 1-1). This should be easy to understand if you think back to the definition of latent heat. For example, at 5°F and 11.79 psi, liquid R-12 contains 9.60 Btus per pound. If it vaporizes, it now contains 77.80 Btus per pound at the same temperature and pressure. Therefore the latent heat absorbed in a change of state at this temperature and pressure is 68.20 (77.80 − 9.60) Btus per pound.

Some of the heat absorbed by the evaporating refrigerant is wasted in cooling the incoming liquid refrigerant (which, in our previous example, was at 100°F). Because of this the liquid should have the lowest possible specific heat so that the minimum amount of heat is absorbed in cooling it. If the liquid R-12 enters an evaporator at 100°F, it will contain 31.10 Btus per pound (column 4 in Table 1-1). At 5°F the liquid contains 9.60 Btus per pound; therefore, in cooling to 5°F the liquid has to give up 31.10 − 9.60 = 21.50 Btus per pound. This heat must be absorbed by the evaporating R-12. In other words, the cooling effect in the evaporator is reduced by this amount. The *net refrigerating effect* of R-12 in this specific situation becomes the latent heat absorbed minus the heat given up by the incoming liquid—i.e., 46.70 (68.20 − 21.50) Btus per pound.

This net refrigerating effect can be calculated another, quicker way. If the liquid R-12 enters the evaporator at 100°F with 31.10 Btus of heat energy per pound, and if the gaseous R-12 leaves the evaporator at 5°F with 77.80 Btus per pound, the R-12 now contains 46.70 (77.80 − 31.10) Btus per pound more than when it entered the evaporator. This is its net refrigerating effect.

The two temperatures of 100°F for the liquid R-12 and 5°F for the gaseous refrigerant would be quite common in a boat refrigerator operating in the tropics. However, for purposes of comparing one refrigerant to another, the industry standards are 86°F for the liquid refrigerant and 5°F for the vapor. Table 1-2 therefore uses these two temperatures to compare certain leading refrigerants.

Ammonia has many more times the net refrigerating effect of the other refrigerants (Table 1-2, column 6), but it is highly toxic and corrosive. It is such a

Table 1-2. *Comparative Table of Common Refrigerants*

1	2	3	4	5	6	7	8
Refrigerant	Btus/lb liquid at 86°F	Btus/lb liquid at 5°F	Btus/lb vapor at 5°F	Latent heat at 5°F	Net refrig. effect, 86°F liquid, 5°F vapor	Boiling point at atmospheric pressure	Condensation pressure at 86°F (psig)
Ammonia (R-717)	138.9	48.3	613.3	565.0	474.4	−28 °F	154.5
R-12	27.77	9.60	77.80	68.2	50.1	−21.6°F	93.34
R-22	34.93	11.75	104.96	93.2	70.03	−41.4°F	158.17
R-502	35.06	11.89	80.75	68.86	45.69	−50.1°F	175.10

powerful refrigerant that in small refrigeration systems it becomes difficult to regulate. Ammonia finds its chief application in large-scale industrial units.

R-22 is an excellent refrigerant for small systems and is considerably more efficient than R-12 (column 6). It is especially useful in low-temperature applications as it has a lower evaporating temperature (column 7). However, it requires considerably higher operating pressures (column 8) and for this reason is not normally used in small units.

R-502 is specially formulated for low-temperature applications (column 7) but once again requires high operating pressures (column 8). It is the low operating pressures that make R-12 so attractive, and pre-eminent, in small boat refrigeration.

Chapter 2

Iceboxes: The Key to Determining What Size Refrigeration Unit You Need

A well-insulated and sealed icebox is central to the success of any refrigeration system. The rate of and amount of heat entering the icebox determines the size and power requirements of the rest of the system. Before you can determine what kind of a refrigeration unit to place in a boat or what size (capacity) unit to use, you must discover the heat loss of the icebox in its anticipated use.

The majority of iceboxes installed in even expensive boats are poorly constructed and inadequately insulated. Almost always far more energy is used in combatting heat losses through the icebox insulation (or lack of it) than is ever used in cooling the contents in the icebox. This chapter outlines the basic principles of icebox construction and insulation, and then explains how to determine the heat leak of any box. In showing how to build an icebox from scratch, I indicate the key factors to consider when assessing the efficiency of an existing box. This should suggest ways to improve inadequate boxes.

Principles of Construction

Heat moves from one body or area to another in three ways:

1. By conduction. For example, the base of a frying pan is heated and the metal of the pan's bottom conducts heat to the handle.
2. By convection. For example, a fan blows air over a heater element and the air picks up the heat and carries it to another area.
3. By direct radiation. For example, the surface of a hot radiator gives off heat directly to the surrounding area. Dark surfaces absorb more heat than do light, shiny surfaces, which tend to reflect heat away from themselves.

The objective in insulating an icebox is to slow to the minimum practical rate the movement of heat from the ambient atmosphere to the interior of the icebox (practicality being largely determined by cost and space considerations). Insulating material should have extremely low conductivity, should prevent the movement of heat by convection, and should radiate very little heat.

Air is a poor conductor of heat. It is plentiful and cheap, which is the reason most insulating materials create a dead air space around the object to be insulated. Common insulating materials of this kind are household fiberglass insulation, cork, and a whole host of foams and foam products. Because of the rela-

10

tively high conductivity of water (15 to 25 times that of air), many of these insulating materials also incorporate a moisture barrier to keep water vapor out of the insulation (e.g., the paper backing on rolls of fiberglass insulation). This moisture barrier is especially important in refrigeration insulation as the low temperatures involved cause condensation and moisture penetration of the insulation, especially in hot, humid environments.

Within dead-air type insulators, distinguishing between those with an open-cell construction, and those with a closed-cell construction is important. Open-cell foams have continuous communication from one part of the insulation to another. A sponge is an example of open-cell construction and if you compress it, place it under water, and release it, the sponge will draw water into every air space. Fiberglass insulation and cork are open-cell.

Every air pocket of closed-cell insulation is completely sealed from the next. When you compress such a material, the air in each pocket is compressed and then re-expands when you release the pressure. No air passes in or out unless the pressure is increased to the point at which the air pockets rupture. Closed-cell foam has two significant advantages over open-cell: (1) It prevents moisture from entering the insulating material, and (2) the individual cells reduce to an absolute minimum the heat movement via convection currents.

Expanded polystyrene (EPS) is a special case. (Note: EPS is often referred to as Styrofoam, which is a trademark of Dow Chemical. Real Styrofoam is a blue insulating foam that is often used in houses.) Its individual pellets are closed-cell, but the method of bonding them together is not. The bonding method allows water vapor to penetrate the structure of the foam. Although it has almost the same thermal efficiency as many other closed-cell foams when it is dry, condensation invariably permeates its structure and reduces its efficiency to around half that of other closed-cell foams. For this reason, although it is frequently used in icebox construction, it should not be part of any well-designed box.

All of the commonly available insulating materials have low heat-radiation properties. These are frequently enhanced by bonding a reflective surface, such as aluminum foil, to the outside of the insulation to reflect direct heat away from the material.

To summarize, effective icebox insulation requires the following:

1. A moisture barrier;
2. A reflective surface to reduce radiated heat;
3. A closed-cell insulating material to maintain a dead-air space, eliminate convection currents, and prevent moisture saturation.

The most commonly available closed-cell icebox foam is urethane foam—*rigid freon expanded polyurethane foam* is its full title. Urethane foam is available in pre-formed sheets of 2 feet by 4 feet and 4 feet by 8 feet and in thicknesses of $1/2$ inch and up. It is also available as a two-part liquid, which is mixed and poured into place (more on this later). *Urethane foam is the only kind of foam that should be used in icebox construction—from this point on its use is assumed.*

How Much Foam?

How much insulation should you wrap around an icebox? The answer is 4 to 6 inches. Now let's see how we arrived at this answer.

The rate of heat loss through the foam is related to the temperature differential between the inside of the icebox and the ambient temperature in the boat, and to the thickness of the insulation. For an equal thickness of insulation, an average freezer with an internal temperature of 20°F to 30°F lower than that of a refrigerator, leaks almost two times more than a refrigerator. Doubling the insulation brings the heat leak more or less in line with that of a refrigerator.

A law of diminishing returns determines the insulation thickness. Let us assume a thickness of 3 inches and a heat leak of 1 Btu per square inch of surface area per 24 hours (not uncommon in a freezer). Doubling the insulation to 6 inches reduces the heat leak to 0.5 Btu per square inch. A further doubling to 12 inches cuts this in half once again—i.e., reduces the heat leak to 0.25 Btu per square inch. Although the first doubling of the insulation decreased the heat leak by 0.5 Btu per square inch, the second only reduced the heat leak by 0.25 Btu per square inch, and a third doubling would only decrease the heat leak 0.125 Btu per square inch. At some point the trade-off of lost icebox volume against reduced heat leakage becomes unacceptable—probably in the region of 4 inches to 6 inches of insulation on a refrigerator and 6 inches on a freezer.

No matter how much insulation an icebox has, any kind of movement of air from the inside to the outside of the box causes the insulation to be ineffective. Although invisible to the naked eye, air masses of different temperatures flow relative to one another, just like rivers. Cold air is denser, and therefore heavier, than warm air, and it seeks to flow below any warm air that it encounters. You can see this when you open a front-opening household freezer door. The cold air, indicated by a light mist, rolls out the bottom of the freezer and along the floor. What you cannot see is the warm air that moves into the top of the freezer to replace it. As often as not, soon after you remove something from a front-opening freezer, it kicks on because the freezer must cool the warm air that invaded it. This kind of a major heat loss by convection is quite unacceptable on most cruising boats.

Another area of heat leak that is frequently overlooked is the drain. All iceboxes need a drain. It should be large enough to prevent it from being too easily plugged up—at least 3/4 inch. If you lead this drain directly downward into a sump or the bilges, cold air will flow down it just like water running out of a hose. To avoid this heat leak either place a valve on the drain or form a U-trap in it. The trap will hold water and prevent the movement of air, just like the U-trap in a drain on a household sink.

An icebox should drain into its own special sump and not into the bilges. Otherwise, on a wooden boat, the fresh water will cause rot in adjacent woodwork; on all boats, bacteria in the water will cause unpleasant odors, while food particles, bits of wrapping paper, and so on may clog bilge pumps.

Given the increased density of cold air over warm air, a top-opening refrigerator or freezer experiences far less heat loss when the door is opened than a front-opening one. The cold air forms a static mass down in the icebox, while the warm ambient air hovers above the opening. Very little mixing of the two air masses occurs. The contents of a top-opening box are less accessible, but this is the only type of box to have in an energy-conscious environment. What is more, a top-opening box will never spill its contents all over the cabin sole—something a front-opening box is liable to do on one tack or another. *From this point on, a top-opening box is assumed.*

Whether the icebox opens from the top or the front, its lid or door must have an effective seal against air movement around its edges when closed. Several approaches to this are indicated in the section on construction details.

However before you construct your icebox, consider its location in the boat. If at all possible put the box in an area out of direct sunlight and away from heat sources—i.e., not close by, or under, a hatch and not up against the engine room bulkhead. Whatever surface you use to finish off the outside of the icebox cabinet, it should be light-colored and reflective to reduce radiated heat to a minimum.

Icebox Construction

It is easiest to consider the construction process from the outside in. Once the exterior cabinet is built, construct the box with the top off. First glue a layer of PVC—the moisture barrier—to the inside of the exterior casing. Seal all seams with tape to make them waterproof. Next, tape in a layer of aluminum foil, reflective side facing out, to reflect back infra-red heat that penetrates the cabinet. Building supply houses generally carry combined reflective and vapor barriers for use in house construction.

If you plan to use sheet urethane foam for insulation, it goes in next. You can build up the thickness with several layers of thin foam glued together, or you can use one thick sheet. Thin sheets do have advantages: They are easier to work with, conform better to curved surfaces, and all the joints can be staggered (step-lapped), which reduces the chances of air leaks and convection currents around the joints (see Figure 2-1). The foam can be stuck together with contact cement, epoxy, or polyester resins—or any number of caulking compounds (silicon, polysulphide, polyurethane, or small spray cans of urethane foam injected into the seams). The caulking compounds reduce the possibility of leaks, especially on corners and where the top is bedded to the sides.

If you use poured, two-part foam for insulation, you will have to suspend the liner in place, and then pour the foam around it. This approach is especially useful if the cavity to be filled contains compound curves or awkward shapes, as is often the case in boats. Approach poured foam with caution because

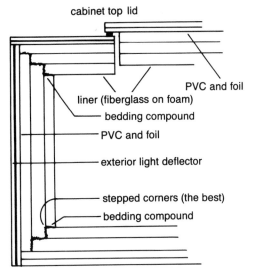

cabinet top lid

PVC and foil

liner (fiberglass on foam)

bedding compound

PVC and foil

exterior light deflector

stepped corners (the best)

bedding compound

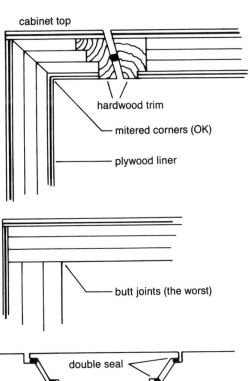

cabinet top

hardwood trim

mitered corners (OK)

plywood liner

butt joints (the worst)

double seal

Figure 2-1. *Details of icebox construction. Note that the icebox lids are illustrated with single seals, but double seals are much better. Mitered corners are hard to make accurately and tend to open with expansion and contraction.*

you must mix two liquids and then pour the mixture into the cavity *immediately*. Within seconds a mass of tiny bubbles forms and starts to grow, and grow, and grow. Although the foam expands outward and upward, it frequently fails to move into awkward or recessed corners, which leaves air spaces in the insulation chamber. It also exerts considerable pressure on large surfaces—a characteristic that often causes icebox liners and cabinets to buckle where excess pressure built up. If the unlucky builder uses too much of the mixture, it creeps over the top of the icebox cabinet like some gooey blob from a 1950s horror movie and sticks to everything in sight. And boy, does it stick! Add to this the noxious fumes given off, and you would be well advised to use sheet foam if at all possible.

If you must use two-part foam, do a little at a time, giving rigorous attention to the manufacturer's instructions. I use the following procedure:

- First I tape plastic all around the top of the icebox cabinet, across the top of the icebox liner, and over the surrounding areas. This will catch drips, spills, and any foam that comes over the top of the box.
- Next I establish a work area and sheet this off with plastic. I buy a large packet of 12-ounce (this is a good size), waxed (not plastic) drinking cups. I set up the two cans of mixture, one on each side of my work area, with a cup in front of each and the rest of the cups in the middle together with a large number of paint stirrers, and a stock of surgical gloves. Off to one side, I have a full-sized plastic garbage bag. I ensure good ventilation and put on a pair of gloves and a respirator-type face mask. It is time to go!
- Now I fill the cup in front of each can about one-third full of mixture and then simultaneously empty the two cups into a cup in the center. I set the two measuring cups back in front of their respective cans. It is vital not to cross them over in the heat of the moment, which is why I keep the two cans widely separated. I stir the mixture vigorously for 30 to 40 seconds, wipe the paint stirrer off across the top of the cup, pour the mixture into the icebox cavity, then lodge the cup somewhere so that it can continue to drain while I start over with a fresh

one. By the time I have poured in the second cup, the first batch of foam is well on the way to being fully risen and the first cup will be fully drained and ready to be thrown into the trash can.

These small batches of foam prevent the process from getting out of control. No undue pressure builds up at any point, and I can see and fill any cavities that start to develop. *If any foam spills or comes out the top, I do not attempt to clean it up until it is fully cured.* To do so would just make a revolting mess, whereas once the foam has cured, you usually can peel it off most surfaces reasonably cleanly.

Icebox liners are most commonly made of stainless steel, fiberglass, plywood, Formica, or a combination of these. They can be assembled in place, or made in the workshop and dropped into place. Stainless steel liners look very professional but have drawbacks. The steel has higher radiation and conduction characteristics than any of the other materials; you cannot easily fasten a cold plate securely (see Chapter 4) to a thin sheet metal liner, and a stainless steel liner is very hard to repair if it gets damaged.

Fiberglass can be laid up directly over closed-cell foam already in the cavity (whereas its resin dissolves EPS), or a liner can be formed over a male mold in the shop. In the former case, a lot of work will be required to obtain a good finish on the liner; in the latter, a lot of wasted effort will go into making the one-off mold. Either way a one-off box in fiberglass involves a surprising amount of work—far more than most amateurs realize—and is rarely worthwhile.

By far the simplest and easiest liner to make is one built of 1/2-inch marine plywood and epoxy glue. Mark out the individual panels on the sheet of plywood and then totally saturate the sheet with epoxy. For additional surface strength, coat the plywood with a layer of fiberglass cloth wetted out with more epoxy. This protects the interior of the finished box against dents and chips. Completely fill the weave of the cloth with epoxy and then sand it to a smooth finish with wet-or-dry sandpaper (80 to 100 grit, used wet—a palm sander works great). Only now cut out the individual panels.

You can assemble the box in the shop or glue the individual panels into an already foamed cavity. The corners need only be butted together since they are now filled out and faired off to make a smooth curve with a fillet of thickened epoxy. This fillet, together with the supporting foam, will provide all the necessary strength. Finally, spraying the box with Awlgrip or Imron will give a very classy, high-gloss finish. Be sure to observe all safety warnings on the paint can (these are highly toxic paints when sprayed) and to use a color with *no lead content* (some whites contain lead).

Whatever form of liner you construct, bear in mind that if the refrigeration system uses cold plates (see Chapter 4), they will eventually be installed in the box. Cold plates weigh up to 60 pounds each and are fastened directly to the liner. The box must be strong enough to support this kind of weight in the most turbulent sea conditions.

Icebox tops do not require the same thickness of insulation as the sides and bottom—2 inches is adequate on refrigerators, 3 inches on freezers. After you have cut the top to fit the cabinet, cut out the icebox lid, or hatch. Lids hinge-open or lift off, and are fitted flush or proud (see Figure 2-2). Note that all hinged lids must be beveled on the side opposite the hinges to allow the insulation on the underside to clear the opening as the lid is raised. Note also that all lids require some form of foam weather stripping, gasketing, or O-ring all the way around to completely seal the lid when it is closed. A double seal, especially on freezers, is much better than a single seal, but it is difficult to construct accurately.

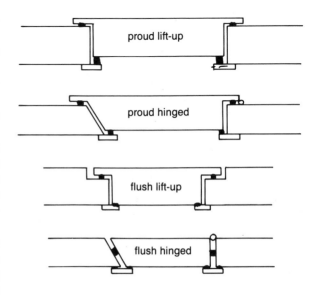

Figure 2-2. *Four types of icebox lids.*

The underside of the cabinet top and icebox lid must be sealed with a moisture barrier and reflective layer of foil, as was done on the cabinet itself. The foam insulation can then be glued onto these surfaces, and finally finished off with a lining of fiberglass, plywood, or whatever you desire. Where the insulation in the lid contacts the foam in the sides, you need to create a tight foam-to-foam joint. The lid is best set in place on a layer of bedding compound to ensure this. Figures 2-3 to 2-16 illustrate the construction of an icebox.

Figure 2-3. *Icebox construction requires the following raw materials: marine plywood, epoxy resin and hardener, acetone for cleaning brushes, a Mason jar to prevent the acetone from evaporating, a roller to apply the epoxy, and fiberglass cloth.*

Figure 2-5. *A finished box (top off) after painting. Note the large drain.*

Figure 2-4. *An odd-shaped freezer box for a sailboat. The inside surfaces were sheathed in fiberglass cloth and sanded before assembly, which is much easier than after assembly. All that remains to do is fair the corners with epoxy paste and paint.*

Figure 2-6. *Close-fitting lids with good seals are hard to make. Here is one method: Start by gluing together the surround, the interior surfaces of which have been covered with fiberglass cloth and sanded. The surround tapers out on all four sides. The tapered blocking pieces are held in place with thickened epoxy, and they stop the sides from falling over while the glue in the corners sets.*

Figure 2-7. *Next glue up the lid inside the surround. This ensures a very close fit. The plastic prevents the lid and the surround from sticking to each other, and the cardboard spacers provide minimal clearance between the lid and the surround.*

Figure 2-8. *The lid has been popped loose from the surround and has been inverted.*

Figure 2-9. *Now add the rim to the surround, using the blocking pieces to support it. (This is from another icebox, hence the different shape.)*

Figure 2-10. *Glue the surround and rim to the icebox top. Cut the opening in the top $^1/_2$ to $^3/_4$ inch less on all sides to provide the ledges (indicated by the arrows). The base of the lid has been routered where it will rest on this ledge. The depth of the cut is just a little bit less than the thickness of the foam that will be used to seal the lid.*

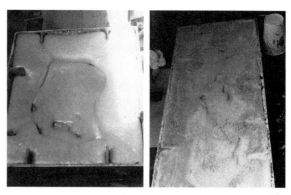

Figures 2-11 and 2-12. *Fill the lid with foam and sand it smooth and even with the sides. Tapered blocking pieces set in place with thickened epoxy provide rigidity and hold the close tolerances.*

Figure 2-13. *The lid and icebox top have been sprayed with Awlgrip (Imron will do as well) and the foam weather stripping has been added as a seal. The lid is upside down to show the seal.*

Figure 2-14. *The cold plate has been installed and the top glued on. Because the plate cannot be removed without taking off the whole top (this is not a good idea!), all of the connections have been soldered to guard against leaks. The lid is in the foreground propped against the box.*

Figure 2-15 (above). *The box and the cold plate have been suspended in the icebox cabinet, all of the tubing connections are completed, and the first batches of foam poured in. This box is unusual because the plate has gone in first and the refrigerant tubes will be foamed into place—they had better not leak! (This, too, is not a good idea!)*

Figure 2-16 (left). *The foam in the cavity will eventually come flush with the top of the upper rim and be smoothed off. The cabinet top will fit onto the outer edge of this rim (below), while the lid will rest on its inner edge, providing a second sealing surface.*

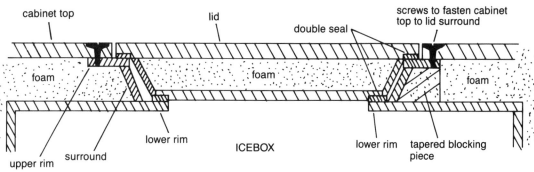

Sizing an Icebox

Sizing in this context does not refer to the volume of the box—that must be chosen by the individual owner. Instead it refers to a determination of the heat losses from any particular box, and therefore of the refrigeration requirements of this box. Remember, we are assuming a well-constructed box (no air leaks), with the use of closed-cell foam and a top-opening lid.

The graph in Figure 2-17 gives an approximate idea of the heat losses from a top-opening box in normal use, relative to its size and thickness of insulation. To determine the heat loss of an icebox, you first must calculate its outside area (i.e., the external cabinet dimensions). Enter the graph on the bottom line at the appropriate thickness of insulation. Move vertically to the appropriate curve (for refrigerator or freezer use), then horizontally to find the heat loss per square foot per 24 hours. Multiply this figure by the square footage to get the total heat loss per day.

When you make these calculations, draw up a worksheet and measure separately each panel of the icebox and the thickness of the insulation on that panel. To calculate the outside area for a combined refrigerator/freezer unit, you must figure the refrigerator and freezer sections individually, using the appropriate curve on the graph. For odd-shaped panels with curved sides, add together the measurements on either side and divide by two to arrive at a close

approximation (see Figure 2-18). Odd-shaped panels with straight sides can be divided up geometrically, as in Figure 2-19.

A typical box of around 6 cubic feet interior volume (see Figure 2-20) requires the removal of 2,508 Btus of heat daily to maintain the interior at a temperature of around 40°F (see Figure 2-21). Figure 2-22 shows the daily heat leak from the same box in freezer use. All figures are the same as those used in the

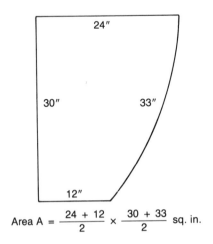

$$\text{Area A} = \frac{24 + 12}{2} \times \frac{30 + 33}{2} \text{ sq. in.}$$

Figure 2-18. *To determine the approximate outside area of odd-shaped panels, add together the measurements on either side and divide by 2.*

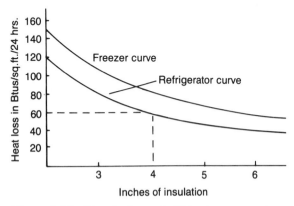

Figure 2-17. *Heat leak graph. This gives approximations of heat losses from a top-opening icebox in normal use, relative to its size and the thickness of its insulation. For example, an icebox in refrigerator use with four inches of insulation will lose 60 Btus of heat per square foot every 24 hours.*

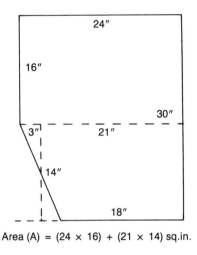

Area (A) = (24 × 16) + (21 × 14) sq.in.

Figure 2-19. *Odd-shaped panels with straight sides can be divided up geometrically.*

previous diagram with the exception of the rate of heat leak per square foot, which is now taken from the freezer curve in Figure 2-17. Note how much larger the heat losses are from a freezer (3,630 Btus). Adler Barbour, a major manufacturer of boat refrigeration units, uses the numbers in Table 2-1 for heat losses from iceboxes insulated with urethane foam. These

figures show the total heat losses as 2,290 Btus per day for a refrigerator and 4,104 Btus per day for a freezer.

While the refrigerator figure corresponds closely to that obtained using the graph, the freezer figure is considerably higher. This reflects different assumptions as to what is normal use. If you have any doubt about the quality of the insulation in an icebox or if you plan to operate your boat in high ambient temperatures, you would be wise to make the calculations on the basis of the more conservative set of figures. Grunert, another major company in this field, provided the heat loss tables given in Table 2-2. The discrepancies between all of these tables indicate that estimating heat losses is a bit of a guessing game. Throughout the rest of this book, I assume a heat loss of 2,400 Btus per day from the sample 6-cubic-foot icebox when in refrigerator use and a heat loss of 4,000 Btus per day when in freezer use.

Although these tables overstate the heat loss from the top of a box, they understate heat loss from the bottom to offset this. In colder ambient temperatures, the heat losses will be less. The tables give a pretty fair average of heat loss based on an average use. They assume that the box is being opened and closed infrequently, and that the contents are already cold. If you constantly stock up with warm beer and regularly dip

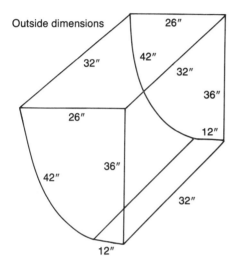

Figure 2-20. *The dimensions for the sample 6-cubic-foot icebox.*

1	2	3	4	5	6	7
Panel	Insulation	Height × Width	Area (sq.in.)	Area (sq.ft.)	Heat Leak (sq.ft.)	Heat Leak 24-Hours (5×6)
Bottom	4"	32 × 12	384			
Outboard face	4"	32 × 42	1,344			
Inboard face	4"	32 × 36	1,152	30	60	1,800
Forward end	4" }	$\frac{12+26}{2} \times \frac{42+36}{2}$	741			
Aft end	4" }		741			
Top	2"	32 × 26	832	6	118	708
						2,508

Figure 2-21. *Worksheet for the sample icebox in refrigerator use. Note that column 6 is taken from Figure 2-17; column 7 is column 5 multiplied by column 6.*

1	2	3	4	5	6	7
Panel	Insulation	Height × Width	Area (sq.in.)	Area (sq.ft.)	Heat Leak (sq.ft.)	Heat Leak 24-Hours (5×6)
Bottom	4"	32 × 12	384			
Outboard face	4"	32 × 42	1,344			
Inboard face	4"	32 × 36	1,152	30	85	2,550
Forward end	4"	$\frac{12+26}{2} \times \frac{42+36}{2}$	741			
Aft end	4"		741			
Top	2"	32 × 26	832	6	180	$\frac{1,080}{3,630}$

Figure 2-22. *The same worksheet, this time for the sample icebox in freezer use.*

into the icebox for a refill, this will drastically alter the calculations. The fresh supplies give off heat as they cool and every time you open the lid, warm air finds its way into the box. For example, a six-pack of 12-ounce cans of beer contains 72 ounces of liquid, plus the metal in the cans. This is $4^1/2$ pounds of liquid, primarily water with a specific heat of 1.00. If the warm beer is at 70°F, and the refrigerator cools it to 38°F, the temperature differential is 70 − 38 = 32°F. We have 4.5 pounds of liquid with a specific heat of 1.00 giving off 32 × 4.5 × 1.00 = 144 Btus of heat energy (the equivalent of one pound of melting ice). All this heat must be absorbed by the refrigerator. Any kind of a riotous party will soon overwhelm the capability of most refrigeration systems. This is sometimes referred to as the WB (warm beer) factor! Table 2-3 gives the specific heat of a number of commonly refrigerated foodstuffs.

If you plan to use your icebox in unusually warm or cold climates, you should dispense with these average-use tables and work the heat loss calculations from scratch. Once again you must establish the outside area of the box and the thickness of insulation. You also need to know the temperature differential between the inside of the box and the ambient temperature. If part of the box is constructed against the side of the hull below waterline, the seawater's temperature becomes the ambient temperature in this area. If the box butts against an engine-room bulkhead, the

engine-room temperature becomes the ambient temperature. Using Table 2-4, calculate the heat loss per square foot. These figures make no allowance for heat infiltration through voids in the insulation, air leaks, icebox use, and so on. Compared to this table, the Adler Barbour figures for a freezer's heat loss indicate a temperature differential of 110 − 120°F. Now clearly they are not working on this basis, but probably something less than an 80°F differential. Adler Barbour's assumptions for other heat losses, assumptions learned after long experience in the field, account for the differences in the figures. It is vitally important to work these heat losses into your calculations.

If you already have an icebox in your boat and wish to determine its rate of heat leak but are unsure of the insulation thickness or quality, you can get a rough idea for a box in refrigerator use by placing a 10- or 20-pound block of ice in the box and seeing how long it takes to melt. Ten pounds of melting ice will absorb 1,440 Btus; 20 pounds will absorb 2,880 Btus. Place the ice as high in the box as possible, otherwise this test will have no validity. To make the test realistic, you should pick a warm day, open the lid from time to time, put things in and take them out, and so on—i.e., simulate normal use. When all the ice is just about melted, divide its Btu content by the number of hours it took to melt, then multiply that figure by 24. This will give the 24-hour rate of heat leak from this box in refrigerator use. If the box is to be

Table 2-1. *Heat Leak Per Square Feet Per 24 Hours*

(Insulation thickness)	2″	2.5″	3″	3.5″	4″	6″
Refrigerator	108	86.4	72	61.92	54.72	36
Freezer	194.4	155.52	129.6	110.88	97.92	64.80

(Courtesy Adler Barbour)

Table 2-2. *Btu Heat Leaks in Refrigerators and Freezers*

Btu heat leak in 24 hours	Refrigerator Box volume in cubic feet				Freezer Box volume in cubic feet			
	6″	4″	3″	2″	6″	4″	3″	2″
5200				14	16	11	8	5
5000				13		10		
4800					14		7	
4600			20	12	12			4
4400			18	11		8	6	
4200			16	10	10			
4000							5	3
3800		20	14		8	6		
3600		18	12	8			4	
3400		16		7	6			
3200	20	14	10			4	3	2
3000	18	13	9	6				
2800		11	8	5	4	3		
2600	14	10	7	4	3		2	
2400	12	8	6					
2200	10	6	5	3	2	2		1
2000	8	5	4				1	
1800	6	4	3	2		1		
1600	4	3			1			
1400	3		2					
1200	2	2		1				
1000			1					

(Courtesy GRUNERT)

Table 2-3. *Specific Heat for Common Foodstuffs*

Substance	Water content	Specific heat
Fruits and vegetables	80-90%	0.8-0.9
Fish	70-80%	0.7-0.8
Beef	50%	0.6
Pork	20-60%	0.4-0.6
Poultry	60-70%	0.7
Butter	20%	0.3
Hard cheese	40%	0.5
Soft cheese	50%	0.6
Cottage cheese	80%	0.8
Milk	90%	0.9
Eggs	70%	0.8

Table 2-4. *Heat Transfer of Closed-Cell Foam—Btus Per Square Feet Per 24 Hours*

Insulation	1°F	10°F	20°F	30°F	40°F	50°F	60°F	70°F	80°F	90°F	100°F	110°F	120°F
						Temperature differential (inside to outside box)							
2"	1.66	16.6	33.2	49.8	66.4	83.0	99.6	116.2	133.0	149.4	166.0	182.6	199.2
3"	1.15	11.5	20.3	34.5	46.0	57.5	69.0	80.5	92.0	103.5	115.0	126.5	138.0
4"	0.89	8.9	17.8	26.7	35.6	44.5	53.4	62.3	71.2	80.1	89.0	97.9	106.8
5"	0.72	7.2	14.4	21.6	28.8	36.0	43.2	50.4	57.6	64.8	72.0	79.2	86.4
6"	0.60	6.0	12.0	18.0	24.0	30.0	36.0	42.0	48.0	54.0	60.0	66.0	72.0

used as a freezer, double the demonstrated rate of heat loss. If the box turns out to have an unacceptably high heat leak and there are no obvious ways to correct this, a book entitled *The Perfect Box—39 Ways to Improve Your Boat's Ice Box*, by the Spa Creek Instrument Company, details numerous ways to improve a box. Their address is in Appendix 3.

Chapter 3

Refrigeration Choices

Once we have determined the daily Btu requirements of an icebox, we must decide what type of refrigeration unit we are going to use to keep it cool. This decision is complex, and getting it right is critically important. On a recent cruise through the West Indies, the farther south we went, the more boats we saw running engines two, three, and even four hours a day to support refrigeration units—sometimes still with unsatisfactory results. Most had the wrong refrigeration units for their type of cruising.

This is a key point: There is no such thing as *the* correct refrigeration unit. Except for air conditioning, *a refrigeration unit is probably the greatest single power consumer on a boat. It must be carefully matched to available power resources, which in turn are frequently a function of boat use.* For example, a powerboat used primarily for running around has its engine operating most of the time it is in use, providing plenty of energy at all times. The same boat used for extended cruising will spend long hours at anchor with the motor shut down, and will depend on other power sources to run its systems. It will quite likely be best served by a radically different type of refrigeration unit. With these points in mind, let's look at some of the options.

Refrigerator/Freezer Combinations

You should think long and hard before installing a freezer in a cruising boat. The tendency is to think of all the advantages and to blithely pass over the disadvantages, some of which are:

1. A freezer requires considerably more space than a refrigerator for the same internal volume in order to accommodate the extra insulation.

2. Even the best-designed and insulated freezer requires approximately twice the energy of a refrigerator of the same volume.

3. If a freezer breaks down, it can result in major food losses quite rapidly, whereas the contents of a refrigerator generally can keep for several days. As a consequence, any decent-sized freezer needs a back-up system.

4. A freezer frequently ties you to your boat, especially if it is in some way powered by the boat's engine, as most are. Someone must stay on board to run the engine daily. A well-built refrigerator, on the other hand, will remain cool for days and allow all of the crew to go on extensive trips ashore.

Constant-Cycling AC Refrigeration Units

Constant-cycling AC units are small units that are left on all the time, just as a household refrigerator is. In fact, on many powerboats household refrigerators are used without modification. On sailboats the common

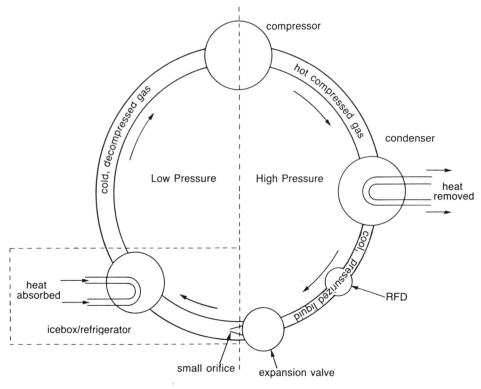

Figure 3-1. *The refrigeration cycle.*

practice is to have the evaporator supplied as a separate unit—a small freezer compartment with the evaporator tubing built into its sides. This is installed in an icebox and then hooked up to an independently mounted condensing unit, which contains the compressor and condenser.

A system of such small capacity needs to operate at frequent intervals—15 minutes per hour or more in hot weather. This means that it needs a continuous source of power, which is why it is called constant-cycling. On a boat, this power generally comes from a dockside hookup when the boat is in a slip, and from an on-board AC generator when the boat is at sea. A regular household refrigeration unit has a low initial cost and is easily installed, but from here on problems arise.

A household refrigeration unit uses an air-cooled condenser to dissipate all the heat absorbed from the cabinet, plus heat generated by the compressor, fans, etc. In the tropics, the condenser will work overtime

because air is a very poor conductor of heat to begin with and hot air is even worse. An air-cooled condenser needs a considerable air flow, but on a boat it often ends up in an engine room with next-to-no air movement and temperatures frequently hotter than 100°F. Even a main cabin is relatively confined and when a boat is closed up, temperatures can climb rapidly. Condenser efficiency declines at the same time that a high ambient temperature increases the heat loss from the icebox. All the variables are moving in the wrong direction. Soon the refrigerator will be operating 30 minutes, 45 minutes, or more every hour. It will use more and more energy, and perhaps even then not cool properly, and the compressor may burn up.

At the dockside, an AC hookup will meet this energy demand. At sea an AC generator running 24 hours a day keeps this constant power drain from being a problem. But when the risk of compressor burnout is considered along with the increased risk of

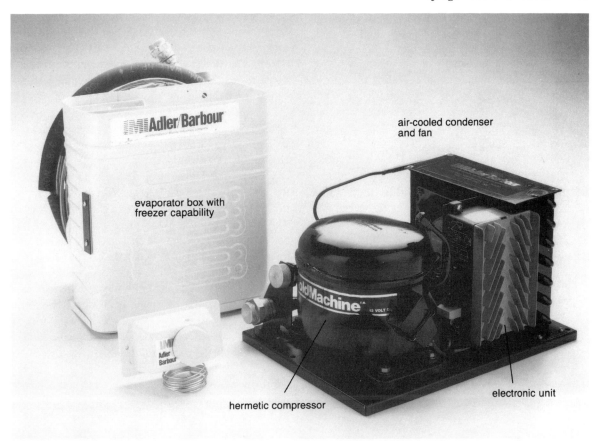

Figure 3-2. *A constant-cycling DC refrigeration unit. The unit on the left is an evaporator box with freezer capability.* ADLER BARBOUR

motor damage, which often arises as a result of AC voltage and frequency irregularities with dockside power and onboard generators, AC refrigeration does not look very attractive. In any case, very few boats have constantly available AC power, which necessitates choosing another refrigeration option.

Constant-Cycling DC Refrigeration Units

Constant-cycling DC refrigeration resembles constant-cycling AC refrigeration in all respects, with the exception of the compressor, which is run from the ship's DC system (see Figure 3-2). The unit runs from the ship's batteries while at sea and from a battery charger when in the slip and connected to shoreside power. Such systems suffer from all the potential inefficiency problems associated with air-cooled condensers. Even the smallest 12-volt units are likely to consume 50 amp-hours of energy a day in the tropics, and most considerably more than this. If boat use is infrequent, this may not be a problem, but to be able to do this day in and day out without problems requires a rather specialized DC electrical system.

Batteries. At the heart of any DC system is a battery. Most batteries are built for engine cranking, which requires a tremendous burst of energy but for just a second or two at most. As soon as the engine fires up, an engine-driven alternator cuts in and meets any further electrical needs, including the recharging of the battery. In a typical cranking application (e.g., an automobile), the battery is rarely discharged more than 5 percent.

Batteries are constructed with alternating negative and positive plates immersed in a solution of sulfuric acid known as the electrolyte. Between the plates are plate separators (see Figure 3-3). A chemical reaction between the acid and active material built into the plates produces energy.

When an engine is first cranked, the acid reacts with the active material on the surface of the plates. As this is used up, the acid must diffuse through the plates to reach less accessible active material, but that takes time. This is why, if you crank an engine until the battery dies and then let it rest for a while, the battery will frequently recover enough to produce another burst of energy. The acid has had time to reach the less accessible plate areas.

Cranking batteries are built with many thin plates to maximize the surface area of active material. The active material itself is of a low density to accelerate acid diffusion. Every time such a battery is deeply discharged, the internal stresses generated weaken the

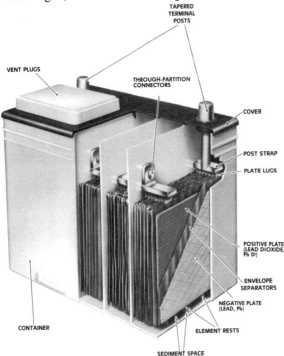

Figure 3-3. *Battery construction. Positive and negative plates have plate separators between them.*

bond between the active material and the plate grids. Such a battery, discharged and then bashed around in a seaway, will soon fall apart internally. This typically occurs after being discharged and recharged (cycled) no more than 30 to 40 times, which might be just four weeks use in a cruising situation.

The power drain of a constant-cycling DC refrigeration unit will, in most situations, cycle a battery on a daily basis. Special deep-cycle batteries are required for this kind of application.

Deep-cycle batteries. Deep-cycle batteries follow the same general principles of construction and operation as cranking batteries, but they are more robust. The plates are thicker, the plate grids stronger, the active material denser, the plate separators sturdier, and the whole thing is tied together more rigidly. Deep-cycle batteries will tolerate repeated discharges in a way that no cranking battery ever will. The best conventional deep-cycle batteries are made by Surrette and Rolls and Rae (see Appendix 4 for addresses).

All constant-cycling DC refrigeration units should be powered by deep-cycle batteries.

Deep-cycle batteries vary enormously in quality. Some are a little better and will not last much longer than cranking batteries. Others, if properly cared for, will last up to 20 years. You get what you pay for.

Battery capacity. What size battery? Even deep-cycle batteries do not like being repeatedly completely discharged. The greater the depth of discharge, the shorter the battery's life (see Figure 3-4). Your refrigeration system in normal use should not discharge the battery more than 50 to 70 percent of its total capacity.

When a battery is recharged, it can be fast charged to around 80 percent of its full charge, but thereafter the rate of charge must be cut back sharply to give the acid time to diffuse to the inner areas of the plates. Failure to cut back the rate of charge will damage the battery. When away from the dock, charging time is generally at a premium, so in cruising use, plan on bringing a battery back up to only 80 percent of its full charge. If a battery is discharged to 30 percent of capacity and then recharged to 80 percent of capacity, however, we are limited to using only half of its rated capacity. If we only discharge to the 50-percent level before recharging to 80 percent, we can only use 30 percent of its capacity.

Over its life span, a battery slowly ages and its output declines. When you calculate how much

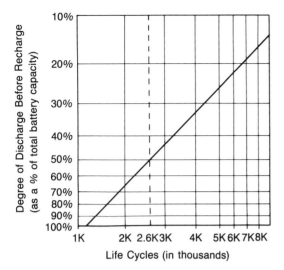

Figure 3-4. *Battery life cycles for a top-of-the-line deep-cycle battery under laboratory conditions.*

capacity your batteries should have, add a 20-percent fudge factor.

This leaves us using somewhere between 30 percent and 50 percent of total battery capacity. For a modest 50-amp daily demand, we need between 125 and 200 amp hours (Ahs) of capacity (and this is without figuring in any other loads). In general, battery capacity needs to be a minimum of 2.5 times anticipated demand between charges—4 times demand if at all possible.

Battery charging. At this point we must distinguish between weekend cruisers and long-term cruisers. Weekend cruisers can bring their batteries back up during the week using their battery charger and the dockside hookup at their slip. However, to gain the maximum life out of their expensive deep-cycle batteries, they ideally should use deep-cycle battery chargers (Balmar and Ample Power Co., see Appendix 4 for addresses). These are also expensive. If deep-cycle batteries and chargers are not already on their boat, the cost of these items must be factored into the total cost of refrigeration for the boat. Long-term cruisers break the dockside connection altogether. The boat's alternator generally becomes the primary means of battery charging. A deeply discharged deep-cycle battery can be recharged at a rate of up to 25 percent of its Ah rating. Let's say we have a well-discharged 400-Ah battery bank. It will readily

accept a rate of charge of 100 amps. To avoid overheating the alternator, you should not run it continuously above 75 percent of its full rating. Therefore, in this situation, we want at least a 130-amp alternator, and this is before figuring in any additional loads pulled off the alternator while the engine is running.

Inefficiencies in the charging process require the recharging to put back 20 percent more amps than were pulled out. If the refrigeration unit has taken out 50 amps, we must put back 60; if 100 amps, we must put back 120. Even with a high-output alternator to replace the energy pulled out by a constant-cycling DC refrigeration unit, we will be looking at a minimum recharging time of 40 minutes to one hour. Complications in the charging process, as explained in the next section, will probably add substantially to that time. Unless the boat has a good-sized wind generator or large array of solar panels, the necessary engine running time is almost always long enough to run a much more powerful engine-driven refrigeration unit. As often as not, the engine-driven unit would have been a better choice.

Voltage regulation. The standard voltage regulator senses the battery's voltage and tapers off output from the alternator as the battery comes up toward full charge. The battery's voltage, however, rises faster than its state of charge, which causes the voltage regulator to cut back the charge rate at around 60 percent of full charge—well before the safety of the battery demands that it be cut back. By the time a battery is 80-percent charged, alternator output is down to a trickle, and it takes hours to bring a battery up the last 20 percent. In practice, very few boat batteries that rely on an alternator for recharging are ever fully charged, and over time this leads to a process of internal damage known as *sulfation*, which is the number-one killer of boat batteries.

In most boating applications, once the craft is away from the dock, charging times are at a premium; therefore, you should accelerate charge rates to the maximum without damaging the battery, and should also periodically push the charge as high as possible to reduce to a minimum damage from sulfation. These two objectives cannot be met with a standard automotive voltage regulator. You need either a manual voltage regulator bypass (Spa Creek, see Appendix 4 for address) or a purpose-built marine voltage regulator (Ample Power Co.).

A Balanced DC System for Constant-Cycling Refrigeration. In reality, most boats are used infrequently—usually weekends only. In such circumstances, the loads of a constant-cycling DC refrigeration system can be handled satisfactorily by a deep-cycle battery, recharged during the week by a battery charger and a shoreside hook-up.

However, during longer trips afloat (a week's vacation, for example) weaknesses in the system will begin to become apparent. The refrigeration unit will run down the battery, and recharging with a typical alternator and voltage regulator will require hours of engine running time. If long-term offshore cruising is contemplated, in order to avoid excessive engine running time, the DC system is going to need a radical restructuring. All of a sudden, a small and apparently economical refrigeration unit can start to look very expensive. *The unit is going to require a substantial bank of deep-cycle batteries (around $2 per Ah of capacity), a high-output alternator to recharge the batteries ($300 to $400) with a voltage regulator bypass ($100) or a purpose-built marine voltage regulator ($200) or all of the above plus a large wind generator (around $1,000) or a substantial bank of solar panels ($300 on up).*

If your boat already has such a high-powered DC electrical system, as more and more do today, then a constant-cycling DC refrigeration unit may be the most economical option. If it does not already have such *a DC system, one that can support constant-cycling refrigeration, independent of a shoreside hookup, costs two to three times more than the refrigeration unit itself. Among long-term cruisers, the failure to match a DC system to a refrigeration system is a major cause of battery failures, unnecessary engine running time, and unsuccessful refrigeration.*

Water-Cooled Condensers

If, after considering all these factors, constant-cycling refrigeration (either AC or DC) is still an appropriate choice, the greatest possible improvement in its efficiency will come from installing a water-cooled condenser in series with the existing air-cooled condenser. Water has 15 or more times the heat-conducting capacity of air (saltwater a little less than fresh).

Even in the tropics, water temperatures rarely rise above 85°F—below ambient air temperatures in many boat cabins. The water will be cooler and many times more efficient than air as a cooling medium.

A water-cooled condenser generally has a pipe that contains the hot compressed refrigeration gas, plus a second, smaller pipe passing through it. Sea water pumped through this inside pipe carries off the heat of the gas and the latent heat of condensation as the gas liquefies. The heat goes overboard with the discharged cooling water instead of raising the ambient temperature in the boat.

Putting a water-cooled condenser in series with an air-cooled condenser allows both to be used at sea. While the boat is dockside, where there is no shortage of power, the air-cooled condenser can be used alone when you leave the boat unattended. This way you can shut down the water circuit and close its seacocks to provide maximum security against an accidental sinking of the boat through the failure of the cooling circuit.

Intermediate-Sized DC Refrigeration Units

Water-cooled condensers provide major energy savings over air-cooled condensers. When using DC refrigeration, installing a larger refrigeration unit will save even more energy. Smaller compressors are inefficient, and every time they kick on, they draw a substantial amount of power during the first minute or two while the unit cools.

A larger compressor consumes much more energy while it runs, but it runs for much less time. It produces the same overall refrigeration output on around two-thirds the total amperage draw of a smaller compressor (see Figure 3-5). The key to energy efficiency in this context is to concentrate all the compressor running time into one sustained operation a day, rather than to have the compressor constantly cycling on and off. The way this is done is by using *cold plates* (holding plates).

Cold Plates. A cold plate is nothing more than a tank with an evaporator coil inside it. The tank is filled with a solution, which has a freezing point below that of water. When the refrigeration unit is running, the solution is frozen. When the unit is shut down, the frozen solution slowly thaws, acting as a super-cooled block of ice in the icebox.

DC refrigeration units of up to $1/2$ h.p., using cold plates, can be run directly from a large enough bank of deep-cycle batteries (minimum 250 Ah). The same considerations of battery-charging capability and voltage regulation that apply to constant-cycling DC units apply to cold-plate units.

The principal advantage of such a system over a constant-cycling unit is the lower power drain for the same amount of refrigeration, or the ability to refrigerate larger spaces for an equal power drain. The principal disadvantage is the horrendous cost. A good quality $1/2$ h.p. unit complete with cold plates will generally cost around $3,000, without figuring in any of the cost of installation or of upgrading the DC electrical system to run it!

receiver

condenser

Figure 3-5. *A large compressor, such as this $1/2$ h.p. 12-volt DC water-cooled one, consumes more energy when it runs than does a small DC unit, but it runs for much less time. It produces the same overall refrigeration at about two-thirds the total amperage draw of a small compressor.* IMI CROSBY

It is possible to install such a system without upgrading the electrical system but only if a large enough battery charger is installed to handle the load at dockside, and only if you run the engine at sea while the refrigeration unit is on so that the engine-driven alternator supplies the necessary power without draining the batteries. Engine running time, however, will be longer than that required for an engine-driven refrigeration unit, and since the DC unit also costs more (while being less powerful) using one in this manner has no rationale. What is more, one of the principal advantages of a battery-driven refrigeration unit is immediately lost. This is the ability to leave the boat for a few days with the refrigeration unit left on, controlled by a thermostat. In fact, most $1/2$ h.p. DC refrigeration units are supplied with a switch that prevents the unit from being run *unless the engine is running. All forms of refrigeration that require the engine to be run tie you to your boat, especially if the system includes a freezer.*

If a boat does not have enough deep-cycle battery power to support the unit, you can find less expensive, more effective ways to refrigerate an icebox. If the boat does have the batteries to support the system, the engine switch should be thrown away or bypassed so that the refrigeration unit can be operated without running the engine.

Large-Capacity DC Refrigeration Units

Large-capacity DC holding plate refrigeration units of from $3/4$ to 1 h.p. are beyond the capability of just about any battery bank and must be powered via an engine-driven alternator. As noted earlier, for the same refrigeration output, the engine generally will have to run longer than in an engine-driven setup. Also the cost will be considerably higher than that of a direct-drive system. In addition, the engine (mechanical power) turns an alternator to produce electrical power, which is used to spin an electric motor, which turns the refrigeration compressor, getting us back to mechanical power. At every conversion step, the system experiences energy losses and has the potential for problems. This has always seemed to me to be an expensive way to look for trouble! The only significant advantage over an engine-driven system is that at dockside, the DC unit can be run from a large, heavy, and expensive battery charger, whereas an engine-driven system requires the engine to be run (unless an auxiliary unit is also fitted).

Engine-Driven Refrigeration Units

Engine-driven refrigeration is yet another variant of cold-plate refrigeration. A refrigeration compressor is directly driven by a belt from the boat's engine. Engine-driven refrigeration units are typically the most powerful of all those readily available for the pleasureboat market, ranging from $^3/_4$ h.p. up to $1^1/_2$ or 2 h.p. For most boats with substantial refrigeration needs, this is the only feasible way to go (see Figure 3-6).

Cost is generally high. For most cruisers who venture offshore for extended periods of time, however, engine-driven systems—especially home-built ones—can begin to look positively economical, taking into account all of the hidden factors in a DC unit. The major drawback is that the engine must still be run at dockside. To get around this, cold plates are frequently built with two sets of evaporator coils. The

second set is connected to a small independent constant-cycling DC unit, which is used at the dockside (via a battery charger) and serves as an emergency back-up at sea. In this case, all the considerations regarding batteries and DC electrical systems previously mentioned should apply, and costs are likely to skyrocket.

Large-Capacity AC Systems with Cold Plates

Boats with AC generators of 5 Kw on up, which are used only intermittently (as opposed to 24 hours a

Figure 3-6. Engine-driven refrigeration systems are the best for boats that have substantial refrigeration needs. IMI CROSBY/FRIGOBOAT

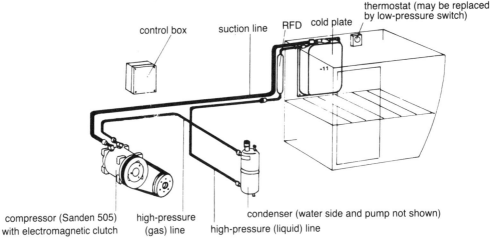

day), can have a high-capacity (1 h.p. on up) AC refrigeration unit coupled to cold plates. Such a unit can be cooled down rapidly while the generator is being run for other purposes (see Figure 3-7). Extremely powerful systems can be installed, limited mostly by the size of the generator. Initial cost is high (even leaving aside the generator), but AC refrigeration has one distinct advantage over engine-driven refrigeration: The unit can be run at dockside via a shore-power cord. Apart from the problems in ensuring a stable AC supply, which have already been referred to, there are certain dangers associated with this type of shoreside approach, which are explained in Chapter 5.

Other Refrigeration Possibilities

You can buy refrigerators that run on kerosene (paraffin) or propane gas, but neither is effective when a boat is pitching and heeling. They do not work too well in the tropics, even on a level keel, and propane can be dangerous in this situation. We ran a propane refrigerator very successfully for years on a houseboat

in England, but the climate was temperate and the boat was always stable.

Solid-state (thermo-electric) refrigeration is another alternative. It cools electronically, without the use of a compressor, condenser, evaporator, or refrigerant. The system has no moving parts, is silent, and requires little or no maintenance. A powerful list of plusses, but it is less efficient than conventional refrigeration, which is reason enough to be unsuitable in most boat applications. You are either limited to a

Figure 3-7. *A large (110-volt) AC system with a hermetic compressor and a water-cooled condenser.* IMI CROSBY/FRIGOBOAT

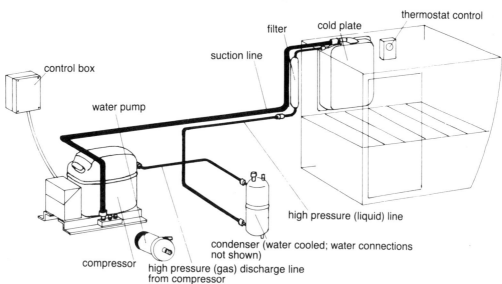

very small unit or stuck with the old problem of massive battery banks and how to charge them.

What Unit for My Boat?

The permutations and possibilities can get quite numerous and confusing, so I intend to draw some broad categories to simplify matters.

A boat with a 24-hour-a-day AC generator can use standard AC refrigerators and freezers. Efficiency will be greatly improved with a water-cooled condenser.

A boat with the light refrigeration needs of weekend cruising (up to 1,500 Btus a day) and with shoreside power in the slip can use a small DC unit, but will need adequate deep-cycle batteries, and preferably a deep-cycle battery charger.

A cruising boat with light refrigeration needs and a powerful DC electrical system can use a constant-cycling DC unit with a water-cooled condenser. *If the electrical system includes a large wind generator, solar panel, or both, the boat so equipped frequently can go days on end without cranking the engine.*

A boat with moderate refrigeration needs (up to 3,500 Btus a day) can use either an intermediate DC holding-plate system or a small engine-driven unit. In the former case, *an adequate DC system is essential* but a wind generator or large solar panel can supply enough electricity to meet all refrigeration needs for days on end without cranking the engine.

Once refrigeration requirements get much above 3,500 Btus a day, an engine-driven cold-plate refrigeration unit is the best option, perhaps with a small constant-cycling DC unit for dockside operation and emergency backup. If the boat has an intermittently operated AC generator, a high-capacity AC system with cold plates may be powered by the generator while at sea, and shore-power at dockside.

Unless AC power is available 24 hours a day, when all the factors are taken into consideration for all but light refrigeration needs, some form of cold-plate arrangement is almost always the most effective refrigeration (see Figure 3-8). The rest of this book focuses on the practical side of such units, but almost all of the information, with the exception of the next chapter on cold plates, is equally applicable to other arrangements.

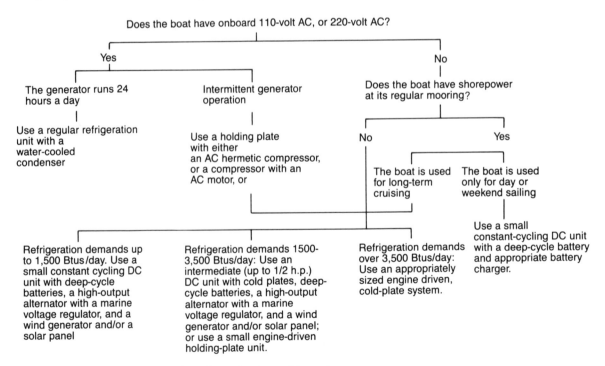

Figure 3-8. *Questions to consider when selecting refrigeration.*

Chapter 4

Cold Plates:
The Limiting Factor

(Note: If you have decided to install a constant-cycling refrigeration unit without cold plates, skip this chapter.)

A discussion of cold plates may seem to be a strange point at which to begin an excursion into the detailed functioning of a refrigeration unit, but I have a good reason for starting here. Most cold-plate systems are engine-driven. *With the exception of the largest refrigeration units, the rate at which a cold plate can be pulled down (frozen) is generally the limiting factor in a system. The rest of the system normally has to be matched to the cold plates rather than vice versa.* However, whereas most engine-driven systems are designed to minimize running time, DC systems, when coupled to cold plates, are limited by power consumption rather than running time. The practical upper limit on these systems is a $^1/_2$ h.p. power draw, which results in a strictly limited compressor capacity (see Chapter 5). This puts much less pressure on the cold plates and alleviates most of the difficulties in cold-plate design dealt with in the next section. On such a system, the compressor capacity should be calculated before making the cold-plate tubing calculations that follow. Before dealing with specific figures, let us first look at some background information.

Basic Requirements

At atmospheric pressure, water freezes at 32°F. Recall from Chapter 1 that on freezing, it gives up 144 Btus per pound of latent heat energy. During the process of freezing, it maintains a more or less constant temperature of 32°F. Only when all the water in a vessel is frozen will the temperature of the ice begin to drop below 32°F as more heat is extracted. Ice exhibits the same behavior in melting—as it steadily absorbs heat and turns into water, it remains at 32°F until it is all melted. Only then does the temperature of the water begin to rise as more heat is added.

From a refrigeration point of view, this property of water and ice enables a constant temperature to be maintained as long as some unmelted ice remains in an icebox, and it absorbs relatively large amounts of heat during the thawing process. The temperature maintained by melting ice, however, is barely adequate for refrigerator use and totally inadequate for freezer use. This is where a *cold plate* comes in.

A cold plate is a tank that contains a special solution, known as a *eutectic solution*. Its freezing point is well below that of water. The evaporator coil runs through the tank and is sealed into it, leaving both ends protruding three or four inches. An expansion

33

valve hooked to one end of the coil receives pressurized liquid refrigerant from a condenser. Within an expansion valve is a tiny nozzle that restricts the flow of refrigerant and causes the refrigeration unit's compressor to try to pull a vacuum on the downstream side. The liquid refrigerant sprays out of this nozzle into the evaporator coil, decompressing and boiling off as it goes (see Chapter 1). Through the absorption of latent heat of evaporation, the refrigerant pulls down the temperature in the evaporator coil, which in turn freezes the solution in the cold plate.

In order for a cold plate to be effective, the solution in it must freeze. Only through utilizing the large amount of heat absorption involved in the melting of solids (latent heat of melting) can cold plates be effective. One pound of melting ice at 32°F absorbs 144 Btus, whereas another liquid with the same specific heat, but which did not freeze, would have to be pulled down to −112°F to have the same refrigerating effect!

A eutectic solution in refrigeration needs to freeze and melt at a specific temperature so that a constant temperature can be maintained in an icebox. It should have the highest possible latent heat of fusion/melting so that the maximum possible Btu capacity can be obtained from the least volume of solution. This enables the smallest possible cold plate to be used.

As icebox temperatures are generally up to 20°F higher than the temperature of a cold plate in the icebox, we want a eutectic solution with a freezing point between 18°F and 26°F in a refrigerator. In a freezer, we want a solution with a freezing point between 0°F and 10°F. The higher the freezing point the more efficient a refrigeration system will be. This once again highlights the importance of good icebox insulation since plates with higher freezing points will only be effective in maintaining a correct icebox temperature if the heat leak into the box is minimized.

Although a freezer icebox temperature of around 20°F (i.e., a cold plate freezing point of 0°F to 10°F) will keep *already frozen* food more or less indefinitely, food that is frozen down in such an icebox freezes slowly. This leads to the formation of large ice crystals, which rupture tissues in the food. When it has defrosted, such food spoils rapidly and frequently loses a great deal of taste. For best results food should be fast frozen (which only allows small ice crystals to form) elsewhere, then placed in the freezer box for storage.

Eutectic Versus Antifreeze Solutions

It is important to distinguish between a eutectic solution and an antifreeze solution. Depending on its initial strength, an antifreeze solution begins to freeze at a certain temperature. Freezing takes the form of ice crystals precipitating out of the solution, which concentrates the remaining antifreeze solution and lowers its freezing point. A further reduction in temperature will cause more ice crystals to form and the remaining solution to become still more concentrated, further lowering its freezing point. This continues until a temperature and level of concentration are reached at which all the solution has frozen.

When this final freeze occurs, the antifreeze solution will have become concentrated to its maximum effective level. At this point, if more water crystalized out of the solution, further increasing its concentration, the freezing point would go no lower. In fact, once the solution passes a certain level of concentration, the freezing point begins to rise. Regular antifreeze (ethylene glycol) has a maximum effective level of concentration of 55 percent glycol by weight, and the freezing point at this level of concentration is −43°F. If the concentration level is raised to 100 percent glycol, the freezing point comes up to +9°F (see Figure 4-1).

If an antifreeze solution is mixed at its maximum effective level of concentration, it will not start to freeze until the temperature falls to −43°F, and then *all of it will freeze at this temperature. This is now a eutectic solution, and this is its eutectic point. At any level of concentration below this eutectic level, we have an antifreeze, not a eutectic, solution.* In other words, we have progressive freezing until the level of concentration reaches the eutectic level. Then the remainder of the solution will freeze at a constant temperature (the eutectic point).

In our cold plate, we do not want a eutectic solution with a freezing point as low as −43°F. If antifreeze is used in cold plates, it is always used with a level of concentration below its eutectic point. An antifreeze solution then suffers from three disadvantages:

1. It is impossible to maintain a constant temperature in an icebox because of the progressively lowering freeze-up point of the antifreeze solution. This is not so important in a freezer, so

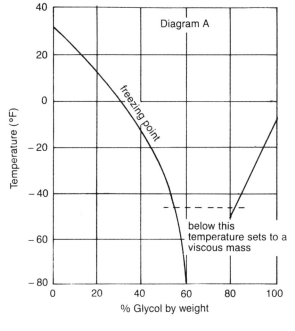

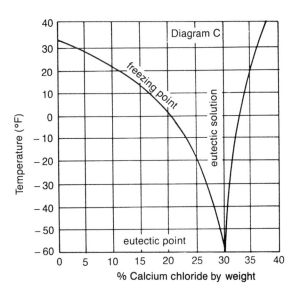

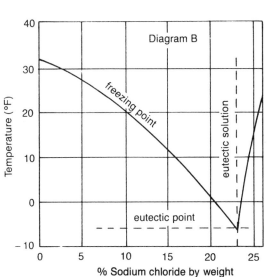

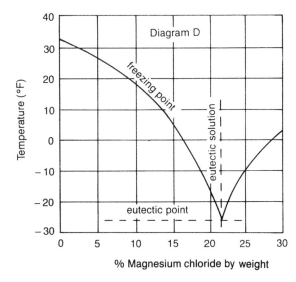

Figure 4-1. *Freezing curves for various solutions.*

long as the plate remains cold enough. In refrigerators, however, when the plate is being pulled down, it freezes vegetables and other sensitive produce.

2. As the freezing point progressively lowers, the system becomes increasingly inefficient because of the extremely low temperatures in-

volved. (Chapter 5 illustrates the marked impact of low-temperature operation on compressor output.)

3. The water that crystalizes out of an antifreeze solution tends to remain separated when the solution thaws. As glycol is heavier than water, over time the glycol has a tendency to settle in

the base of the cold plate while the water floats at the top. This is particularly the case in large cold plates.

Eutectic Solutions

The trick with cold plates is to find a chemical that when mixed with water, has a eutectic point within the ranges we want (18°F to 26°F for refrigerators, 0°F to 10°F for freezers). This chemical must then be added in the exact amount to produce a true eutectic solution so that freezing and melting take place at a precisely controlled temperature. A list of chemicals with their eutectic strengths and freezing points appears in Table 4-1.

Once you have selected the right chemical and mixed it in the correct proportions, the following factors have to be taken into consideration in the manufacture of cold plates:

1. When solutions freeze, they expand and can exert more than enough pressure to burst pipes and tanks. For this reason, certain other chemicals have to be added to cold plates to keep the eutectic solution from freezing hard.
2. The solutions used in cold plates are frequently extremely corrosive. All materials used in cold-plate construction have to be compatible with the solution. The better manufacturers leave a certain percentage of the cold plate empty, and then pull a vacuum on the plate before sealing it. This removes oxygen from the plate and so reduces the risk of corrosion. The empty volume on which the vacuum is pulled also serves as an expansion chamber for the solution as it freezes.

3. When a cold plate starts to freeze, ice forms around the evaporator coil. This ice has an insulating effect and slows down the rate of heat removal from the rest of the plate. To improve the efficiency of the plate, fins should be added to the coil, just as is done with an automobile radiator. As the rate of heat removal from a cold plate is frequently *the* limiting factor on the overall efficiency of a system, this is of some importance.
4. A cold plate is liable to be subjected to considerable shocks when a boat is pounding into a head sea. The evaporator coil in it needs to be well supported in a grid to prevent undue flexing and the possibility of eventual rupture. If the plate is to have a vacuum pulled on it, a pretty solid internal framework will in any case be necessary in order to prevent the sides from collapsing inward.

The Dole Refrigeration Company is the largest manufacturer of cold plates in the United States. They say that they may add an inhibitor to prevent electrochemical anaerobic corrosion; a freezing starter to prevent sub-cooling of the liquid phase; a softening agent to prevent hard freezing, which might damage the plate; and other additives for special purposes. The vacuum holds the assembly solidly together and prevents internal anaerobic corrosion. The channels are designed and located to transmit heat in a specific manner during the freezing or melting of the eutectic.

Commercial Cold Plates

Dole plates are made for refrigerated trucks, which are generally hooked up to a refrigeration unit overnight to freeze up the plates. On the road during the day, the plates maintain the necessary temperatures. These plates are designed to be pulled down over a number of hours, instead of with the speed often needed in marine refrigeration. Nevertheless, Dole plates have been proven to work in most boat refrigeration situations, though with some qualifications (see "Limitations of Commercial Plates" later in this chapter).

Dole plates are solidly made and extremely durable (see Figure 4-2). The evaporator coil is fully supported in a grid inside the plate. The plates are made

Table 4-1. *Eutectic Strength of Five Chemicals*

Chemical	Eutectic strength (% by weight)	Eutectic point
Calcium Chloride	30%	−59°F
Magnesium Chloride	22%	−27°F
Sodium Chloride	23%	−6°F
Propylene Glycol	50%	−24°F
Ethylene Glycol	55%	−43°F

Figure 4-2. *A well-constructed cold plate.* DOLE REFRIGERATION CO.

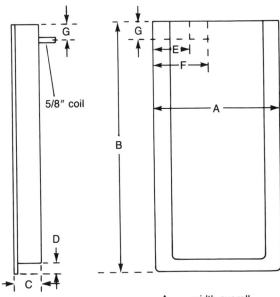
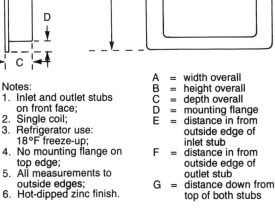

Notes:
1. Inlet and outlet stubs on front face;
2. Single coil;
3. Refrigerator use: 18°F freeze-up;
4. No mounting flange on top edge;
5. All measurements to outside edges;
6. Hot-dipped zinc finish.

A = width overall
B = height overall
C = depth overall
D = mounting flange
E = distance in from outside edge of inlet stub
F = distance in from outside edge of outlet stub
G = distance down from top of both stubs

Figure 4-3. *Cold plate ordering information. See the text for explanation.*

of galvanized steel (stainless steel is available at extra cost). All the tubing, fins, etc., are steel because the eutectic solutions used in them would probably set up galvanic corrosion in dissimilar metals. Adler Barbour and Grunert have a line of stainless steel plates filled with eutectic solutions, but in general, stainless steel tanks are filled with glycol solutions and will not perform as well as tanks filled with a eutectic solution.

It is possible to order twin coils in a plate. This provides the capability to add a completely independent, parallel system as a backup or to run on shoreside power when at the dock. The trade-off is that these plates will cost approximately 10 percent more than single-coil plates. The extra coil reduces the internal volume, therefore the Btu capacity of the plate.

Cold plates have to be specially ordered for most boat applications. Although Adler Barbour and Grunert have a pretty good range of shapes and sizes, sometimes a special plate is needed, and very few standard truck plates are the optimum shape for use on a boat. Dole will manufacture to just about any specification but the company charges a setup fee, which is frequently as much as the cost of an individual plate. The base price on two plates I ordered was $168 each, and the one-time setup charge was an additional $165. The setup charge is constant, regardless of the number of plates of the same size that are made, and is only charged once. Thus, while the cost

of one of these plates would have been $168 + $165 = $333, the cost for two plates was (2 × $168) + $165 = $501, or $250.50 each. That is a saving of $82.50 on each plate. Ten plates would have cost (10 × $168) + $165 = $1,845, or $184.50 each. Obviously, you can benefit from combining with other boat owners and ordering a batch of identical plates. They can have different solutions in them for freezer or refrigerator use—only the physical dimensions need be the same to keep to the one-time setup charge.

Ordering Cold Plates. The manufacturer needs to know the following (see Figure 4-3):
1. The required freeze-up temperature.
2. The overall dimensions (see "Cold-Plate Volume")—length, height, and width, including the width of a rim around the edges through

which holes will be drilled to fasten the plate. This rim should be a minimum of 3/4 inch wide, but need not be run on all four sides.

3. The location of the evaporator coil inlet and outlet stubs.
4. The size of the evaporator coil—1/2-inch or 5/8-inch tubing—and its length (see Tables 4-2 and 4-3; also "Limitations of Commercial Plates").
5. Whether the plate is to have an auxiliary coil and whether the plate is to be mounted horizontally or vertically.

Note: When calculating the size of a cold plate, make sure that it is not too big to fit through the lid of the icebox!

If you ordered a galvanized steel cold plate, prime it with a zinc-compatible paint and then apply a finish coat. Although R-12 is non-corrosive, when it is mixed with water it forms hydrochloric acid, which eats up zinc in no time at all. If the cold-plate connections leak when the unit is in use, the R-12 may mix with moisture in the icebox and destroy galvanizing on unpainted surfaces.

Placement of Cold Plates

Cold plates have little cooling effect above the level of their tops because cold air sinks. To keep a whole icebox cool, the cold plate must be placed as high in the box as possible. This is especially important in a freezer.

When a cold plate is pulled down, the temperature on the surface of the plate frequently falls close to the temperature in the evaporator coil because the coil is generally placed against the plate's surface. Consequently even in refrigerators, the plate surface will be well below freezing. Refrigerators have to be designed to keep fresh produce away from the cold plate so that the food will not freeze.

Freezers, on the other hand, must remain well below freezing at all times. If a single plate is placed in a large icebox, there will be a gradual rise in temperature across the box, moving away from the plate. The far upper side of the icebox is likely to rise above freezing and cause food to spoil. The best design for freezers is to have more than one plate, with the plates widely spaced in the box.

Table 4-2. *Cold-plate Pull-down Rates (as a function of cold-plate Btu capacity and refrigeration unit run time)*

| Plate Btu capacity | Minimum volume of eutectic solution (US gal) | Approx. final volume of cold plate (cu.ft.) | Refrigeration unit run time (in hours) | | | | | | |
			1/2	3/4	1	11/2	2	3	4
1,000	1	0.2	2,000	1,333	1,000	666	500	333	250
1,500	11/2	0.3	3,000	2,000	1,500	1,000	750	500	375
2,000	2	0.4	4,000	2,666	2,000	1,333	1,000	666	500
2,500	21/2	0.5	5,000	3,333	2,500	1,666	1,250	833	625
3,000	3	0.6	6,000	4,000	3,000	2,000	1,500	1,000	750
3,500	31/2	0.7	7,000	4,666	3,500	2,333	1,750	1,166	875
4,000	4	0.8	8,000	5,333	4,000	2,666	2,000	1,333	1,000
4,500	41/2	0.9	9,000	6,000	4,500	3,000	2,250	1,500	1,125
5,000	5	1.0	10,000	6,666	5,000	3,333	2,500	1,666	1,250

Rate of pull-down (in Btus per hour)

Enter table on the left with the cold-plate capacity (established in Chapter 2). Move across to read off:
1. Minimum volume of eutectic solution;
2. Minimum overall cold-plate volume;
3. Necessary rate of pull-down in Btus per hour for any given refrigeration unit running time.
Enter Table 4-3 to find the necessary size and length of evaporator tubing in the cold plate.

Refrigerator/freezers are sometimes engineered using freezer plates. Cold air is allowed to spill from the freezer compartment to the refrigerator side. Various methods can be used: placing the freezer below the refrigerator where the air is coldest; using a thinly insulated partition between a freezer and a refrigerator compartment; using just a partial partition, which allows cold air to spill over the top; using thermostatically operated spill-over fans; etc. The product literature of most of the major boat refrigeration companies has many ideas. In general, however, units with sepa-

rate boxes and plates and independent controls yield more satisfactory results (see Chapter 9).

Sizing Cold Plates

If you already know the necessary capacity for your cold plate (i.e., how many Btus it must absorb in melting) and how long you plan to run on an engine-driven unit, you can skip all the following calculations and go to Tables 4-2 and 4-3 to find out what volume

Table 4-3. *Cold-plate Evaporator Tubing Sizes and Lengths*

Rate of pull-down (Btus/hr)	Plate used for a refrigerator (26°F eutectic; 0°F evaporator temperature)		Plate used for a freezer (0°F eutectic; −20°F evaporator temperature)	
	Tubing size	Tubing length (feet)	Tubing size	Tubing length (feet)
200	1/4″ (1)	6.5 (1)	1/4″ (1)	8.5 (1)
300	1/4″ (1)	9.8 (1)	1/4″ (1)	13 (1)
400	1/4″ (1)	13 (1)	1/4″ (1)	17 (1)
500	1/4″ (1)	16 (1)	1/4″ (2)	11 (2)
600	1/4″ (1)	20 (1)	1/4″ (2)	13 (2)
750	1/4″ (2)	12 (2)	3/8″ (1) or 1/4″ (3)	21 (1) or 11 (3)
1,000	3/8″ (1) or 1/4″ (2)	22 (1) or 16 (2)	3/8″ (1) or 1/4″ (4)	28 (1) or 11 (4)
1,250	3/8″ (1) or 1/4″ (3)	27 (1) or 14 (3)	1/2″ (1) or 3/8″ (2)	27 (1) or 18 (2)
1,500	3/8″ (1) or 1/4″ (4)	33 (1) or 12 (4)	1/2″ (1) or 3/8″ (2)	32 (1) or 21 (2)
1,750	3/8″ (1) or 1/4″ (4)	38 (1) or 14 (4)	1/2″ (1) or 3/8″ (2)	37 (1) or 25 (2)
2,000	1/2″ (1)	33 (1)	1/2″ (1)	43 (1)
2,500	1/2″ (1)	41 (1)	5/8″ (1)	42 (1)
3,000	1/2″ (1)	49 (1)	5/8″ (1) or 1/2″ (2)	51 (1) or 32 (2)
3,500	5/8″ (1)	46 (1)	1/2″ (2)	37 (2)
4,000	5/8″ (1) or 1/2″ (2)*	52 (1) or 33 (2)*	1/2″ (3)	28 (3)
4,500	5/8″ (1) or 1/2″ (2)	59 (1) or 37 (2)	5/8″ (2) or 1/2″ (3)	38 (2) or 32 (3)
5,000	5/8″ (1) or 1/2″ (2)	65 (1) or 41 (2)	5/8″ (2) or 1/2″ (3)	42 (2) or 35 (3)
6,000	1/2″ (2) or 1/2″ (3)*	49 (2) or 33 (3)*	5/8″ (2) or 1/2″ (4)	51 (2) or 30 (4)
7,000	5/8″ (2) or 1/2″ (3)	46 (2) or 38 (3)	5/8″ (3) or 1/2″ (5)	40 (3) or 30 (5)
8,000	5/8″ (2) or 1/2″ (3)	52 (2) or 44 (3)	5/8″ (3) or 1/2″ (6)	45 (3) or 28 (6)
9,000	5/8″ (2) or 1/2″ (4)	59 (2) or 37 (4)	5/8″ (4) or 1/2″ (6)	38 (4) or 32 (6)
10,000	5/8″ (3) or 1/2″ (4)	44 (3) or 41 (4)	5/8″ (4) or 1/2″ (7)	42 (4) or 30 (7)

* = a refrigerant flow rate a little below the recommended minimum rate.
Assumptions: Type-L refrigeration tubing; R-12 use; net refrigerating effect is 45 Btus/pound.
Notes: 1) The numbers in brackets are the number of plates needed *in parallel*.
2) Individual tubing lengths (e.g., 60′) can be broken up between two plates if the plates are *in series* (e.g., 2×30′ in series).
3) Where there is a choice, elect more circuits *in parallel* and shorter individual evaporator coil lengths.
Example: 5,000 Btus/hr rate of pull-down in freezer use. The table calls for tubing size 5/8-inch (2) or 1/2-inch (3); tubing length, 42 feet (2) or 35 feet (3). We can either use two circuits of 5/8-inch tubing in parallel with 42 feet of tubing in each circuit, or three circuits of 1/2-inch tubing with 35 feet each.

of solution you need in the plate, the necessary size of the evaporator tubing, and the length of tubing. All you have to do once this information has been extracted is to determine the best shape of cold plate to accommodate the solution and tubing within the context of your icebox. If you are building a DC system with cold plates, first go to Chapter 5 to find the rate of pull-down your chosen compressor will give, then enter the tables.

The larger a cold plate, the longer it will take to pull down, but also the longer it will hold down the temperature in its icebox. Sizing a plate is a function of:

1. The size of the icebox, its thermal efficiency, and its use as a refrigerator or freezer. These three factors broadly determine the heat loss of the icebox (see Chapter 2).
2. How often you want to run the engine or how often you want the refrigeration unit to run if it is not engine-driven. This becomes critically important for engine-driven systems when the engine is run intermittently (e.g., cruising sailboats) and for any other system when you want to keep run time to a minimum (e.g., a high-capacity AC system powered by an intermittently operated AC generator).

Let us return to our sample 6-cubic-foot icebox with a daily heat loss of 2,400 Btus in refrigeration use, or 4,000 Btus in freezer use (see Chapter 2).

If we intend to run our refrigeration unit just once a day, we need cold plates that have a minimum holdover capacity of 2,400 Btus in refrigeration use; 4,000 Btus in freezer use. If we only want to run the unit every other day, we need a minimum holdover capacity of 4,800 Btus in refrigeration use; 8,000 Btus in freezer use.

Cold-Plate Volume. Cold-plate manufacturers invariably specify the Btu capacity of their plates in different applications, but if you need to get an approximate idea of the size of a plate for a given capacity, here is a rough and ready method.

Assume we need a 24-hour holdover capacity of 2,400 Btus. The latent heat of freezing water is 144 Btus per pound. Eutectic solutions are less efficient, so taking a purely arbitrary and conservative figure of, say, 100 Btus per pound, we need to freeze 24

pounds of solution. Water weighs approximately 64 pounds per cubic foot, and there will be up to 12 pounds of chemical per cubic foot of solution in the kinds of cold plates we are dealing with, giving a total weight of approximately 75 pounds per cubic foot. A cubic foot contains roughly 7.5 gallons, so each gallon of solution weighs in at around 10 pounds. We need approximately 2.4 gallons of solution in our cold plate for a holdover capacity of 2,400 Btus—i.e., one gallon of solution, in round figures, provides 1,000 Btus of holdover capacity.

As mentioned previously, Dole plates have a vacuum pulled on 15 percent of the volume of the plate, and we also need to make allowance for the volume of the evaporator coil in the plate, say another 15 percent. As a result, the total internal volume will be 30 percent more than the 2.4 gallons—i.e., 3.12 gallons, which is close to $1/2$ cubic foot. This gives a cold-plate size of 24 inches high by 12 inches wide by 3 inches deep, or some variant thereof. A freezer requires a cold-plate volume of approximately $3/4$ cubic foot—i.e., a plate around 24 inches high by 18 inches wide by 3 inches.

Notice how conveniently all these numbers worked out! None of these figures are very precise. The objective is to indicate the general approach. In any case, cold plates should be oversized rather than undersized. There is nothing more disappointing than cutting the calculations fine and discovering that the unit will only hold over for 18 hours.

Pull-Down Rate. It is not sufficient to simply have adequate volume of solution in a cold plate. For the refrigeration system to be effective, it must be able to freeze this solution in a strictly limited amount of running time.

The formula for calculating the rate at which a cold plate can be pulled down (i.e., how fast heat can be taken out of it) is as follows:

Plate eutectic freezing capacity (in Btus per hour)

$$= A \times K \times (t_1 - t_2)$$

where:

A = the surface area, in square feet, of the evaporator coil in the plate

K = the rate of heat transference from the eutectic solution to the refrigerant in Btus per hour, per square foot of evaporator coil, per 1°F temperature differential between the solution and the refrigerant

t_1 = the temperature of the refrigerant (i.e., $[t_1 - t_2]$ is the temperature differential between the refrigerant and the eutectic solution)

t_2 = the temperature of the solution in the cold plate.

The key to the formula is to discover the K factor for a cold-plate evaporator using eutectic solutions. This is no easy matter because so many variables are at work, the principal one being that as the solution freezes around the cold-plate evaporator coil, it insulates the coil and reduces the rate of heat transfer from the remaining solution. After years of practical experience, the Dole Company has determined that an average K factor of 18 Btus per square foot of coil area per 1°F temperature differential between the solution and the refrigerant is a good approximation for the performance of their plates *as used in refrigerated trucks with a temperature differential of maybe 10°F to 15°F between the evaporator coil and the eutectic solution.*

Boat refrigeration systems sometimes have temperature differentials of more than 40°F, and as far as I know, no research has been done to discover the practical consequences of this. We do know, however, that *as the differential increases, the rate of pull-down does not increase in a straight line. The K factor drops lower than 18.* As no concrete figures are available, the following calculations are based on a K factor of 18; therefore, you must bear in mind that the rate of pull-down is probably exaggerated by some unknown amount. The greater the temperature differential between the eutectic solution and the refrigerant, the greater the degree of exaggeration.

Since the limiting factor in the rate of pull-down is the build-up of ice around the evaporator coil, it makes little difference whether the coil is made of steel, aluminum, copper, or any other metal. The rate of heat transfer through any metal will greatly exceed the rate of transfer through the first layer of ice. Even the number of internal fins has a strictly limited effect once the first icing occurs. It therefore becomes extremely important to have the coil as well distributed as possible throughout the solution so that all parts of the solution are the minimum possible distance from the coil. We end up with a couple of contradictory requirements:

1. The need to increase the surface area of the evaporator tubing without reducing the volume of solution in the plate, since any reduction in volume will reduce the plate's holdover capacity.

2. The need to reduce the spacing between the coils of the evaporator tubing without reducing the volume of the solution in the plate or increasing the number of the bends in the coil because bends can impair system performance by creating an excessively high pressure drop from one end of the coil to the other (see later in this chapter and Chapter 8). We have to find a satisfactory compromise between these different requirements.

Let us return to our sample icebox in refrigerator use. Let us assume the plate contains a 25-foot coil of $1/2$-inch tubing—probably about par for commercially made plates of this capacity. The surface area A of this tubing is:

$$\pi \times D \times L$$

where:

π = 3.14

D = $1/2$ in. (the diameter of the evaporator coil)

L = the length of the coil in feet (25 ft.)

Since D is in inches and L is in feet, convert L to inches by multiplying by 12. L is now (25 × 12). Therefore:

$$A = (3.14 \times 0.5 \times 12 \times 25) \text{ sq.in.}$$

Now we need to convert this back to square feet, so we divide by 12^2 or (12 × 12), which gives us:

$$A = (3.14 \times 0.5 \times 12 \times 25) \div (12 \times 12)$$
$$= 3.27 \text{ sq.ft.}$$

If we assume a refrigerator plate with a freezing point of 26°F, and we also assume an evaporator coil temperature of 0°F (which, as we shall see later, is a fair assumption), then:

$$(t_1 - t_2) = 26 - 0 = 26$$

We already know K = 18. Therefore, the plate freezing capacity is:

$$3.27 \times 18 \times 26 = 1,530.36 \text{ Btus per hour}$$

This means it will take 2,400 ÷ 1530.36 = $1^{1}/_{2}$ hours to pull the plate down. This is unacceptably long in most engine-driven applications because we must keep engine running time to a minimum. We have come up against the limiting factor of most engine-driven systems.

Since the K factor is fixed at 18, *pull-down can only be speeded up by either increasing the surface area A of the evaporator coil (a longer coil and/or a larger size of tubing), or increasing the temperature differential between the freezing point of the eutectic solution and the temperature of the evaporator coil.*

Temperature Differential and Evaporator Coil Calculations.

If we raise the temperature differential between the freeze-up point of the eutectic solution and the evaporator coil temperature, the rate of heat removal—the K factor—declines by some unknown amount. Raising this differential becomes an increasingly inefficient way of speeding up the rate of pull-down on a cold plate. There are, in any case, other limits on how far we can increase this differential.

Since the freezing point of the eutectic solution in our cold plate is fixed, the only way to increase the temperature differential between this freezing point and the evaporator coil is to drop the temperature in the coil. The only way to do this is to reduce the pressure in the coil (see Chapter 1, Table 1-1). For example, using R-12, to obtain an evaporator temperature of 0°F, we need a pressure of 9.15 psi. To drop the temperature to −20°F, the pressure must be brought down to around 0 psi. The pressure in an evaporator coil is determined by the suction pressure on the compressor. For reasons which will become clear in the next chapter, pulling a compressor into a vacuum is not desirable. A temperature of −20°F therefore becomes the practical lower limit in the evaporator coil.

In a refrigerator with a 26°F cold plate, −20°F would give a temperature differential of 46°F. This is unacceptably high and therefore inefficient, in most applications. The practical choice in refrigeration work is generally an evaporator temperature of around 0°F, giving a differential of 26°F (which is why I chose these figures in the first place!). In a freezer with plate freeze-up temperatures as low as 0°F, we need to pull down the evaporator temperature to −20°F, giving a temperature differential of 20°F.

These are the figures I started with, which means we are no nearer reducing our plate pull-down time. We will have to try tackling the problem from the other end. Assume that we wish to freeze our plate in 45 minutes (not an unreasonable target in a well-designed engine-driven system). Because we have a plate capacity of 2,400 Btus in refrigerator use, we need a rate of pull-down of:

$$2,400 ÷ 45 × 60 = 3,200 \text{ Btus per hour}$$

A plate freeze-up point of 26°F and an evaporator temperature of 0°F gives us a differential ($t_1 − t_2$) of 26°F. The K factor is still 18. We re-enter our formula as follows:

$$3,200 = A × 18 × 26$$

Therefore:

$$A = 3,200 ÷ (18 × 26) = 6.838 \text{ sq.ft.} = 984 \text{ sq.in.}$$

Since $^{1}/_{2}$-inch tubing has a circumference of ($\pi ×$ D), the tubing length must be:

$$984 ÷ (3.14 × 0.5) = 627 \text{ in.} = 52 \text{ ft.}$$

If we had used $^{5}/_{8}$-inch tubing for the evaporator coil, the circumference would be (3.14 × 0.625) inches and the tubing length, therefore:

$$984 ÷ (3.14 × 0.625) = 501 \text{ in.} = 42 \text{ ft.}$$

What about a freezer? We now need a plate capacity of 4,000 Btus in our 6-cubic-foot box, with a plate eutectic point of 0°F. To pull down this plate in 45 minutes, we need a pull-down rate of:

$$4,000 ÷ 45 × 60 = 5,333 \text{ Btus per hour}$$

We do not want our compressor to pull into a vacuum, so we are not going to allow the suction pressure to fall below 0 psi, giving an evaporator temperature of −20°F (Table 1-1 in Chapter 1), and a temperature differential ($t_1 − t_2$) of 20°F.

We can now enter the formula to find the necessary length of evaporator tubing, using $^{1}/_{2}$-inch and $^{5}/_{8}$-inch tubing:

$$5,333 = A × 18 × 20$$

Therefore:

$$A = 14.8 \text{ sq.ft.} = 2,133 \text{ sq.in.}$$

Using $^{1}/_{2}$-inch tubing, the length of the evaporator coil must be:

$$2{,}133 \div (3.14 \times 0.5) = 1{,}359 \text{ in.} = 113 \text{ ft.}$$

Using 5/8-inch tubing, the length of the evaporator coil must be:

$$2{,}133 \div (3.14 \times 0.625) = 1{,}087 \text{ in.} = 91 \text{ ft.}$$

Multiple Plate Systems. These long lengths of tubing will not fit into single plates, so you must build up the total plate volume and tubing surface area with multiple plates. Even doing this, you still may not be able to fit a sufficient tube surface area into the plates to achieve the 45-minute pull-down time, especially for a freezer. Unless a longer pull-down time is acceptable, the only way to reach your goal is to put in oversized plates. The unit then can be just partially frozen in 45 minutes, to give a 24-hour holdover, or completely frozen with a longer compressor running time, giving a holdover period of more than 24 hours.

At this point, however, we run into another problem. Long tubing runs result in a considerable pressure drop through an evaporator coil, which seriously impairs performance (see Chapter 8). To lessen this problem, you can build up longer evaporator coil lengths by running more than one cold plate in parallel. The parallel cold plates branch out from a common refrigerant supply line and then connect back into a common compressor suction line. A total length of 90 feet of evaporator coil could be built up by running three plates, each with a 30-foot coil, in parallel. A limit on how many plates can be run in parallel is largely determined by the speed of the refrigerant flow through the evaporator coil. This is the next variable that you must consider.

Speed of Refrigerant Flow. Refrigeration units operate with flow rates through the evaporator tubing of 800 feet per minute to 5,000 feet per minute. The higher the flow rate, the greater the scrubbing action of the refrigerant on the walls of the evaporator coil. Scrubbing helps promote heat transfer through the coil, which results in a high K factor. But higher flow rates also increase friction, therefore the pressure drop through an evaporator coil, and this seriously impairs performance (see Chapter 8).

A low flow rate keeps down the pressure drop, but an oil film tends to coat the inside of the evaporator coil. The oil reduces the rate of heat transfer, which lowers the K factor. What is more, since the oil that lubricates a refrigeration system is carried by the refrigerant, a low flow rate, especially at low temperatures, can cause the oil to settle out in the tubing, resulting in oil starvation and compressor failure.

The system needs a balance among the flow rate, pressure drop, oil circulation, and the rate of heat transfer. I know of no studies of the optimum flow rates for boat refrigeration, but a rate of 1,500 feet per minute is needed for effective oil circulation through a vertical tube (there will be many sections of vertical tubing in a cold plate). I have taken this as a good average figure in the following calculations, then arbitrarily selected 1,800 feet per minute as a maximum flow rate, and 1,100 feet per minute as a minimum.

Tubing has a cross-sectional area (CSA) of:

$$\pi \times R \times R$$

where:

R is the *internal* radius of the tubing

Half-inch refrigeration tubing (type-L) has a wall thickness of 0.032 inch; 5/8-inch type-L tubing a wall thickness of 0.035 inch. The *inside diameter (ID)* of 1/2-inch tubing is:

$$0.5 - (2 \times 0.032) \text{ in.} = 0.436 \text{ in.}$$

The inside radius is:

$$0.436/2 = 0.218 \text{ in.}$$

The inside CSA is:

$$3.14 \times 0.218 \times 0.218 = 0.15 \text{ sq.in.}$$

The internal volume of 1/2-inch tubing is:

$$0.15 \times 12 = 1.8 \text{ cu.in./ft. of length.}$$

To maintain a flow rate of 1,500 feet per minute, we must circulate $1.8 \times 1{,}500 = 2{,}700$ cubic inches of refrigerant per minute.

For a flow rate of 1,800 feet per minute, we must circulate 3,240 cubic inches of refrigerant per minute. For a flow rate of 1,100 feet per minute, we must circulate 1,980 cubic inches of refrigerant per minute.

The same calculations for 5/8-inch tubing yield an inside CSA of 0.24 square inches, a volume of 2.88 cubic inches per foot of length, and a requirement to circulate between 3,168 and 5,184 cubic inches of refrigerant per minute.

Quarter-inch tubing has an inside CSA of 0.34 cubic inches per foot of length, and a requirement to circulate between 374 and 612 cubic inches of refrigerant per minute. Three-eighths-inch tubing has an inside volume of 0.917 cubic inches per foot of length, and a requirement to circulate between 1,008 and 1,650 cubic inches of refrigerant per minute.

Where plates are fitted *in series*, the volume of refrigerant needed to maintain proper flow rates will be as above regardless of the number of plates. Where plates are fitted *in parallel*, volume must be doubled for two plates, trebled for three, etc.

Maximum Evaporator Coil Length. Friction in refrigerant lines, therefore pressure drop, is a function of the cross-sectional area (i.e., tubing size), the length of the line, the number of the bends, and the speed of the refrigerant flow. Tests have shown that a straight length of $^1/_2$-inch tubing creates a pressure drop of around one psi per 80 feet of length at a refrigerant flow rate of 1,000 feet per minute. Every 90-degree bend introduces approximately the same resistance as an extra foot of length.

Keeping the pressure drop through an evaporator coil to 2 psi or less (see Chapter 7) is desirable. This translates to 160 feet, or less, of *straight* $^1/_2$-inch tubing at 1,000 feet per minute of refrigerant flow. As flow rates increase, resistance, therefore pressure drop, increases disproportionately. At 1,800 feet per minute, resistance is more than doubled, reducing the overall desirable evaporator coil length to less than 80 feet, even without bends. A typical evaporator coil in a cold plate will have one 180- degree bend (i.e., two 90-degree bends) for every one to two feet of length. This means the bends introduce as much, if not more, resistance as the tubing length itself. To keep within a 2-psi pressure drop at typical flow rates, an evaporator coil of $^1/_2$-inch tubing should be kept shorter than 30 feet. With $^5/_8$-inch tubing, the desirable upper limit would be around 40 feet. Keeping within these limits is not always possible, in which case, the system requires an externally equalized expansion valve, which is explained in Chapter 7.

Putting the Calculations Together. Now is the time to tie all these considerations together. A pretty fair generalization in boat refrigeration says that the *net refrigerating effect* per pound of R-12 circulated through a system is 45 Btus. In some refrigeration applications, it may go as high as 50 Btus per pound; in some freezer applications, as low as 40 Btus per pound. Forty-five Btus is a good working average.

To achieve a 45-minute pull-down on our sample cold plate, we have determined that in refrigeration use we need a system capacity of 3,200 Btus per hour. With a net refrigerating effect of 45 Btus per pound, we must circulate:

$$3,200 \div 45 = 71 \text{ lbs. of R-12/hr.}$$

We intend to hold our evaporator temperature at 0°F. Referring back to Table 1-1 in Chapter 1, column 3 tells us that, at this temperature, R-12 vapor has a volume of 1.6 cubic feet per pound. Since we are circulating 71 pounds an hour, this gives us a total vapor volume of:

$$71 \times 1.6 = 114 \text{ cu.ft./hr.}$$

This is:

$$114 \times 12 \times 12 \times 12 = 196,992 \text{ cu.in./hr.}$$

which is:

$$196,992 \div 60 = 3,283 \text{ cu.in./min.}$$

This is just above the upper recommended limit for the speed of refrigerant flow through $^1/_2$-inch tubing (the limit is 3,240 cu.in./min.) and just within the lower recommended limit for $^5/_8$-inch tubing (3,168 cu.in./min.). We could use either 52 feet of $^1/_2$-inch tubing in the evaporator coil or 42 feet of $^5/_8$-inch tubing. The $^5/_8$-inch tubing is preferable because it reduces the amount of pressure drop through the evaporator coil. Our cold plate will have to be sized to accommodate the chosen coil length. If we use more than one plate, they must be *in series* to maintain the rate of flow.

Note that both evaporator coil lengths are above the maximum recommended length of 30 feet. What about using two cold plates in parallel with 25 feet of $^1/_2$-inch evaporator coil in each? The speed of refrigerant flow would fall to 3,283 ÷ 2 = 1,641.5 cu.in./min. through each coil. This translates into a flow rate of 1,641.5 ÷ 1.8 = 912 ft./min., which is well below the minimum recommended speed of refrigerant flow. Whatever course we choose, we are bound to run into certain inefficiencies—shooting for a 45-minute pull-down is pushing the limits of practicality on this system.

The same calculations *for a freezer* produce the following results:

Rate of pull-down: 5,333 Btus.

With a net refrigerating effect of 45 Btus per pound, we must circulate:

5,333 ÷ 45 = 118.5 lbs. of R-12/hr.

In freezer applications, we will have an evaporator temperature of −20°F, which Table 1-1 tells us gives a vapor volume of 2.5 cubic feet per pound of R-12. We will therefore have a total vapor volume of:

118.5 × 2.5 = 296.25 cu.ft./hr.
            = 511,920 cu.in./hr.
            = 8,532 cu.in./min.

This is three or four times the desirable rate of flow through the 1/2-inch tubing, and two times the rate of flow through 5/8-inch tubing. We can arrive at the desired rate of flow with three plates with 1/2-inch tubing in parallel (each with 113 ÷ 3 = 38-foot evaporator coils); four plates with 1/2-inch tubing in parallel (each with 29-foot evaporator coils); or two plates with 5/8-inch tubing in parallel (each with 91 ÷ 2 = 45.5-foot evaporator coils). All but the four 1/2-inch plates in parallel have overly long evaporator coils for optimum performance. Once again we are straining at the limits of practicality.

Step-By-Step Summary of Plate Sizing Procedure.

1. Establish the minimum plate Btu capacity. This is a function of the heat leak from the icebox (Chapter 2) and the length of time between pull-downs.
2. Assuming 1,000 Btus per gallon, calculate the minimum *volume* of eutectic solution to provide the holdover capacity in step 1.
3. Decide *how long* the refrigeration unit will be run to pull down the plate. This will be related to the type of usage the boat gets and the type of refrigeration system that is being used (AC; DC; or engine-driven).
4. Using the plate capacity (step 1) and the pull-down time (step 3), calculate the required *rate of pull-down* (capacity ÷ time [in hours]). Note that on most DC systems, the rate of pull-down will be limited by the compressor capacity, which will be the determining factor in the calculations from this point on. The upper limit on a 1/2-h.p. DC unit is approximately 2,250 Btus per hour in refrigerator use and 1,500 Btus per hour in freezer use. On engine-driven systems using automotive compressors, the practical upper limits on the rate of pull-down are 8,000 Btus per hour in a refrigerator and 5,000 Btus per hour in a freezer. Beyond these points, the compressor becomes the limiting factor.
5. Assume a K factor of 18 and a differential $(t_1 - t_2)$ of 26°F in refrigeration use, or of 20°F in freezer use. Calculate the *surface area* of tubing needed to achieve the required rate of pull-down (A = required rate of pull-down ÷ 18 × $[t_1 - t_2]$)
6. Assume a net refrigerating effect of 45 Btus per pound. Calculate the weight of refrigerant that must be circulated per hour (rate of pull-down ÷ 45 = lbs./hr.).
7. In a refrigerator, assume a vapor volume of 1.6 cubic feet per pound; in a freezer, a vapor volume of 2.5 cubic feet per pound. Convert the figure in step 6 to *cubic inches per minute* ([lbs./hr. × vapor volume × 12 × 12 × 12] ÷ 60).
8. Assume the following flow rates: 1/2-inch tubing 1,980 to 3,240 cubic inches per minute; 5/8-inch tubing 3,168 to 5,184 cubic inches per minute. Compare the figure in step 7 to these figures and determine what *tubing size* and if necessary how many plates *in parallel* you will need to handle the flow rate in step 7 while remaining within these flow rates.
9. Calculate the *length of tubing* required to produce the tubing surface area determined in step 5, using the tubing diameter determined in step 8 and using D = 0.5 for 1/2-inch tubing; D = 0.625 for 5/8-inch tubing (L [in feet] = [A × 12] ÷ [3.14 × D]).
10. If the length of tubing determined in step 9 cannot be accommodated in the plate volume determined in step 2, either increase the plate volume to accommodate the tubing or settle for a longer pull-down time and recalculate. This may, in any case, be necessary to keep evaporator coil lengths within reasonable limits.

Now we have all the necessary information to design a cold plate, namely the minimum volume of solution and the size and length of the evaporator tubing. All that remains is to figure out the best physical configuration to accommodate these requirements with respect to your icebox. It looks complicated, but in reality it is pretty straightforward. Tables 4-2 and 4-3 summarize these procedures for all normal cold-plate sizes found in boat refrigeration. Why don't you give it a shot?

One Final Calculation. Once we have designed a cold plate, we have to make sure it has enough surface area exposed within the icebox to maintain a sufficient rate of cooling between pull-downs. The formula is:

$$\text{Rate of cooling (Btus/hr.)}$$
$$= \text{plate surface area(sq.ft.)} \times 2 \times (t_1 - t_2)$$

where:

t_1 is the temperature of the interior of the icebox and t_2 is the temperature of the cold plate.

A cold plate of 24 inches by 12 inches by 3 inches fastened directly to an icebox liner (so that one surface is not exposed) has an exposed surface area of:

$$(12 \times 24) + (2 \times 24 \times 3) + (2 \times 12 \times 3)$$
$$= 504 \text{ sq.in.} = 3.5 \text{ sq.ft.}$$

It is normal to assume a temperature differential between the cold plate and the box of 20°F. We enter the formula as follows:

$$\text{Rate of cooling (Btus/hr.)} = 3.5 \times 2 \times 20$$
$$= 140 \text{ Btus/hr.}$$
$$140 \text{ Btus/hr.} = 3,360 \text{ Btus/24 hrs.}$$

Since we only need a heat absorption capability of 2,400 Btus/24 hours, this is more than adequate in this situation. Had it not been enough we could have set the plate in the box on stand-offs so that its rear surface was not up against the liner. This would have given us an extra 248 square inches of plate surface area absorbing heat from the icebox.

The formula can be turned around to determine the plate surface area that must be exposed in any given icebox. This is done as follows:

$$\text{Required 24-hour holdover capacity} = 2,400 \text{ Btus}$$
$$= 100 \text{ Btus/hr.}$$

The temperature differential $(t_1 - t_2)$ is assumed to be 20°F

$$100 = A \times 2 \times 20$$

Therefore:

$$A = 2.5 \text{ sq.ft.}$$

For a freezer with a daily heat loss of 4,000 Btus, the same calculation yields a plate surface area of 4.17 square feet. A 24-inch by 18-inch by 3-inch plate fastened directly to the icebox liner has an exposed surface area of 4.75 square feet, which is adequate. However, the better an icebox is insulated, the lower the temperature differential between the cold plate and the box interior $(t_1 - t_2)$. This differential can, in exceptionally well-built iceboxes, drop to as low as 5°F, in which case the flush-mounted plate would not be adequate. In general, *it is a good idea to mount plates in freezers on stand-offs*.

Limitations of Commercial Plates

I noted previously that commercial plates are built primarily for refrigerated trucks, in which they are pulled down slowly over a number of hours. The designed rate of pull-down is therefore generally much slower than we want in boat refrigeration. As a result the size of the evaporator tubing in the plates and the length of the tubing is almost always less than called for in all the foregoing calculations.

If you are buying a cold plate off-the-shelf, you have to find out the plate's overall Btu capacity and the rate at which it can be pulled down at an evaporator coil temperature of 0°F for a refrigerator plate and a temperature of −20°F for a freezer plate. Alternatively, ask for the size and the length of the tubing in the plate and check it against Tables 4-2 and 4-3 to see if it is suitable in your application. If the plate manufacturer cannot accommodate the tubing specifications you want, you have three options: downgrade the whole system to fit the plates; attain the desired tubing specifications by fitting oversized plates; or build your own plates.

Building a Cold Plate

Use 16-gauge, or heavier, stainless steel sheet metal. To keep welding to a minimum, form the front and sides out of one piece, cutting out the corners and folding up the sides as shown in Figure 4-4. Build the pan for $1/2$-inch tubing $2^1/2$ inches deep; for $5/8$-inch tubing $2^3/4$ to 3 inches deep. Weld the corners to form a pan. Cut the back a little oversize to provide a mounting flange.

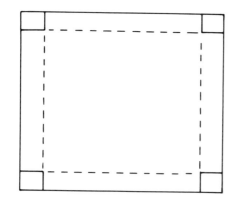

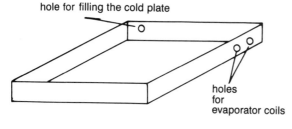

hole for filling the cold plate

holes
for
evaporator coils

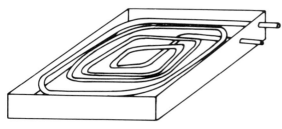

Figure 4-4. *Simple cold-plate construction. Step 1: Cut out the corners and bend up on the dotted lines. Step 2: Weld the corners to form a pan. Step 3: Put in the coil. Step 4: Weld on the back, overlapping the sides by 3/4 inch to provide a mounting flange.*

Copper tubing is used for the evaporator coil. It can be bent with tubing benders (see Figure 4-5), cut and soldered using standard fittings, or coiled by carefully and slowly tightening down a spiral of soft copper refrigeration tubing (see Figure 4-6). The latter is preferable—because it does not create sharp bends that restrict flow or joints that may leak. Take an appropriate length of tubing (up to 50 feet). Spread the coils slightly with one of the ends on each side of the roll. Grasp approximately half the roll in each

hand and slowly tighten the coil by rotating your hands in opposite directions. With care you can pull the center of the roll into quite a small loop (6 inches to 8 inches in diameter). Work out the rest of the coil in a spiral in both directions, slowly squaring off the outer loops to form corners that will fit neatly into the plate. Keep the individual rings in each spiral within 1 inch to 1 1/2 inches of each other. Take your time—copper rapidly work-hardens when you bend it, and if you try to rework sections of the coil, it will soon become unworkable and kink. If it kinks, you will have to junk it, or cut out the kink and splice the tubing.

Coiling tubing in this manner will generally get more tubing into a plate, and with closer spacing, than with any other method. What is more, it will not have joints or sharp bends. To hold the spirals in place, slide lengths of 1-inch OD copper tubing between the two spirals and solder each loop of each spiral to the tubing. This will also help in heat transfer within the plate. With 1/2-inch tubing, this will produce an assembly that is 2 inches deep; with 5/8-inch tubing, 2 1/4 inches deep. Drill holes in the pan sides for the inlet and outlet tubes, then slip the two ends of the tubing through these holes. Silver solder (see Chapter 8) the coil to the pan in a number of places to hold it rigidly in place. Also silver solder the tubing where it passes through the sides so that the pan is sealed at these points. Don't forget to add a fill fitting to the pan while you are at it! Weld on the back of the cold plate. Finally, silver solder a length of 1/4-inch copper tubing down the face or the side of the plate. A thermostat sensing line will be slipped in here to control the unit (see Chapter 9). Figures 4-7 to 4-10 illustrate cold-plate construction.

If a cold plate is built like this, no part of the eutectic solution will ever be more than 1/2 inch to 3/4 inch from a section of the evaporator tube (with the exception of a small volume in the center of the coil). In a given size cold plate, the closer the spacing of the evaporator tubes, the faster the rate of pull-down but the less the volume of eutectic solution, therefore overall plate capacity. If the minimum pull-down time is a major priority, as it is on many boats, this is likely to be an acceptable trade-off. Reducing the spacing between evaporator coils by half more than doubles the rate of freeze-up, assuming the rest of the system has the capacity to take advantage of the greater surface area of the evaporator coil. In multiple plate units

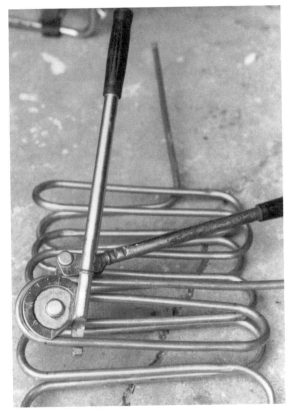

Figure 4-5. *Using $^1/_2$-inch tubing benders to make an evaporator for a cold plate takes quite a lot of skill, especially when you deal with long lengths of tubing.*

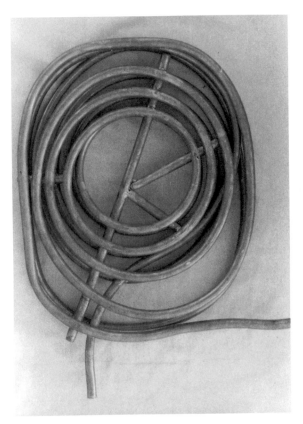

Figure 4-6. *This hand-coiled evaporator has five spirals working out from the center of a roll of $^1/_2$-inch tubing. Some lengths of $^1/_2$-inch tubing soldered between hold everything in place. This plate was designed for a very fast pull-down, but the $^1/_2$-inch spacing is too close for most applications; 1-inch spacing would be better.*

with a considerable length of evaporator tubing this may not be the case.

Home-built plates will have to be filled with an antifreeze solution (eutectic solutions are too corrosive and complex). Automotive antifreeze is made from *ethylene glycol*, which is poisonous. *Propylene glycol* is preferable. This has much the same properties as ethylene glycol but is not poisonous; therefore leaks will not pose a health hazard. A refrigerator plate should have a solution with 30-percent glycol; a freezer plate, 40-percent glycol. Any efficiency lost through not having a proper eutectic solution is likely to be more than compensated for with extra tubing in the plate as compared to most commercially made plates.

Although I have described the construction of a simple oblong-shaped plate, one of the principal advantages of building them yourself is that you can make odd-shaped plates to fit into what would otherwise be dead spaces in many iceboxes. This is especially true on sailboats with iceboxes built up against the hull sides.

Final Note

Using the information in this chapter, you should now have determined the size and number of cold plates in your refrigeration system. In doing this, you have used a certain rate of pull-down in Btus per hour. Since this

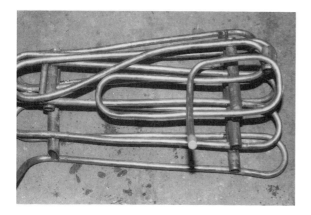

Figure 4-7. *Note the 1-inch spacers and the properly capped ends of the tubing on this evaporator coil made for an odd-shaped plate. It is ready for installation.*

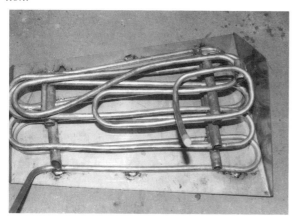

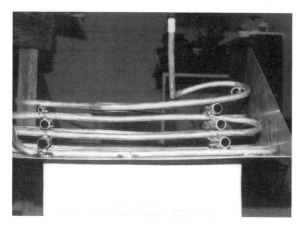

Figures 4-8 and 4-9. *Two views of the same evaporator coil soldered to its cold plate. The unusual shape takes advantage of the shape dictated by having an icebox built against the side of a boat's hull.*

Figure 4-10. *A completed cold plate. Note the fill fitting (***top right***), the in and out refrigerant lines, and the copper tube (***far left***), which will hold the thermostat's sensing line.*

Figure 4-11. *The cold plate is installed in its freezer box. Note the thermostat capillary tube at the far left. This plate has a very large volume for this box; it is designed to provide 48-hour holdover in the freezer.*

figure determines the capacity of all the other components in the system, it is worth reiterating what it is and is not. It is **not** the cold-plate holdover capacity nor the daily heat leak from the icebox, except when the daily running time of the refrigeration unit happens to be exactly one hour a day. It **is** the daily heat leak from the icebox *divided by the running time in hours.* For example, 30 minutes of running time equals $1/2$ hour—the daily heat leak figure must be *doubled* to find the rate of pull-down.

Chapter 5

Compressors:
The Heart of a System

The compressor is the pump that keeps the refrigerant flowing through a refrigeration system. It has to be matched to the cold plates (where fitted) and other components in a system so that it is capable of moving the required amount of refrigerant *at the temperatures and pressures that prevail in the system.* It must also provide reliable, trouble-free service for many years.

Types of Compressors

The two broad types of compressors in widespread use are *hermetic* and *belt-driven (open).*

Hermetic compressors have an electric motor directly coupled to a compressor and the whole unit sits inside a sealed canister (see Figure 5-1). The compressor suction and discharge lines hook up to fittings on the outside of the canister.

Belt-driven compressors have an external pulley fastened to the end of the compressor's crankshaft. This pulley is turned either by a separate electric motor or by an engine. Usually the boat's main engine turns the compressor, but any engine with sufficient power will do, even a lawnmower engine.

Hermetic Compressors. Hermetic compressors have one significant advantage over belt-driven compressors, and one significant disadvantage. The

advantage is that the sealed unit prevents refrigerant leaks to the atmosphere from around the drive shaft, which is a fairly common problem of belt-driven compressors. The disadvantage is that if a hermetic compressor is pulled into a deep vacuum on its suction side, an electric arc (a *corona*) can occur between electrical terminals or between a terminal and ground. This arcing sometimes leaves a trace of carbon, which electrical current may follow in subsequent operation. This in turn can lead to compressor failure.

Because of the low temperatures necessary to pull down cold plates, compressors in cold-plate refrigeration often pull into a deep vacuum (see Table 1-1 in Chapter 1, showing the relationship between temperature and pressure for R-12). This is especially so at the bottom end of a cycle when the plates are almost frozen and a heavy layer of ice has formed around the evaporator tube in the cold plates. The rate of heat removal slows, and the compressor responds by pulling an ever lower pressure. A similar problem arises where two or more plates are installed in parallel with separate shut-down controls on each plate (see Chapter 9). As the plates freeze up and shut down, the whole compressor output is concentrated on the last plate, frequently resulting in a deep vacuum.

Hermetic compressors are generally used only on constant-cycling refrigeration units. *If a hermetic compressor is used on a cold-plate system, careful*

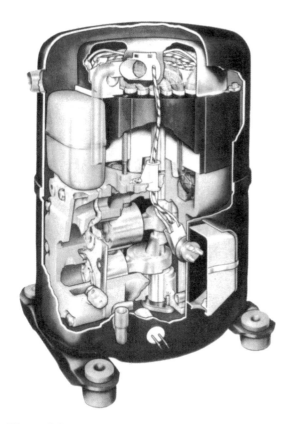

Figure 5-1. *A typical hermetic compressor.*
TECUMSEH PRODUCTS CO.

engineering and control will be needed to protect the compressor from excessive vacuums.

Belt-Driven Compressors.

The overwhelming majority of belt-driven compressors used in pleasure-boat refrigeration are automotive air-conditioning compressors, driven directly from the boat's main engine. These are readily available and relatively inexpensive because they are produced by the millions. Given the proper application, they work well in this field. Apart from these compressors, a few small industrial compressors find their way into boat refrigeration. These are generally driven by an electric motor but can just as easily be driven off the boat's engine so long as they are set up to run at the correct speed.

All the common industrial compressors are reciprocal compressors. They have an arrangement of pistons connected to an offset crankshaft in just the same way as the pistons are connected to the crankshaft in a car engine. An external belt-driven pulley keyed to the crankshaft turns the shaft, which drives the pistons up and down in their cylinders. At the top of each cylinder are suction and discharge valves to allow the refrigerant in and out of the cylinder (see Figures 5-2A and 5-2B).

Many automotive compressors are also reciprocal but quite a number are not. Variations include *radial* (scotch yoke) compressors (a modification of reciprocal action—see Figures 5-3A and 5-3B), *rotary vane*, and *swash-plate* (wobble plate). Of these, only the swash-plate compressors are common in boat refrigeration.

A swash-plate compressor has a number of cylinders (generally from five to seven) arranged in a circle. In each cylinder is a piston with a connecting rod. All the connecting rods are attached to a plate (the *swash plate*), which is held at its center in a way that prevents it from rotating but allows it to wobble up and down around this central point. Beneath the swash plate is a lopsided rotor (the cam), which does rotate. As the rotor turns, it drives first one side of the swash plate up, and then the other, causing the plate to oscillate around its pivot point. This in turn drives the pistons up and down their cylinders (see Figure 5-4).

Some swash-plate compressors have all the pistons set on one side of the plate. Double-sided swash plates have the pistons at opposite ends of the compressor, interconnected with the swash plate and rotor between. When one piston is driven up its cylinder, the piston at the other end of the compressor is dragged down its cylinder. On all swash-plate compressors, suction and discharge valves are set in a cylinder head at the top of the cylinders.

Lubrication of Compressors

Lubrication on all the refrigeration systems considered in this book is achieved by circulating specially blended refrigeration oils with the refrigerant in the system.

The lower the temperature in a refrigeration system, the lower the evaporator pressure. At lower temperatures and pressures, the volume of vapor per pound of refrigerant sharply increases (see Table 1-1 in Chapter 1). A compressor has a certain fixed *displacement*—the volume of vapor moved through its

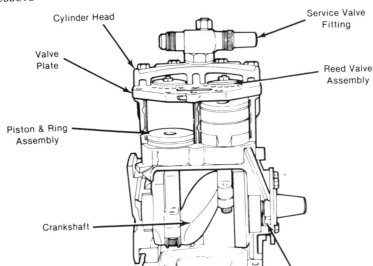

Figure 5-2A. *A reciprocal compressor—this one is a 2-cylinder in-line model.*
FOUR SEASONS

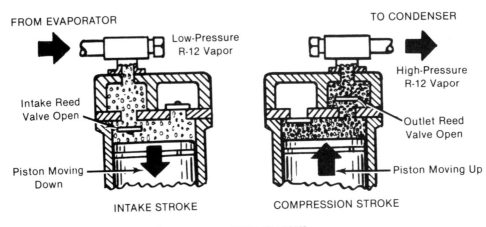

Figure 5-2B. *The action of a reciprocal compressor.* FOUR SEASONS

cylinders in one revolution. So, for any given size of compressor, the greater the volume of refrigerant vapor per pound of refrigerant, the less the *weight* of the refrigerant that will be circulated—i.e., the lower the operating temperatures and pressures, the less the refrigerant that will be moved through the system.

Less refrigerant pumped through a compressor means *less lubricant circulated*. What is more, at colder temperatures and with the long tubing runs of cold-plate evaporator coils, oil tends to coalesce and puddle out in the system, especially at low spots in the tubing. These low spots are almost impossible to avoid in boat refrigeration.

Reciprocal compressors generally have a sizable sump that holds oil, but swash-plate compressors do not. *If operating pressures on a swash-plate compres-*

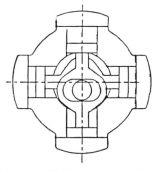

Figure 5-3A. *A radial, or scotch-yoke, compressor.* TECUMSEH PRODUCTS CO.

Figure 5-3B. *The action of a scotch-yoke compressor: The scotch-yoke mechanism allows the four cylinders of a large-capacity compressor system to be assembled in a radial arrangement of very small axial and diametral dimensions.* TECUMSEH PRODUCTS CO.

sor are allowed to pull into a sustained vacuum, the compressor may burn out from a lack of lubrication. These compressors are therefore limited in their application. *When swash-plate compressors are used on cold-plate systems, careful engineering is needed to avoid sustained vacuums.*

Mounting Compressors

Hermetic compressors are generally bolted to a base plate (a skid) to which is also fastened a condenser (air- or water-cooled) and other parts of the system. This is all quite straightforward. Belt-driven compressors require a little more thought.

A compressor in automotive use needs up to a maximum of 15 h.p. to drive it. In a boat, the lower

operating temperatures sharply reduce output because the vapor volume per pound of refrigerant circulated increases with lower temperatures, so the weight of refrigerant pumped by a compressor decreases. The overall system capacity is reduced correspondingly. Automotive compressors used in boat refrigeration systems generally require no more than 2 h.p. to drive them. (I deal with the calculations later in this chapter in the section on sizing). Even so, 2 h.p. is a pretty good load, and compressors need to be solidly mounted to avoid excessive belt wear and the problems caused by vibration. Reciprocal compressors, in particular, set up pulsating loads, which frequently cause vibration problems.

Compressors can be mounted either directly to an engine, using standard automobile mounts, or on a separate base fastened to a boat's hull or a bulkhead

service ports   clutch bearings   field coil (clutch)

cylinder head   rotor with cam (rotates)

valve plate   pistons   "wobble" plate (moves up and down but does not rotate)

Figure 5-4. *A swash-plate compressor.*

(see Figure 5-5). The latter should only be done when the engine is rigidly mounted. If the engine has flexible feet (most do nowadays), the loads of a hull-mounted compressor can flex the engine sideways and cause misalignment of the propeller shaft, leading to premature failure of the Cutless bearing or transmission oil seal.

The driving pulley, generally on the front of the engine's crankshaft, or on an electric motor, needs to be precisely aligned with the driven pulley on the compressor. Check this by removing the pulley belt and dropping a length of wooden doweling into the two pulley grooves. Misalignment will be immediately obvious (see Figure 5-6).

Whatever way the compressor is mounted, it should be as close to its driving pulley as possible—long belt runs frequently cause problems.

Some means of tensioning a drive belt must be provided. Setting the compressor on an adjustable mount is one way. A spring-loaded or adjustable *idler* pulley set up to bear against the belt is another (see Figure 5-7). Such pulleys should be on the *slack* side of the belt run. Compressor belts need to be set up tightly—in general, no more than 3/8-inch belt depression under moderate finger pressure in the center of the longest stretch of belt run.

Long belt runs, especially on reciprocal compressors, occasionally experience excessive vibration between pulleys. Additional idler pulleys will be needed in these long belt runs.

When a compressor is driven by an engine that has other belt-driven equipment mounted to it (e.g., an alternator), attempt to have the loads pulling from opposite sides—i.e., counterposed—so that the side-

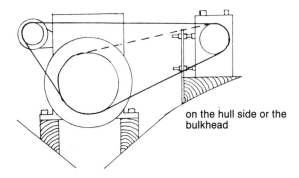

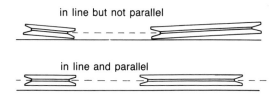

Figure 5-6. *Pulley alignment.*

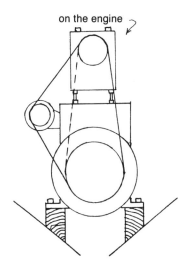

Figure 5-5. *Compressor mounting arrangements. The drive belts are tensioned with adjustable feet or using the alternator, or with an idler pulley (not shown).*

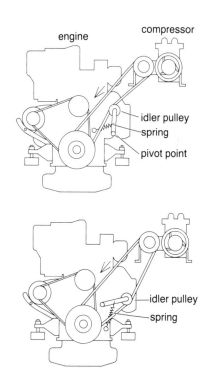

Figure 5-7. *Idler pulley arrangements. The idler pulley goes on the slack side of the belt. (In most setups, the belt from the engine pulley would drive the compressor assembly directly, without the intermediate pulley shown here.)*

ways pulls on the crankshaft tends to cancel out. *Excessive side loading of crankshafts can lead to failure of the oil seal and bearing.* Before making any installation, always check the manufacturer's specifications on the engine to ensure that it can handle the load of a refrigeration compressor.

The drive pulley and the compressor pulley must be sized to produce the correct compressor speed. All automotive compressors are designed for minimum operating speeds of 500 to 1,000 revolutions per minute (rpm); normal operating speeds of 3,000 to 4,000 rpm; and maximum operating speeds of 6,000 to 7,000 rpm. Industrial compressors run much more slowly—300 rpm to a maximum of 1,750 rpm. The larger the compressor, the slower it turns.

The faster a compressor spins, the lower its efficiency, and in boat use, automotive compressors never run anywhere near their maximum speed. Keeping them between 1,000 and 2,000 rpm is best. (Note: In the first edition of this book, I outlined a system based on a compressor speed of 3,000 rpm.

Table 5-1. *Sizing an Engine-driven Pulley*

Normal engine speed when refrigerating	Desired compressor speed (rpm)							
	500	750	1,000	1,250	1,500	2,000	2,500	3,000
1,000	3" (2 1/4")	4 1/2" (3 3/8")	6" (4 1/2")	7 1/2" (5 5/8")	9" (6 3/4")	12" (9")	15" (11 1/4")	18" (13 1/2")
1,500	2" (1 1/2")	3" (2 1/4")	4" (3")	5" (3 3/4")	6" (4 1/2")	8" (6")	10" (7 1/2")	12" (9")
2,000	1 1/2"	2 1/4" (1 5/8")	3" (2 1/4")	3 3/4" (2 3/4")	4 1/2" (3 3/8")	6" (4 1/2")	7 1/2" (5 5/8")	9" (6 3/4")
2,500		1 4/5"	2 2/5" (1 4/5")	3" (2 1/4")	3 3/5" (2 7/10")	4 4/5" (3 3/5")	6" (4 1/2")	7 1/5" (5 2/5")
3,000			2" (1 1/2")	2 1/2" (1 7/8")	3" (2 1/4")	4" (3")	5" (3 3/4")	6" (4 1/2")

Engine pulley size for a 6-inch compressor pulley or, in brackets, for a 4 1/2-inch compressor pulley.

This works, but it drives the compressor hard.) Industrial compressors should be set up to run at the speeds shown in the manufacturer's specifications.

Automotive compressor pulleys generally come in diameters of 4 1/2 inches and 6 inches, varying the size of the driving pulley on the engine is the easiest way to adjust the compressor's speed. You can determine the size of the pulley by the following procedure:

1. Decide on the necessary normal operating speed for the compressor (see the "Compressor Sizing Procedures"). This will generally be between 1,000 and 2,000 rpm.
2. Determine the normal operating speed of the engine during refrigerating. This is **not** the maximum engine speed, or necessarily the normal cruising speed. For example, if a cruising boat spends long hours using its engine to refrigerate at anchor, the normal operating speed during refrigerating may be little more than idle speed.
3. Size the engine-driven pulley to produce the desired compressor speed at the normal engine operating speed when refrigerating (see Table 5-1).
4. Check to see that the compressor does not overspeed at maximum engine speed. This is unlikely but should be checked anyway.

An example: We want a compressor speed of 1,500 rpm. Normal engine operating speed when refrigerating is 1,000 rpm. The compressor has a 6-inch pulley, so the engine will need a 9-inch pulley. Maximum engine speed is 3,500 rpm, producing a maximum compressor speed of 5,250 rpm, which is within tolerable limits for an automotive compressor.

Compressor Sizing Procedures

Let's recap where we are in sizing our system at this point. In Chapter 2, we determined the 24-hour rate of heat leak of our icebox in its intended use. If we use a constant-cycling unit, we need to keep running time down to approximately 20 minutes in an hour. To do this, the compressor capacity must be three times the hourly icebox heat leak. An additional 25 percent must be added to this capacity to allow for inefficiencies introduced by heat from the compressor and other extraneous sources, which are collectively known as *mechanical heat*. In our sample refrigerator with a daily heat loss of 2,400 Btus, the hourly heat leak is 100 Btus. Compressor capacity must therefore be [(100×3) + 25 percent] = 375 Btus per hour. In our freezer with a daily heat leak of 4,000 Btus, the figure is 625 Btus per hour.

Rather than constant-cycling refrigeration, we chose cold plates and an engine-driven compressor run just once a day. The next thing we decided was how long we wished to run our unit each day. We fixed on 45 minutes, giving us a pull-down of 3,200 Btus per hour in refrigerator use and 5,333 Btus per hour in freezer use. We designed our cold plates to achieve this rate of pull-down. Now we must size our compressor to give us the necessary Btu output. Remember that we are assuming a compressor suction temperature (evaporator temperature) of 0°F in refrigerator use and −20°F in freezer use, and a net refrigerating effect of 45 Btus per pound of R-12 circulated through the system.

First, we need to divide our rate of pull-down by the net refrigerating effect per pound of R-12. This will tell us how many pounds of R-12 we must circulate in an hour (3200 ÷ 45 = 71; 5,333 ÷ 45 = 118.5). Using Table 1-1 in Chapter 1, we can see that R-12 has a vapor volume of 1.6 cubic feet per pound at 0°F; 2.5 cubic feet per pound at −20°F. We can now calculate the *volume* of refrigerant we must circulate to get the refrigeration we want. In a refrigerator with an evaporator temperature of 0°F, it will be 71 × 1.6 = 114 cubic feet per hour; in freezer use, with an evaporator temperature of −20°F, it will be 296.25 cubic feet per hour. Finally, we need to convert this figure to cubic inches per minute by multiplying by [(12 × 12 × 12) ÷ 60]. We arrive at 3,283 cubic inches per minute for a refrigerator, and 8,532 cubic inches per minute for a freezer. Adding 25 percent for mechanical heat, our totals are 4,104 cubic inches per minute for a refrigerator, and 10,665 cubic inches per minute for a freezer. Table 5-2 summarizes these procedures for refrigerators and freezers.

We now have to pick a compressor that, at a certain operating speed, will circulate this required volume of vapor. All compressors have a certain displacement given in cubic inches. This is the *theoretical volume* of vapor moved through the compressor at each revolution. If this figure is multiplied by a specific compressor speed, given in rpm, we have the theoretical volume of vapor in cubic inches moved by this compressor in one minute. In practice, things are not quite this simple.

Volumetric Efficiency (VE).

There are certain unavoidable inefficiencies in operating any compressor. For example, when a piston is pushed up a cylinder, a small pocket of gas will always be left at the top of the stroke. It stops the piston from hitting the cylinder head. During a compression stroke, the gas compressed into this space is not driven out of the cylinder. During a suction stroke it re-expands, occupying cylinder space and reducing the volume of fresh gas drawn into the cylinder. Other inefficiencies include losses due to inertia in moving the refrigerant into and out of the cylinders, especially at higher compressor speeds; leaks through valves and down the sides of pistons; and heat from the operation of the compressor warming the incoming vapor. Warming causes it to expand and occupy more space, which reduces the amount (weight) of refrigerant pumped through the compressor.

The net result of all these losses is that compressors only move between 40 percent and 75 percent of the refrigerant they are theoretically capable of moving. This is the *volumetric efficiency* of a compressor. The lower the suction temperature (evaporator temperature) and the faster a compressor operates, the lower its volumetric efficiency. In boats, I like to assume a conservative volumetric efficiency of 50 percent. For a freezer or at high operating speeds, volumetric efficiency may even go as low as 40 percent. Given a 50 percent volumetric efficiency, we must divide by 2 the theoretical volume of vapor moved by a compressor at any given speed in order to find the actual volume of vapor moved. Table 5-3 summarizes these calculations for compressors of varying displacement at a variety of operating speeds. This table understates compressor performance at slow speeds. It will be excessively conservative if a system is built around a slow-turning industrial compressor.

Compressor Size and Speed.

From Table 5-2, we take the volume of refrigerant that we need to move through our compressor. We enter the body of Table 5-3 with this figure and read off the compressor displacements and operating speeds that will meet this

Table 5-2. *Volume of Refrigerant That Must Be Circulated for a Given Rate of Pull-down*

Rate of pull-down (Btus/hr)	Refrigerator (0°F evaporator temperature; 1.6 cu.ft./lb. of refrigerant)		Freezer (−20°F evaporator temperature; 2.5 cu.ft./lb. of refrigerant)	
	Volume in cu.in./min.	+25% for mechanical heat	Volume in cu.in./min.	+25% for mechanical heat
200	204.8	256	320	400
300	307.2	384	480	600
400	409.6	512	640	800
500	512	640	800	1,000
600	614.4	768	960	1,200
750	768	960	1,200	1,500
1,000	1,024	1,280	1,600	2,000
1,250	1,280	1,600	2,000	2,500
1,500	1,536	1,920	2,400	3,000
1,750	1,792	2,240	2,800	3,500
2,000	2,048	2,560	3,200	4,000
2,500	2,560	3,200	4,000	5,000
3,000	3,072	3,840	4,800	6,000
3,500	3,584	4,480	5,600	7,000
4,000	4,096	5,120	6,400	8,000
4,500	4,608	5,760	7,200	9,000
5,000	5,120	6,400	8,000	10,000
6,000	6,144	7,680	9,600	12,000
7,000	7,168	8,960	11,200	14,000
8,000	8,192	10,240	12,800	16,000
9,000	9,236	11,545	14,400	18,000
10,000	10,240	12,800	16,000	20,000

Assumptions: R-12 use; net refrigerating effect is 45 Btus/lb.
Enter the table on the left with the required rate of pull-down on a system in Btus/hr and read off the volume of refrigerant that must be circulated in cu.in./min. for either refrigerator or freezer use.

Table 5-3. *Volume of Vapor Moved By a Compressor With Volumetric Efficiency of 50%* (cu.in./min.)

Compressor swept volume (cu.in.)	Compressor speed (rpm)											
	250	500	750	1,000	1,250	1,500	1,750	2,000	2,250	2,500	2,750	3,000
1	125	250	375	500	625	750	875	1,000	1,125	1,250	1,375	1,500
2	250	500	750	1,000	1,250	1,500	1,750	2,000	2,250	2,500	2,750	3,000
3	375	750	1,125	1,500	1,875	2,250	2,625	3,000	3,375	3,750	4,125	4,500
4	500	1,000	1,500	2,000	2,500	3,000	3,500	4,000	4,500	5,000	5,500	6,000
5	625	1,250	1,875	2,500	3,125	3,750	4,375	5,000	5,625	6,250	6,875	7,500
6	750	1,500	2,250	3,000	3,750	4,500	5,250	6,000	6,750	7,500	8,250	9,000
7	875	1,750	2,625	3,500	4,375	5,250	6,125	7,000	7,875	8,750	9,625	10,500
8	1,000	2,000	3,000	4,000	5,000	6,000	7,000	8,000	9,000	10,000	11,000	12,000
9	1,125	2,250	3,375	4,500	5,625	6,750	7,875	9,000	10,125	11,250	12,375	13,500
10	1,250	2,500	3,750	5,000	6,250	7,500	8,750	10,000	11,250	12,500	13,750	15,000

cu.in./min. assuming a 50% VE

Search in the body of the table for the volume of vapor that was determined in Table 5-2. Then read off the different-size compressors and operating speeds that will move this volume of vapor.
Note: This table understates compressor performance at slow speeds. It will be excessively conservative if a system is built around a slow-turning industrial compressor.

requirement. We then compare these figures to those given in the manufacturers' specifications on various compressors to find one suitable for our application. Remember, Table 5-3 is already corrected for a volumetric efficiency of 50 percent—no further correction is needed. If you want to work with a different volumetric efficiency, you will have to make the calculations yourself. Remember also to avoid swash-plate and hermetic compressors on systems that are likely to pull into a sustained vacuum—in particular, freezers and parallel cold-plate installations with independent shut-down controls on the individual plates.

Horsepower (H.P.) Requirements.
In order to calculate the amount of horsepower you will need to drive any given compressor, use the following formula:

$$\text{HP} = \{[(\text{Btus added} \times \text{weight of refrigerant circulated}) \div 2546] \times 100 \div \%\text{VE}\} + 20\%,$$

where:

Btus added = (Btu content of the R-12 vapor at the compressor discharge temperature − Btu content of the vapor at the suction temperature),

and

weight of refrigerant circulated = (Btus per hr. ÷ net refrigerating effect)

The additional 20 percent is a fudge factor to compensate for friction losses in the driving belt, etc.

The only information we do not currently have is the discharge temperature of the compressor and the Btu content of the vapor at the compressor suction and discharge temperatures. In most boat refrigeration applications *with a water-cooled condenser,* the discharge temperature is going to be 100°F to 125°F. A compressor with an air-cooled condenser is likely to have a discharge temperature around 130°F in the tropics, but sometimes as high as 160°F. If we refer to Table 1-1 in Chapter 1, we can find the Btu content of R-12 *vapor* at these temperatures (column 5), as well as at the temperature in our evaporator. (In *constant-cycling* refrigeration, the evaporator temperature will be around 20°F for a small refrigerator only, and around 0°F for a refrigerator with a freezer box. In *cold-plate* refrigeration, the evaporator temperature will be around 0°F in a refrigerator; −20°F in a

Table 5-4. *Btu Content of R-12 Vapor*

Evaporator temperature	Btus/lb
+20°F	79.4
0°F	77.3
−20°F	75.2
100°F	87.6
125°F	89.0

freezer.) Table 5-4 gives the Btu content of R-12 vapor at these temperatures. We are now ready to enter the formula in relation to our sample icebox.

1. Cold-plate refrigerator. We need to circulate 71 pounds of R-12 per hour. Assuming a VE of 50 percent, an evaporator temperature of 0°F, and a compressor discharge temperature of 125°F (the highest likely), our h.p. requirement will be:

$$\{[(89.0 - 77.3) \times 71 \div 2,546] \times 100 \div 50\} + 20\% = 0.65 + 0.13 = 0.78 \text{ h.p.}$$

Adding 25 percent for mechanical heat, we need a total of 0.98 h.p.

2. Cold-plate freezer. We need to circulate 118.5 pounds of R-12 per hour. Assuming a VE of 40 percent (the lowest likely), an evaporator temperature of −20°F, and a compressor discharge temperature of 125°F (the highest likely), our h.p. requirement will be:

$$\{[(89.0 - 75.2) \times 118.5 \div 2546] \times 100 \div 40\} + 20\% = 1.6 + 0.32 = 1.93 \text{ h.p.}$$

Adding 25 percent for mechanical heat, we need a total of 2.41 h.p.

If we succeed in holding the compressor discharge temperature to 100°F, we arrive at the following requirements: in a refrigerator, 0.81 h.p.; in a freezer, 2.06 h.p. Keeping the compressor cool has obvious benefits.

Compression Ratio.
Calculate the compression ratio of a compressor in refrigeration use by dividing the suction pressure into the discharge pressure, but *first convert the pressures to absolute pressure (psia).* Do this by adding 14.7 psi to the given pressures (see Chapter 1).

Where suction pressures fall into a vacuum, convert a reading in inches of mercury ($''$ Hg) to psi by dividing by 2. Then add 14.7 to convert this figure to psia. For example:

$$-5.4'' \text{ Hg} = \text{approximately } -2.7 \text{ psi} = -2.7 + 14.7 = 12 \text{ psia.}$$

Returning to our sample system, we must change our compressor suction and discharge temperatures to psi (Table 1-1), then convert psi to psia. We get:

1. Refrigerator:

suction temperature of 0°F = 9.2 psi = 23.9 psia
discharge temperature (maximum) = 125°F
   = 169.1 psi = 183.8 psia

The compression ratio is:

$$183.8 \div 23.9 = 7.7{:}1$$

2. Freezer use:

suction temperature of −20 F = 0.6 psi = 15.3 psia
discharge temperature (maximum) = 125°F
   = 183.8 psia

The compression ratio is:

$$183.8 \div 15.3 = 12.0{:}1$$

At a discharge temperature of 100°F, the compression ratios are 5.5:1 for a refrigerator; 8.6:1 for a freezer.

It is not a good idea to allow the compression ratio to go above 10:1 because it overloads the compressor. This example illustrates the importance of keeping down the compressor discharge temperature, therefore pressure (known as *head pressure*), especially in freezer work. This subject is covered in the next chapter.

Compressor Choices

Hermetic Compressors. In almost all instances, a hermetic compressor is the best choice for constant-cycling refrigeration units. If this is your choice, simply calculate the Btu requirements of your icebox, add 25 percent to allow for mechanical heat, then buy a complete condensing unit (a compressor, condenser, and other components properly matched and neatly packaged on a skid) that matches your requirements.

The 24-hour capacity of the condensing unit should be at least twice, preferably three times, the figure calculated above so that the unit runs no more than 20 to 30 minutes in the hour. What is more, *the Btu capacity of the condensing unit must be rated in the kind of conditions found on a boat.* In particular, an air-cooled condensing unit for a boat that will be cruised in the tropics needs to be rated in ambient air temperatures of up to 110°F and *condensing* temperatures from 130°F up to 160°F. A water-cooled condensing unit needs to be rated in ambient water temperatures of 85°F to 94°F and condensing temperatures from 105°F to 125°F. For rating purposes, a typical evaporator temperature, without cold plates, in a small refrigerator would be 20°F. It would be 0°F to −10°F if the unit is to have a freezer compartment. *A water-cooled condenser must have a water tube of cupronickel in order to resist corrosion from saltwater.*

These are not typical rating temperatures for refrigeration units in either household or commercial use. Most air-cooled units are rated in an ambient temperature of 90°F and a condensing temperature of

Table 5-5. *Danfoss 12-Volt DC and 24-Volt DC Hermetic Compressors*

Compressor	Evaporator temperature				
	−20°F	−10°F	0°F	10°F	20°F
BD2	95	143	202	256	315
BD2.5	124	185	240	300	362
	Output in Btus/hr				

Assumptions: R-12 use; an ambient temperature of 90°F; a condensing temperature of 130°F; 90°F suction gas temperature.

Notes
1. Given the condensing temperature (no sub-cooling) and the suction-gas temperature, the net refrigerating effect is 47.6 Btus/lb. (see Chapter 1). This is probably a little on the high side and overstates the system's performance by 5 to 10 percent.
2. For every 10°F rise in ambient temperature, output will decline by approximately 8 percent. At an ambient temperature of 110°F in the condensing space, output will be 16 percent lower than stated.
3. Together, points 1 and 2 will reduce output by up to 25 percent in many tropical conditions.
4. The dramatic loss of output at lower evaporator temperatures illustrates the problem of running a freezer from a small hermetic unit.

130°F. Most water-cooled units are rated in an ambient water temperature of 75°F to 85°F. The suction gas temperature is frequently given as 90°F, whereas in reality, it will be much closer to the evaporator temperature (i.e., +20°F to as low as −20°F). The effect of overstating the suction gas temperature is to overrate the unit's capacity by as much as 25 percent. An air-cooled unit will generally lose around 8 percent of its rated output for every 10°F rise in the ambient air temperature. You will have to buy a more powerful unit than is apparently necessary to compensate for these losses. How much more powerful will depend on the actual rating conditions.

The predominant 12-volt and 24-volt DC hermetic compressor and condensing unit manufacturer is Danfoss. Table 5-5 gives some sample specifications for their widely used BD 2.5 unit. When it comes to AC hermetic compressors there are a number of manufacturers competing in this field because hermetic compressors are used in household refrigerators and freezers. Table 5-6 gives some data for Tecumseh compressors.

Hermetic compressors can also be used in certain cold-plate refrigeration applications, but if a hermetic compressor is used, it should have some kind of a low-pressure shut-down built into the system so that the compressor will not pull into a deep vacuum. Similar considerations apply to the use of swash-plate automotive air-conditioning compressors, which can be additionally protected with a high-temperature cutout fastened to the compressor housing. If the compressor begins to overheat—as it will if it starts to burn up—the system will shut down. When sizing hermetic compressors for use with cold plates, assume an evaporator temperature of 0°F for a refrigerator and −20°F for a freezer, and a compressor discharge temperature of 105°F to 125°F. The condenser must be water-cooled, and assume that the ambient water temperature is 85°F to 94°F.

AC hermetic compressors are designed for high-temperature use (air conditioners); medium-temperature use (refrigerators); and low-temperature use (freezers). In almost all instances, boat refrigeration requires a low-temperature compressor. *Use of high- and medium-temperature compressors may result in compressor burnout.*

Belt-Driven Compressors.

Within the general category of automotive compressors, three brands predominate. These are Tecumseh, York, and Sanden (Sankyo). To my mind, the best compressor is the Tecumseh HG 1000. This is a very rugged, cast-iron

Table 5-6. *Sample Air-Cooled Hermetic Condensing Units; Tecumseh Range*

Model #	H.P.	AC volts	Amps	Btu/hr output at select evaporator temperatures				
				−20°F	−10°F	0°F	10°F	20°F
AE1336AA	1/8	115	2.2	320	450	590	740	900
AE1343AA	1/6	115	2.8	400	545	700	855	1,025
AE1360AA	1/5	115	3.0	525	700	885	1,090	1,315
AE2410AC	1/4	115	5.0	900	1,250	1,600	2,000	
AE2415AC	1/3	115	6.5	1,380	1,800	2,200	2,600	
AJ2425AC	1/2	115	8.7	2,160	2,780	3,400	4,160	
AH2435AC	3/4	230	6.8	3,050	4,100	5,200	6,300	
AH2445AC	1	230	9.1	3,750	4,900	6,200	7,600	
AH2466AC	1 1/2	230	10.8	5,200	6,900	8,800	10,950	

Assumptions: R-12 use; ambient air temperature of 90°F; suction-gas temperature of 90°F.

Note: Assuming a suction-gas temperature of 90°F is unrealistic in boat refrigeration. It results in overstating the system's capacity by as much as 25 percent. To be safe, downgrade all output figures by that percentage. Divide by 4 and multiply by 3. For example, 320 Btus/hr becomes (320×3)÷4=240. Now downgrade this 240 Btus/hr by another 10 to 15 percent for a system to be used in the tropics.

(and therefore heavy!) reciprocal compressor, which has proven over many years to be outstanding in boat refrigeration. It is also made in a smaller size—the HG 850. York compressors are very similar in design, essentially substituting an aluminum case for cast iron, therefore being somewhat lighter. York builds three sizes of this compressor: the 206; 209; and 210. Where possible, the heavy-duty (HD) is to be preferred over the standard compressor. The heavy-duty is built for trucks and has a reinforced crankcase.

Sanden (Sankyo) is the leading swash-plate compressor manufacturer, with a number of sizes available: the SD 505, SD 507, SD 508, SD 508 HD (heavy-duty), SD 510, SD 510 HD, SD 708, and SD 709. Table 5-7 gives the actual displacement and typical operating speeds of all these automotive compressors.

Then there are a whole range of belt-driven industrial compressors admirably suited to boat refrigeration. Table 5-8 gives a few sample specifications drawn from the Tecumseh range. Other manufacturers have similar products.

Buying a Compressor

In most states, retail outlets for *commercial* refrigeration equipment do not exist, and wholesale stores will

Table 5-7. *Automotive Compressors in Widespread Boat Refrigeration Use*

Make	Model #	Displacement (cu.in./rev.)	Operating speeds		
			Minimum	Typical in boat refrig.	Maximum
Tecumseh	HG850	8.54	500	1,000–2,000	6,000
	HG1000	10.35	500	1,000–2,000	6,000
York	206	6.1	500	1,000–2,000	6,000
	209	8.7	500	1,000–2,000	6,000
	210	10.3	500	1,000–2,000	6,000
Sanden	SD505	5.3	500	1,000–2,000	6,000
	SD507	6.59	500	1,000–2,000	6,000
	SD508	8.42	500	1,000–2,000	6,000
	SD510	9.82	500	1,000–2,000	6,000
	SD708	7.9	500	1,000–2,000	6,000
	SD709	9.5	500	1,000–2,000	6,000

Note: The Tecumseh and York compressors are reciprocal compressors; the Sanden are swash-plate. The series 5 Sanden has five cylinders; the series 7 has seven cylinders.

Table 5-8. *Small Industrial Belt-driven Tecumseh Compressors*

Model #	H.P.	Operating speed		Displacement (cu.in.)	Weight (lb.)
		Minimum	Maximum		
CB	$1/8$	475	850	1.53	30
CA	$1/6$	475	850	2.33	30
CD	$1/4$	475	850	3.06	37
CC	$1/3$	475	850	4.66	37
CE	$1/2$	475	950	5.06	37
CG850	$3/4-1$	500	1,750	8.54	37
CG1000	$1^1/2$	500	1,750	10.35	37

only sell to licensed refrigeration experts. This is to protect the public from untrained people. However, very often these stores will sell items for cash if you know what you want and look like you are in the business! Otherwise you will have to find a licensed person to make purchases for you.

Automotive equipment, on the other hand, is available from any good automotive parts store. All of the automotive compressors mentioned in the text are widely available. Rebuilt compressors can be bought for around half the cost of new ones. They are reliable and offer good value for the money.

Compressors (and other equipment) can also be salvaged from low-mileage junked cars for very little cost. Never take equipment from a system that has been opened (e.g., hoses cut or other components removed). The slightest bit of dirt in the compressor will likely cause major problems later on. Make sure the compressor is not seized. Do this by gripping the center of the compressor drive pulley (not its rim) and turning the compressor over by hand. When removing the compressor, be sure to cap all openings to keep out dirt. After the compressor is installed in your system, check the oil level before you run it (see Chapter 8).

When all is said and done, the compressor is generally no more than 20 percent of the cost of a holding-plate refrigeration system. Unless your budget is very tight, avoid using salvaged equipment.

Chapter 6

Condensers: Ensuring Liquidity

When a refrigeration unit first kicks on, the compressor begins to compress the vapor in the system. The pressure, and therefore the temperature, builds up on the discharge (high) side of the compressor. The hot compressed gas pumped out of the compressor is passed to a condenser. Here the gas begins to lose heat to the cooling medium (air or water). The higher the pressure, and therefore the temperature, of the gas discharged from the compressor, the greater the temperature differential between this gas and the cooling medium in the condenser. The greater the temperature differential, the greater the rate of heat removal from the gas.

After a while the increasing discharge pressure, and therefore temperature, of the refrigerant coupled to the increasing rate of heat removal in the condenser brings the refrigerant to a point at which it starts to condense—the refrigerant starts to liquefy. The compressor discharge pressure (its head pressure), and therefore the temperature of the discharged gas, continues to rise *until the rate at which the refrigerant liquefies equals the output from the compressor*. At this point the system stabilizes. Heat is being removed from the gas in the condenser as fast as the compressor is pumping in fresh heat with new gas.

If the cooling medium rises in temperature, the temperature differential decreases between the hot compressed gas in the condenser and the cooling medium. The compressor drives up the head pressure until the temperature differential in the condenser is restored. At this point the rate of heat removal returns to what it was previously, and the system stabilizes at this new discharge pressure and discharge gas temperature. If the cooling medium falls in temperature, the head pressure and discharge gas temperature fall correspondingly.

The function of a condenser is to remove heat at a rate that allows the refrigerant to liquefy at the desired compressor head pressure. The biggest compressor in the world, and the best cold plate, will be worthless if the condenser cannot remove at an adequate rate the heat absorbed from the cold plate.

Since air temperatures in the enclosed spaces of a boat in the tropics can rise to well above 100°F, the efficiency of an air-cooled condenser is frequently minimal, even with small constant-cycling refrigeration units. The standard air-cooled refrigerator condenser just cannot handle the loads of any substantial refrigeration system. *There is no substitute for a water-cooled condenser.* The only time an air-cooled condenser is really justified in boat refrigeration is where a small auxiliary AC or DC hermetic refrigeration unit runs from shorepower when the boat is docked and the owners are away. If the owners close the seacocks for safety's sake, an air-cooled condenser must be used.

Air-Cooled Condensers

Two things are critical to the performance of an air-cooled condenser: (1) the temperature differential in the condenser between the hot gas discharged from the compressor and the air flowing through the condenser; (2) the rate at which air flows through the condenser. We know from this that a condenser must be located in the coolest spot possible (not an engine room!) and with adequate ducting to ensure a good airflow. You should lead the inlet duct to the bottom of the condenser compartment and the exit duct from the top (hot air rises). If you can duct in cooler air from outside the boat without interfering with its watertight integrity, so much the better.

Condenser fans are best placed inside a *shroud* that directs all the airflow over the condenser cooling fins. Be sure the fan is operating in the correct direction! Some DC fans will operate backwards if the positive and negative leads are crossed. Condenser fins must be kept clean and unobstructed to work effectively.

Water-Cooled Condensers

Water-cooled condensers are of two basic types—*the water chamber or shell type* and the *tube-in-a-tube* condenser.

Shell-Type Condensers. The shell-type condenser consists of a coil, through which the cooling water passes, inserted in a cylinder, through which the refrigerant circulates. The refrigerant is cooled and liquefies, and the bottom of the condenser then acts as a storage chamber for the liquid refrigerant (see Figure 6-1).

Because of the pressure of the refrigerant gas on the walls of a shell-type condenser it must be strongly constructed. Steel is best, but bronze or naval brass are essential for a marine environment. But if the refrigerant is passed through the coil and the water circulated in the cylinder, very little pressure is exerted on the walls of the cylinder. This has led some people to construct shell-type condensers by inserting a copper or cupronickel coil inside a plastic pipe,

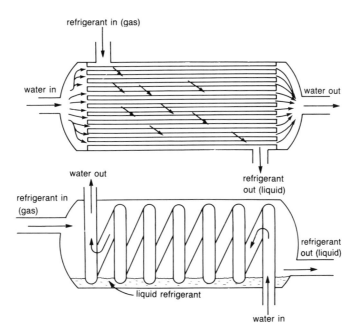

Figure 6-1. *Shell-type condensers. The shell-type condenser consists of a coil inserted into a cylinder. Cooling water passes through the coil and refrigerant circulates through the cylinder. As the refrigerant condenses, it collects in the receiver at the bottom of the condenser.*

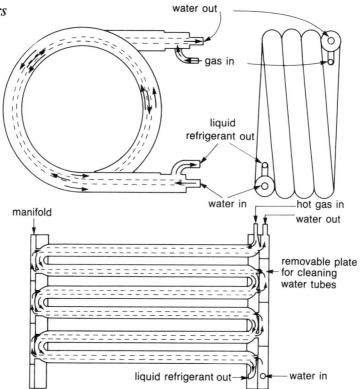

Figure 6-2. *Tube-in-tube condensers have a coil running through a larger coil. Water runs through the inner one and gas through the outer one. Hot gas enters the condenser at the same end from which cooling water exits. This promotes a uniform rate of cooling throughout the length of the condenser. The manifold on the bottom condenser makes cleaning the inside of the coil easier.*

sealing the ends of the pipe and making the appropriate connections with readily available plumbing fittings. A very inexpensive condenser can be made easily. One of the key factors in condenser efficiency, however, is the *speed of the water flow through the condenser*. In the plastic condenser, this rate of flow is greatly reduced, compared to a regular shell-type condenser. A boundary layer of stagnant water forms around the refrigerant coil, substantially reducing efficiency. Despite its low cost and ease of fabrication, such a condenser should not be used, and none of the calculations in the section on sizing apply to it.

Tube-in-a-Tube Condensers. The tube-in-a-tube condenser consists of a coil, through which water passes, inserted in a larger coil, through which

the refrigerant circulates. This type of condenser can be further broken down into those with or without a *manifold* (see Figure 6-2).

Tube-in-a-tube condensers are the most efficient, and I strongly recommend them for marine refrigeration. Key features in design and installation are a water tube of *cupronickel* (not just of copper, since copper corrodes in saltwater), a zinc *pencil anode* installed in the cooling circuit to protect against electrolytic corrosion, and having the water pass through the condenser in the opposite direction to the refrigerant gas. This way the warmest water is alongside the warmest gas, and the coldest water alongside the coldest refrigerant, which promotes a uniform rate of cooling throughout the length of the condenser (see Figure 6-3).

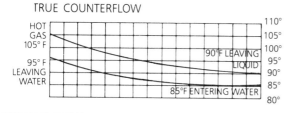

TRUE COUNTERFLOW

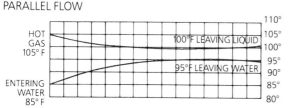

PARALLEL FLOW

Figure 6-3. *The relationship of the direction of water flow to cooling rates in condensers.* STANDARD REFRIGERATION CO.

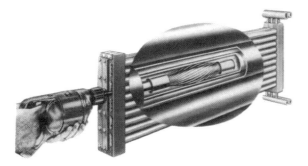

Figure 6-4. *Cleaning a manifold-type condenser.* STANDARD REFRIGERATION CO.

Over time, the water tube is liable to become plugged with scale and sludge deposits. Manifold-type tube-in-a-tube condensers have the distinct advantage of being relatively easily opened and rodded out (see Figure 6-4). A spiral-type tube-in-a-tube condenser can be cleaned with a flexible brush, but this is much harder.

Installation of a Water-Cooled Condenser

The refrigerant is almost always in the *external* tube on a water-cooled condenser, with the water in the *internal* tube. As a consequence, the exterior surface of the condenser interacts to a certain extent with the surrounding ambient atmosphere, and a condenser placed in a hot engine room will pick up a certain amount of extraneous heat. Apart from the obvious consideration of not placing a condenser next to a hot exhaust pipe, the location is not too critical. The main thing is to place it where it is most convenient to running water and refrigerant lines, and where you can get at it for cleaning and draining (very important in the winter).

You should keep water and refrigerant lines as short and as straight as possible. Long lines and bends introduce friction, which reduces performance (see Chapter 8). A condenser must also be so placed that it can be fully drained in freezing temperatures. If the water side freezes and ruptures, the entire refrigeration system will be extensively damaged.

Water Circuits. Many engine-driven refrigeration units use the raw-water cooling pump on the boat's engine to circulate water through the condenser. The condenser is placed in the engine cooling circuit before the engine so that water first passes through the condenser. When an engine has greater water requirements than a condenser, some sort of a bypass line is also fitted so that only a portion of the engine cooling water passes through the condenser. After cooling the engine, the water generally passes through a water-cooled silencer (muffler) and out of the engine exhaust. Such a system is inexpensive because it saves on the cost of a water pump for the condenser and on the cost of a separate overboard discharge seacock. I do not like it for several reasons:

1. Most small marine diesels have a limited flow of cooling water—frequently no more than two gallons a minute. This will severely limit the rate of flow through a condenser, which in turn will sharply reduce the efficiency of the condenser.
2. The condenser may raise the temperature of the cooling water entering the engine by as much as 10°F. In warm tropical waters this may be enough to cause a fully loaded engine to overheat.
3. If the condenser plugs up, it will cut off the water supply to the engine altogether and may lead to engine failure. For this reason, *connecting a condenser in series with an engine cooling circuit will void most engine warranties.*

I prefer to give a condenser its own water pump and overboard discharge, although the suction side may be Teed off the engine's water-suction seacock. Even this can cause a couple of problems in exceptional circumstances:

1. If the raw-water filter becomes plugged, the condenser water pump may suck water out of the engine.
2. When the refrigeration unit is shut down, the engine water pump may suck air through the condenser circuit.

In either case the engine warranty is likely to be voided. The owner must weigh the cost of an additional suction seacock and raw-water strainer, plus the risk posed by the extra hole in the hull, against the slim chance of engine damage arising from a shared seacock.

What is not in question is the advantage of a separate overboard discharge seacock set high in the hull. Whenever the refrigeration unit runs, the water flow will be clearly visible. Various flow rate and temperature tests can also be made, which are very useful in monitoring system performance and troubleshooting (see Chapters 10 and 11).

Water Pumps. Two types of pumps predominate in boat refrigeration: rubber impeller pumps (see Figure 6-5) and centrifugal pumps (see Figure 6-6). Each type has distinct advantages and disadvantages.

Rubber impeller pumps, which I call impeller pumps from here on in, are self-priming, which is to say they will draw up water to themselves. Centrifugal pumps are not; they must be installed below the waterline at all angles of heel with the suction piping making a steady run to the pump so that no air gets trapped. If a centrifugal pump is installed above the water level, a check valve will be needed on the suction line in order to maintain its prime. Any time the valve leaks back, the pump will need to be primed manually to get it going again.

An impeller pump cannot be run dry for more than a few seconds because the impeller will tear up. A centrifugal pump, depending on the nature of its shaft seal, may be able to run dry indefinitely.

Even if the suction and discharge lines of an impeller pump are partly clogged, the pump will attempt to shift the same volume of liquid. It will work harder and harder until the vanes strip off the impeller. A centrifugal pump, on the other hand, responds to restrictions by pumping less and less fluid, and doing less and less work.

The volume of flow through a condenser should be sized for the highest ambient water temperature anticipated (normally 85°F in the tropics, but sometimes as high as 94°F). If you cruise into significantly colder waters (e.g., 40°F), the condenser will be greatly oversized. This will drag down the compressor discharge temperature and pressure (head pressure). In extreme circumstances the reduction in discharge temperature and pressure will reduce performance since it cuts down the pressure drop across, and the rate of refrigerant flow through, the expansion valve. It could also result in liquid slugging at the compressor (see Chapter 8), a condition which can do serious damage. The best way to avoid such problems is to simply reduce the rate of water flow through the condenser by closing down a valve on the suction side. Such a restriction in the flow, however, may damage an impeller pump. For this reason a centrifugal pump is preferred.

A cooling circuit would consist of: the suction-side seacock (or a shared seacock with the engine cooling water); a raw-water filter; a valve to control the rate of flow; a check valve if the pump will be above the water level at any angle of heel; a centrifugal pump; the condenser; and the overboard discharge set high in the hull. The circuit will need a drain at its lowest point, placed so that it drains the whole condenser. Somewhere you must place a renewable zinc anode to protect against electrolytic corrosion (see Figure 6-7).

Sizing a Condenser

Air-Cooled Condensers. If you have to use an air-cooled condenser you should buy a complete condensing unit package. This includes the compressor and other components mounted on a common skid. Remember that *normal rating conditions for such a unit do not apply to most boats in the tropics.* Ambient air temperatures in condenser-unit compartments frequently climb to 110°F, perhaps even higher. Most condensing units are rated at an ambient air temperature of 90°F, *so these units will not put out anywhere near their rated capacity in high ambient tempera-*

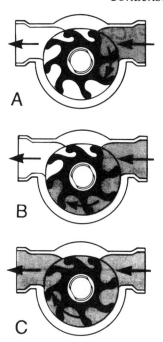

Figure 6-5. *A typical flexible impeller pump and its operation.* (A) *Upon leaving the offset cam, the flexible impeller pump blades expand, creating a vacuum which draws liquid into the pump body.* (B) *As the impeller rotates, each successive blade draws in liquid and carries it to the outlet port.* (C) *The remaining liquid is expelled when the flexible impeller blades are again compressed by the offset cam, creating a continuous uniform flow.*

Below is an exploded view of the flexible impeller pump shown above. 1. Pump cover. 2. Gasket. 3. Impeller (splined type). 4. Wear plate. 5. Pump cover retaining screws. 6. Cam (mounted inside pump body). 7. Cam retaining screw. 8. Pump body. 9. Slinger (to deflect any leaks away from the bearing).

10. Bearing. 11. Bearing retaining circlip. 12. Shaft retaining circlip. 13. Outer seal. 14, 15, 16. Inner seal assembly, lip-type, or 17. Inner seal assembly, carbon-ceramic type. 18. Pump shaft. 19. Drive key. ITT/JABSCO

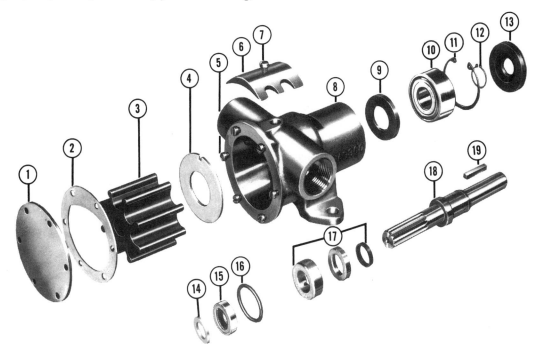

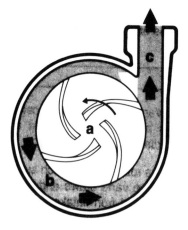

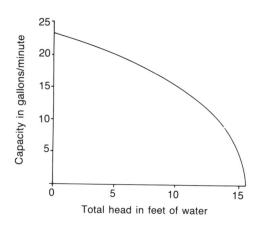

Figure 6-6. *Operation of a centrifugal pump.* **(A)** *Liquid enters the inlet port in the center of the pump. The level of the liquid must be high enough above the pump for gravity to push it into the pump, or the pump must receive an initial priming.* **(B)** *Centrifugal force generated by rotating a curved impeller forces fluid to the periphery of the pump casing, and from there toward the discharge port.* **(C)** *The velocity of the fluid discharge translates into hydraulic pressure in the system downstream from the pump. The flow rate is dependent upon restrictions in the inlet and outlet piping, and the height that the liquid must be lifted.* **(Right)** *Typical performance curve for a centrifugal pump.*

tures. You will have to buy a unit with a larger rated capacity.

Even many condensing units sold specifically for marine use are rated at an ambient air temperature of 90°F. A few are rated at an ambient temperature of 100°F, but none, so far as I know, are rated at 110°F. No wonder so many people have refrigeration problems in the tropics! A rise of just 10°F in the ambient air temperature not only cuts the output from the condensing unit but, at the same time, increases the heat loss from the icebox. All the key factors are moving in the wrong direction.

Water-Cooled Condensers.

The following calculations assume a tube-in-a-tube condenser. The two primary considerations in sizing a water-cooled condenser are the *volume* of water required to carry off the heat of the refrigerant, and the *diameter and length* of the water tube needed to conduct heat out of the refrigerant at the required rate.

Volume of water. Calculate the volume of water required by a condenser using this formula:

$$\text{Btus per hour} = MC(t_1 - t_2),$$

where:

M = the mass of water in pounds per hour
C = the specific heat of the cooling water—
        1.00 for fresh water—0.80 for saltwater
$(t_1 - t_2)$ = the temperature rise in the cooling water
        from one end of the condenser to the
        other. This is normally assumed to be
        10°F.

In the earlier example, our refrigerator needed a system capacity of 3,200 Btus per hour; the freezer, 5,333 Btus per hour. So we get:

  1. Refrigerator:

$$3200 = M \times 0.80 \times 10$$

Therefore:

$$M = 3200/(0.80 \times 10) = 400 \text{ lb/hr}$$

Since one US gallon of seawater weighs 8.3 pounds, this is:

$$400/8.3 = 48.2 \text{ gal/hr} = 0.80 \text{ gal/min}$$

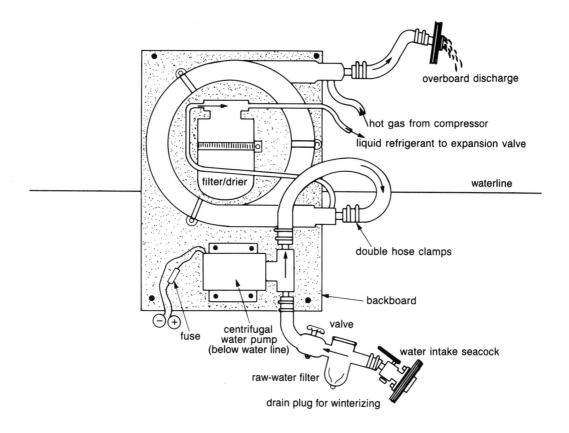

Figure 6-7. *A condenser installation.*

Add 25 percent to this figure to account for *mechanical heat.* This gives a total water requirement of:

$$0.80 + 0.20 = 1.00 \text{ gal/min.}$$

2. Freezer:

$$5333 = M \times 0.80 \times 10$$

Therefore:

$$M = 5333 \div (0.80 \times 10) = 666.6 \text{ lb/hr} =$$
$$666.6/8.3 = 80.3 \text{ gal/hr} = 1.34 \text{ gal/min.}$$

Making a 25-percent allowance for mechanical heat, we have a total water requirement of 1.68 gallons per minute.

Most popular water pumps (flexible impeller and centrifugal) circulate around 4 gallons of water a min-

ute, which is more than adequate. As the volume of water increases the temperature differential decreases for a given Btu condenser capacity between the incoming and outgoing water. For example, a flow of 4 gallons per minute = 240 gal/hr = 1992 lb/hr:

1. Refrigerator:

$$3200 = 1992 \times 0.8 \times (t_1 - t_2)$$

Therefore:

$$(t_1 - t_2) = 3200 \div (1992 \times 0.8) = 2°F.$$

Adding 25 percent for mechanical heat, we arrive at a temperature rise through the condenser of 2.5°F.

2. Freezer:

$$5333 = 1992 \times 0.8 \times (t_1 - t_2)$$

Therefore:

$(t_1 - t_2) = 5333 \div (1992 \times 0.8) = 3.35°F.$

Adding in 25 percent for mechanical heat, we arrive at a temperature rise through the condenser of 4.2°F.

Diameter and length of the water tube. *The rate of heat transfer* in a water-cooled condenser is a function of *the speed of the water flow* through the condenser; *the surface area* of the water tube, and *the temperature differential* between the refrigerant and the water. The refrigerant temperature is taken to be the condensing temperature (CT) of the gas at the compressor's given head pressure (discharge pressure as given by Table 1-1). The water temperature is sometimes taken to be that of the entering seawater (EWT). Sometimes we use the average temperature of the water (AWT) going into and coming out of the condenser—i.e., $(t_1 + t_2) \div 2$.

We already know what rate of heat transfer we need and that tropical seawater is around 85°F, sometimes rising to 94°F. Furthermore, we have based all of our calculations on a compressor discharge temperature of between 100°F and 125°F, giving us a head pressure of 117 psi to 169 psi (see Table 1-1).

A temperature differential between the entering seawater temperature (EWT) and the refrigerant condensing temperature (CT) of around 20°F (105°F CT − 85°F EWT) would be typical. If the temperature (85°F) of the cooling water rises 10°F as it passes through the condenser the average water temperature (AWT) will be 90°F.

Only two variables remain in this situation: the speed of the water flow through the condenser and the surface area of the water tube in the condenser. Given either one, we can calculate the other. Put another way, given a known water pump capacity we can calculate the necessary size and length of the water tube in a condenser for any given rate of heat removal. Or, given a known size and length of water tube, we can calculate what water pump capacity is needed to maintain a given rate of heat removal.

Known pump capacity. Assume a pump flow rate of 4 gallons per minute. There are 7.5 gallons in a cubic foot. Four gallons per minute translates into a flow rate of:

$$4 \div 7.5 = 0.53 \text{ cu.ft./min.} =$$
$$0.53 \times (12 \times 12 \times 12) =$$
$$922 \text{ cu.in/min.}$$

The internal volume of a tube is given by $\pi \times R \times R \times L$, where:

$$\pi = 3.14$$
$$R = \text{inside radius of the tube}$$
$$L = \text{length of the tube}$$

As we saw in Chapter 4, the internal volume of 1/2-inch type-L refrigeration tubing is 1.8 cubic inches per foot of length, and that of 5/8-inch type-L tubing 2.88 cubic inches per foot of length. The same calculations for 3/4-inch type L tubing yields an internal volume of 4.36 cubic inches per foot of length. Given a pump output of 4 gallons per minute the speed of flow through these various tubing sizes is going to be:

1/2-inch tubing: $922 \div 1.8 = 512$ ft/min
5/8-inch tubing: $922 \div 2.88 = 320$ ft/min
3/4-inch tubing: $922 \div 4.36 = 211$ ft/min

In the real world, the rate of heat removal in a water-cooled condenser made of type-L tubing bears the relationship to the speed of the water flow through the condenser shown in Table 6-1.

This rate of heat removal is the K factor for a condenser, much the same as we had a K factor in sizing a cold plate. If the pump output is 4 gallons per minute, a 3/4-inch water tube will remove heat at the rate of 330 Btus per square foot per 1°F temperature differential. A 5/8-inch water tube will result in an even higher K factor, but with greater resistance to flow, therefore

Table 6-1. *Relationship of the Rate of Heat Removal to Speed of Water Flow Through Water-Cooled Condenser*

Speed of water flow (ft/min)	Rate of heat removal*
50	185
150	250
200	330

*(Btus/hr./sq./ft. of condenser water tube surface area, per 1°F temperature differential between CT and AWT.)

CT = condensing temperature
AWT = average cooling water temperature

pressure drop, through the condenser. Pressure drop causes a reduction in the volume of flow. A compromise between *speed of flow* and *volume of flow* is necessary and a good point at which to make this compromise is 200 feet per minute or less. (Since I do not have any figures for faster rates of flow than 200 feet per minute, in the following calculations whenever the water speed exceeds this rate of flow I assume a K factor of 330 Btus. In reality the K factor is likely to be higher, so the calculations will be on the conservative side.)

The formula used to find the length of the water tube in the condenser is the same as the one we used to find the length of the evaporator coil in a cold plate:

$$\text{Capacity of the condenser (Btus/hr)}$$
$$= K \times A \times (t_1 - t_2),$$

where:

K = as defined above
A = the external surface area of the water tube, in square feet
$(t_1 - t_2)$ = the temperature differential between the condensing temperature (CT) of the refrigerant and the average water temperature (AWT) or 15°F in a typical situation.

We are set to enter the formula:
1. In a refrigerator:

$$3200 = K \times A \times (t_1 - t_2)$$

Therefore (using 3/4-inch or smaller tubing):

$$A = 3200/(330 \times 15) = 0.65 \text{ sq.ft.}$$

Add 25 percent for mechanical heat losses and this gives a total of 0.81 square feet.
2. In freezer:

$$5333 = K \times A \times (t_1 - t_2)$$

Therefore (using 3/4-inch or smaller tubing):

$$A = 5333/(330 \times 15) = 1.06 \text{ sq.ft.}$$

Add 25 percent for mechanical heat losses and this gives a total of 1.35 square feet.

To find the length of tubing necessary to provide this surface area, we must divide the surface area by the circumference ($\pi \times D$) of the tubing (see Chapter 4). The relevant figures for circumferences are:

1/2-inch type-L tubing: 1.57 in. = 0.13 ft.
5/8-inch type-L tubing: 1.96 in. = 0.16 ft.
3/4-inch type-L tubing: 2.36 in. = 0.2 ft.

Therefore:
1. In a condenser for a refrigerator:

$0.81 \div 0.13$ = 6.2 feet of 1/2-inch tubing.
$0.81 \div 0.16$ = 5 feet of 5/8-inch tubing.
$0.81 \div 0.2$ = 4 feet of 3/4-inch tubing.

2. In a condenser for a freezer:

$1.35 \div 0.13$ = 10.4 feet of 1/2-inch tubing
$1.35 \div 0.16$ = 8.44 feet of 5/8-inch tubing
$.35 \div 0.2$ = 6.75 feet of 3/4-inch tubing

Condensers are generally made longer than called for in most of these calculations, enabling them to be used with a smaller volume of water, or giving considerable excess capacity in the situation illustrated. In time the water tube in a condenser will develop a coating of slime and perhaps a build-up of scale, which will seriously impair the rate of heat transfer through it. *An oversized condenser is the best possible insurance against future problems.*

Known condenser tube. Given a certain size and length of water tube in a condenser, we can readily calculate the surface area of the tube, and from this work backwards to calculate the K factor needed in this condenser for any given capacity. From the K factor, we can work back to find the flow rate of the water and therefore water pump capacity, for this size of tubing. For example, a 10-foot long, 5/8-inch OD type-L water tube's area is:

$$\pi \times D \times L, \text{ where } \pi = 3.14, D = 0.625,$$
$$\text{and } L = 10 \text{ ft.} = 120 \text{ in.}$$

Therefore:

$$A = 3.14 \times 0.625 \times 120 = 235.5 \text{ sq.ins}$$
$$= 1.64 \text{ sq.ft.}$$

In our refrigerator we have:

$$3200 = K \times A \times 15$$

Therefore:

$$K = 3200/(1.64 \times 15) = 130$$

In our freezer we have:

$$5333 = K \times A \times 15$$

Therefore:

$$K = 5333/(1.64 \times 15) = 217$$

Referring back to the K factors for various speeds of water flow, we can see that we need no more than 50 feet per minute in the refrigerator condenser, and 150 feet per minute in the freezer condenser. Since the internal volume of 5/8-inch type-L refrigeration tubing is 2.88 cubic inches per foot of length, a flow rate of 50 feet per minute will move a volume of:

$$2.88 \times 50 = 144 \text{ cu.in./min.}$$

A flow rate of 150 feet per minute will move:

$$2.88 \times 150 = 432 \text{ cu.in./min.}$$

$$144 \text{ cu.in./min.} = 144 \div (12 \times 12 \times 12) =$$
$$0.083 \text{ cu.ft./min.} = 0.083 \times 7.5$$
$$= 0.62 \text{ gal./min.}$$

Add 25 percent for mechanical heat and the total is 0.78 gallons per minute. This is the minimum volume of water we must pump through this condenser to achieve the necessary rate of pull-down in a refrigerator and still keep within the parameters outlined for the ambient water temperature and compressor head pressure. The same calculations for our freezer yield a minimum flow rate of 2.35 gallons per minute.

Size of Refrigerant Tube. In the kind of condenser under consideration the water tube is inside the refrigerant tube. Adequate clearance between the two tubes is essential for the refrigerant to flow without undue restriction. Whatever size of water tube is used, the next larger size of tubing will provide the necessary clearance.

Summary of Condenser Sizing Procedures. Determine necessary condenser capacity in Btus per hour (e.g., 3200 Btus/hr in refrigerator use or 5333 Btus/hr in freezer use in our two examples).

Assuming a known pump capacity.

1. Take the pump capacity and enter Table 6-2 to find a flow rate between 50 and 200 feet per minute. Read off the tubing size necessary to achieve this flow rate.
2. From Table 6-1, find out the nearest K factor corresponding to the rate of flow selected in step 1. Enter Table 6-3 with this K factor, find the required overall condenser Btu capacity, and read off the necessary tubing area.

Table 6-2. *Speed of Water Flow (ft/min) Based on Pump Capacity and Tubing Size*

Pump capacity		Tubing size, type-L refrigeration tubing					
gal/min	cu.in/min	1/4"	3/8"	1/2"	5/8"	3/4"	
0.5	115	338	125	64			Speed of water flow (ft/min)
1.0	230		251	128	79		
1.5	346		377	192	119	80	
2.0	461			256	159	107	
2.5	576			320	199	134	
3.0	691				238	161	
4.0	922				318	214	
5.0	1,152					268	
6.0	1,382					321	

Table 6-3. *Condenser Tube Surface Area*

Condenser water tube surface area (sq.ft.)	K Factor			
	185	250	330	
0.40	1,110	1,500	1,980	
0.50	1,388	1,875	2,475	
0.60	1,665	2,250	2,985	Btus/hr capacity (assuming CT – AWT = 15°F)
0.75	2,081	2,812	3,712	
1.00	2,775	3,750	4,950	
1.25	3,468	4,687	6,187	
1.50	4,162	5,625	7,425	
1.75	4,856	6,562	8,662	
2.00	5,550	7,500	9,900	
2.25	6,243	8,437	11,137	
2.50	6,937	9,375	12,375	
2.75	7,631	10,312	13,612	
3.00	8,325	11,250	14,850	
3.50	9,712	13,125	17,325	
4.00	11,100	15,000	19,800	

3. Enter Table 6-4 with the tube size determined in step 1, read down to the tube area determined in step 2, and read off the necessary water tube length for this condenser. Add 25 percent for mechanical heat. This is the *minimum* desirable length.

Assuming a known condenser.

1. Enter Table 6-4 with the water tube size and length and read off its surface area.

Table 6-4. *Condenser Tube Length*

Condenser water tube length (ft.)	Tube diameter, type-L refrigeration					
	1/4″	3/8″	1/2″	5/8″	3/4″	
6	0.392	0.589	0.785	0.978	1.177	
8	0.523	0.785	1.047	1.304	1.568	
10	0.654	0.981	1.308	1.630	1.960	Surface area of condenser water tube (sq.ft.)
12	0.785	1.177	1.570	1.956	2.352	
14	0.916	1.373	1.832	2.282	2.744	
16	1.046	1.570	2.093	2.608	3.136	
18	1.177	1.766	2.355	2.934	3.528	
20	1.308	1.962	2.617	3.260	3.920	

2. Enter Table 6-3 with the tube surface area, move across to the required overall condenser Btu capacity, then up to find the condenser K factor.

3. Use Table 6-1 to convert the K factor to speed of flow. Enter Table 6-2 with the tube size, move down to the speed of flow, then across to read off the necessary water pump capacity. Add 25 percent for mechanical heat. This is the *minimum* desirable water pump capacity.

Building a Condenser

Commercial cupronickel condensers are expensive, whereas a tube-in-a-tube condenser can be fairly easily made for around $25. The big problem is finding soft cupronickel tubing for the water tube. I have not discovered a source and instead have made a number of condensers of copper tubing in the knowledge that they only have a limited life (several years in normal use). After I have installed the condenser, I make sure it is electrically isolated from the rest of the system by using rubber hoses on all connections (refrigerant and water). This helps to reduce the risk of electrolytic corrosion. If you can find cupronickel tubing, it should be 90/10 (i.e., 90 percent copper; 10 percent nickel); 5/8-inch, or 3/4-inch OD; with a wall thickness of around 0.030 inch (thirty-thousandths of an inch). Type-L soft copper refrigeration tubing is used for the external tube in the condenser.

The homemade condenser consists of an outer refrigerant tube with the water tube inside it and suitable fittings soldered or brazed onto the ends. The outer tube needs to be one size larger than the inner tube. Open the outer tube into a semicircle of the length determined in the sizing procedures. Eleven feet will be adequate for all but the largest boat refrigeration units. Cut the inner tube two feet longer, open it out to the same curvature, and slide it inside the outer tube. This may prove to be quite awkward and may require a fair amount of rattling, banging, and shaking to keep it from jamming. When it is in, it will stick out by 12 inches at each end.

The outer tube is going to be the refrigerant tube in the condenser. Any contamination in it, especially moisture, will cause numerous problems further down the road. *The ends of this tube and all other parts of the refrigerant system must always be kept sealed as far as this is possible with a cap or piece of tape until you make the final hook-up.*

For a professional-looking condenser, you can rent a pair of tubing benders to fit the outside tube and make a neat coil out of the condenser. Otherwise the two tubes can be bent around a suitably sized pylon into a coil of whatever diameter is desired. The smallest feasible without kinking is approximately 12 inches in diameter. To do this, nail a bracket to the pylon and slot one end of the condenser into it. Now walk the rest around and around. While you do this, pull the tubing hard as if you were trying to stretch it. This will help to stop it from kinking. If it kinks, it will have to be junked, so take it slowly and carefully. Do not try to rework any sections—copper rapidly work hardens, after which it is sure to kink if bent again. The tube will flatten out somewhat, but this is acceptable.

Now is the time to fit the various inlet and outlet stubs to the condenser. Here we run into some plumbing anomalies. All of the tubing referred to so far has

Table 6-5. *Tubing Sizes*

Nominal size	Actual size (OD)		Wall thickness			
	Water	Refrigeration	Water K	Water L	Water M	Refrigeration L
1/8	0.250"	——	0.032"	0.025"	0.025"	——
1/4	0.375"	0.250"	0.035"	0.030"	0.025"	0.030"
3/8	0.500"	0.375"	0.049"	0.035"	0.025"	0.032"
1/2	0.625"	0.500"	0.049"	0.040"	0.028"	0.032"
5/8	0.750"	0.625"	0.049"	0.042"	0.030"	0.035"
3/4	0.875"	0.750"	0.065"	0.045"	0.032"	0.035"
7/8	1.000"	0.875"	0.065"	0.045"	0.032"	0.040"
1	1.250"	1.000"	0.065"	0.050"	0.035"	0.040"

been refrigeration tubing, which is measured by its outside diameter (OD) and wall thickness (e.g., type-L). Water tubing is measured by a purely nominal size, which is *not* its OD (see Table 6-5). The various plumbing fittings we need to finish our condenser are for water piping. Do not look for a 5/8-inch fitting to fit 5/8-inch refrigeration tubing. We have the following correlation:

- 3/8-inch refrigeration tubing needs 1/4-inch water fittings;
- 1/2-inch refrigeration tubing needs 3/8-inch water fittings;
- 5/8-inch refrigeration tubing needs 1/2-inch water fittings;
- 3/4-inch refrigeration tubing needs 5/8-inch water fittings;
- 7/8-inch refrigeration tubing needs 3/4-inch water fittings;
- 1.0-inch refrigeration tubing needs 7/8-inch water fittings.

The fittings we need are called *reducing Tees*. One end of each Tee has to fit the external pipe of the condenser; the other end of the same Tee has to fit over the water pipe. The third exit from the Tee needs to be

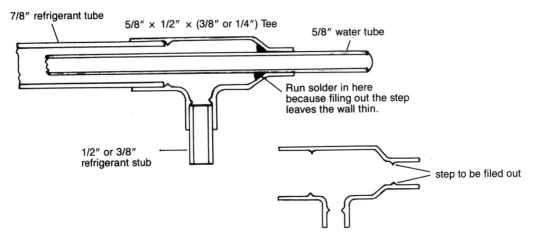

Figure 6-8. *Attaching a reducing Tee to the condenser. Note: You may not be able to get a reducing Tee with the necessary refrigerant outlet. If you cannot, buy a larger one (e.g., 1/2-inch) and reduce the size with readily available fittings (see the condenser in Figure 6-9).*

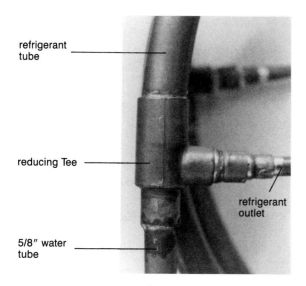

refrigerant tube

reducing Tee

refrigerant outlet

5/8″ water tube

Figure 6-9. *A reducing Tee used in condenser construction.*

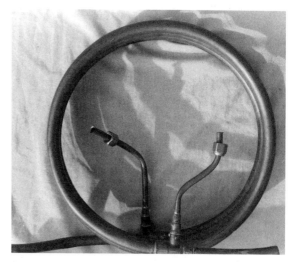

Figure 6-10. *A completed condenser. The tubing stubs with flare nuts are the refrigerant lines. The other two stubs are the water lines.*

for $3/8$-inch water pipe at one end of the condenser and $1/4$-inch water pipe at the other end of the condenser. For example, if we have a condenser with an external (refrigerant) tube of $3/4$-inch type-L refrigeration tubing, and a water tube of $5/8$-inch type-L refrigeration tubing, we will need one $5/8$-inch-by-$1/2$-inch-by-$3/8$-inch Tee, and one $5/8$-inch-by-$1/2$-inch-by-$1/4$-inch Tee.

The Tees come with a small step inside each exit. On both Tees we need to file out the step on the inside of the $1/2$-inch exit until we can slide the Tee over the water tube in our condenser and down onto the refrigerant tube (see Figure 6-8). The various tubes and the Tee are cleaned and fluxed, and the Tee is soldered in place (see Chapter 8). Solder a 6-inch stub of $1/2$-inch refrigeration tubing into the remaining exit from the Tee at one end of the condenser, and a 6-inch stub of

$3/8$-inch tubing into the remaining exit at the other end of the condenser. These are for the refrigerant inlet and outlet connections—the $1/2$-inch tubing is for the hot gas from the compressor; the $3/8$-inch tubing for the liquid line to the receiver and expansion valve (see next chapters). The condenser is complete (see Figures 6-9 and 6-10).

(Note: On some Tees, the step inside the various exits is formed by compressing the wall of the Tee inwards. When the step is filed out, it leaves the wall thin and weakened. If this is the case, before soldering on the refrigerant stub, run a good bead of solder down *inside* the Tee around the water tube (see Figure 6-8). It would be preferable, however, to find a Tee in which the steps are made without compressing the wall, and in which no weakening occurs when the Tee is filed out.)

Chapter 7

Expansion Valves: The Brain of a System

How an Expansion Valve Works

The expansion valve is the brain of a refrigeration unit. It is nothing more than a restriction in the refrigerant line, causing high pressure to build upstream of it (on the compressor discharge side) while the compressor suction attempts to pull a vacuum on the downstream side. In fact, some small constant-cycling units do not have an expansion valve as such, but merely have a very fine length of tubing, known as a *capillary tube*, which feeds the liquid refrigerant into the evaporator.

An expansion valve is mounted on a cold plate (or evaporator) inlet, where it receives liquid refrigerant at high pressure from the condenser and liquid receiver. The expansion valve is set to control precisely the rate of flow of the liquid refrigerant into the evaporator coil, relative to the speed with which the liquid boils off in the coil. An expansion valve can be set to allow liquid refrigerant into the coil more slowly than it boils off, at the same rate, or more quickly than it boils off. In the latter case, some of the liquid will emerge from the evaporator coil un-evaporated.

Figure 7-1 illustrates schematically the operation of an expansion valve connected to a cold plate. Let us assume the compressor suction is holding the pressure

in the evaporator coil at 10 psi. At this pressure, liquid R-12 boils off at any temperature above 2°F (see Table 1-1 in Chapter 1)—10 psi is the *saturation pressure* for R-12 at 2°F. The cold plate is for a refrigerator and has a plate eutectic temperature of 20°F. It is currently at this temperature and is in the process of freezing. The expansion valve allows a stream of liquid R-12 into the evaporator coil. The R-12 rapidly boils off as it moves along the evaporator coil, and in the process absorbs latent heat of evaporation from the eutectic solution. After a while, all the liquid refrigerant boils off, and the vapor continues down the coil, warming as it goes, until its temperature equals that of the eutectic solution—i.e., 20°F. (For the purpose of this argument, we assume that the cold-plate temperature remains constant, and that the R-12 equalizes with it, neither of which are likely to be true in practice.)

Superheat Settings. Since the compressor holds the pressure in the evaporator coil at 10 psi, the R-12 vapor is now 18°F above its evaporation temperature at this pressure (20°F − 2°F = 18°F). This is known as its degree of *superheat*. The *saturation pressure* for R-12 at 20°F is 21 psi (Table 1-1, Chapter 1). If a separate bulb containing an independent charge of R-12 is strapped to the evaporator coil exit line, it too will

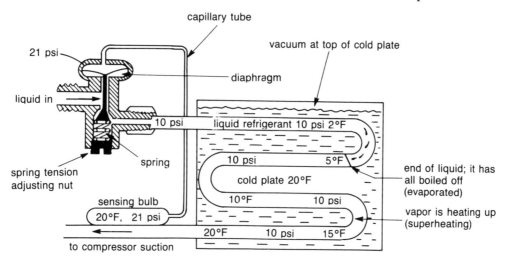

Figure 7-1. *Expansion valve operation.*

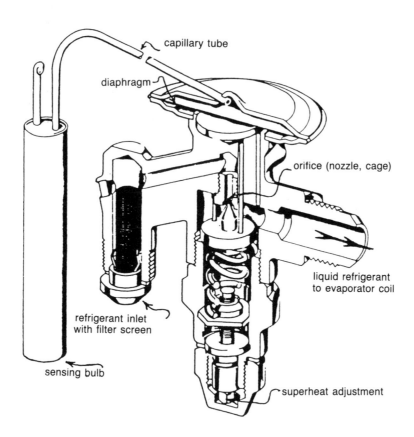

Figure 7-2. *A cutaway view of an expansion valve.* ALCO Controls

equalize at 20°F. However, since it is not affected by the compressor suction, its pressure will stabilize at 21 psi. The R-12 in the bulb is now 11 psi above that in the evaporator coil, and this pressure differential operates an expansion valve.

In the top of an expansion valve is a diaphragm, which is opposed by a spring at its base. The pressure from the *sensing bulb* strapped to the evaporator coil exit line acts on this diaphragm via a length of capillary tubing. This pressure pushes the diaphragm down, opening a *needle valve* in the *orifice* of the expansion valve. This allows more refrigerant to flow through. Adjusting the spring tension controls the amount of pressure differential between the refrigerant in the evaporator coil and the refrigerant in the bulb that is required to open the needle valve.

Let us assume the valve has opened, increasing the flow of R-12. This makes more liquid R-12 available for heat removal from the cold plate. A layer of ice now forms around the evaporator coil, and the temperature in the coil falls to 6°F while the pressure remains constant at 10 psi. When the R-12 vapor equalizes with the temperature of the evaporator coil (6°F), the vapor is now only 4°F above its evaporation point at 10 psi—i.e., it now has only 4°F of superheat. The R-12 in the sensing bulb will also fall to 6°F, at which temperature the saturation pressure is 12 psi (see Table 1-1, Chapter 1). There is now only a 2 psi pressure differential between the pressure in the evaporator coil and that in the sensing bulb. The spring tension in the expansion valve will close the valve, restricting the flow of refrigerant.

Adjusting this spring tension makes an expansion valve open and close at different superheat settings. The valves are designed to start opening at a specific superheat setting, generally around 6°F to 10°F, and to be wide open by the time the superheat has risen by another 4°F to 6°F. In other words, response is fairly rapid.

Superheat is very important to the safe operation of a refrigeration unit. If, for example, the evaporator coil was to be pulled down to a temperature of 2°F while the compressor suction pressure remained constant at 10 psi, the evaporator coil would now be at the evaporation temperature of R-12 at this pressure and there would be 0°F of superheat. If the expansion valve continued to allow liquid R-12 into the evaporator coil, not all of it would boil off. The remaining liquid would be drawn back into the compressor, where it would most probably damage the valves because liquids are incompressible. This is known as *liquid slugging*.

An expansion valve must maintain a minimum working superheat of 6°F to provide a margin of safety against liquid slugging. On the other hand, if the superheat setting is too high, less refrigerant circulates than will boil off in the evaporator and the unit operates below its peak efficiency.

Sizing an Expansion Valve

The principal expansion valve manufacturer is ALCO Controls, St. Louis, Missouri. The company manufactures two series of valves that are ideally suited for boat refrigeration—the HC and RC series—and from this point on, the selection of a valve will be made by reference to these two. If you use another brand, you need to cross-reference it with the ALCO valve. The principal difference between an HC and an RC valve is that the latter has a removable orifice (*cage*). The size of this orifice determines the maximum rate at which refrigerant can flow through an expansion valve. If the valve does not operate satisfactorily, you can change its capacity by changing the orifice, instead of the entire valve. For this reason, if you are unsure what size of valve to use, the RC series is a better choice as long as the sensing bulb charge is correct for the temperature range of the evaporator coil.

Internally or Externally Equalized. Expansion valves are internally or externally equalized. An expansion valve is at one end of an evaporator coil, its sensing bulb at the other end. The valves are designed to operate with a pressure drop from one end of the coil to the other of no more than 2 psi (even less in freezer applications). An evaporator coil that is too small in diameter, excessively long, or has too many tight bends can easily exceed this pressure drop (see Chapter 4). If this happens, a pressure sensing line has to be connected from the expansion valve body to the evaporator coil exit line, close to the sensing bulb. This is an *externally equalized* valve. A properly sized evaporator coil should not require an externally equalized valve. An *internally equalized* valve can be used. This simplifies installation.

Capacity. Expansion valves are rated in tons, which reflects the volume of refrigerant that they can handle at their rated temperature and pressure. The term ton is a unit of measure for heat absorption over a 24-hour period. In the old days, ice was the primary means of refrigeration, and suppliers sold it by the ton (a U.S. ton equals 2,000 pounds), or some fraction thereof. The latent heat of fusion of water is 144 Btus; therefore, one ton of ice at 32°F absorbs 288,000 (2,000 × 144 = 288,000) Btus in melting. This converts to 12,000 Btus per hour. A standard automotive compressor with a nominal rating of 36,000 Btus per hour is a 3-ton unit. A condenser with a nominal rating of 6,000 Btus per hour is a $1/2$-ton unit, and so on.

Just as a 36,000-Btu automotive compressor ends up putting out no more than 6,000 Btus in the low temperatures and pressures of boat refrigeration, so too expansion valves have a lower-than-rated capacity. Table 7-1 converts the nominal rating of ALCO's HC and RC valves into actual capacities at a variety of evaporator temperatures (using R-12 only).

Our 6-cubic-foot icebox needs a system capacity of 3,200 Btus per hour, or 3,200 ÷ 12,000 = 0.27 tons. We are assuming an evaporator temperature of 0°F (see Chapter 4). This corresponds to a compressor suction pressure of 9.16 psi (Table 1-1, Chapter 1). With a water-cooled condenser we have been assuming a compressor discharge pressure (head pressure) of 117 to 169 psi (Chapters 5 and 6). This gives us a pressure drop across the expansion valve of 108 to 160 psi. (This assumes no pressure losses in the lines to the expansion valve and from the evaporator coil; both assumptions will prove false.)

Taking our lowest pressure-drop figure (108 psi) and making an allowance for pressure losses in the lines, we look for the capacity we need (0.27 tons) in Table 7-1, under the section for an evaporator temperature of 0°F, under the column for a pressure drop of 100 psi. We find that a $1/4$-ton valve has a capacity of 0.21 tons at this temperature and pressure, and a $1/2$-ton valve has a capacity of 0.42 tons. Given that 0.21 is closer to what we want, it might be best to choose the smaller valve. A larger-than-necessary valve causes a surging situation to develop. Known as *hunting*, it occurs as the valve first lets in too much refrigerant, over-reacts and clamps down too much, and then opens again, and so on. This installation might be a good place for an RC valve, so that if the valve is

Table 7-1. *Expansion Valve Capacity Chart (R-12 Use)*

Nominal valve capacity	+20°F			0°F			-10°F			-20°F			-40°F		
	80	100	125	80	100	125	80	100	125	80	100	125	80	100	125
	Pressure Drop Across The Valve														
Hc,Rc $1/4$	.24	.27	.30	.19	.21	.23	.16	.18	.20	.14	.16	.17	.10	.11	.12
Hc,Rc $1/2$	.48	.54	.60	.38	.42	.46	.32	.36	.40	.28	.32	.34	.19	.21	.24
Hc,Rc 1	.96	1.1	1.2	.74	.83	.93	.64	.72	.80	.56	.62	.69	.38	.43	.48
Hc,Rc $1 1/2$	1.4	1.6	1.8	1.1	1.2	1.4	.96	1.1	1.2	.83	.93	1.0	.58	.64	.72
Hc,Rc 2	1.9	2.2	2.4	1.5	1.7	1.9	1.3	1.4	1.6	1.1	1.2	1.4	.77	.86	.96
Tons	Actual valve capacity (Tons)														

(Courtesy ALCO Controls)

too small, we can change to a larger ($1/2$-ton) orifice (cage).

Our freezer needs a system capacity of 5,333 ÷ 12,000 = 0.44 tons. It has an evaporator temperature of −20°F; a compressor suction pressure of 0 psi and a head pressure of 117 psi to 169 psi, giving a pressure drop of 117 to 169 psi. We look for a capacity of 0.44 tons in Table 7-1 under the section for an evaporator temperature of −20°F, using either the column for a pressure drop of 100 psi or 125 psi (since our lowest pressure drop, after some allowance for pressure losses, will fall somewhere between the two). In both columns, the closest valve is a 1-ton valve, so this will be our choice.

Temperature Corrections.

The figures in Table 7-1 have been drawn up assuming 100°F liquid entering the expansion valve. This is a fair assumption for boat refrigeration using a water-cooled condenser, but the liquid temperature of an air-cooled condenser is likely to be around 130°F in the tropics. Table 7-2 indicates the correction factors to be applied to ALCO valves for different liquid temperatures (R-12 use only).

Liquid temperatures of 80°F to 120°F have at most a 12-percent correction, and most of the time, these factors can be safely ignored. At higher and lower temperatures, there is a significant impact. If we were using an undersized air-cooled condenser, the condensing temperature might climb to 140°F. The 0.21− and 0.42-ton capacities we extracted from Table 7-1 now become 0.21 × 0.769 = 0.16, and

Table 7-2. *Expansion Valve Correction Factors*

Liquid temperature °F	Correction factor
60	1.224
70	1.168
80	1.112
90	1.056
100	No correction
110	0.943
120	0.885
130	0.828
140	0.769

(Courtesy ALCO Controls)

0.42 × 0.769 = 0.32 tons. If all other factors remained the same, in this case, we would definitely want to install the $1/2$-ton, rather than the $1/4$-ton valve. However, as the condensing temperature climbs, the head pressure also will rise (on air-cooled units, it is likely to run between 180 and 250 psi), as will the evaporator coil temperature and pressure (to 20°F and 20 psi or higher). This will give us a 150-psi pressure drop (or greater) across the expansion valve, which requires the use of the 150-psi pressure-drop column in Table 7-1. Any temperature corrections must now be applied to valve capacities extracted from this column.

Power Element Charge.

By varying the chemical composition of the charge in the sensing bulb and capillary tube attached to an expansion valve, you can alter the range and operating characteristics of the valve. This charge is known as the *power element charge*. Whereas in a regular household refrigeration unit an expansion valve is operating continuously over a narrow temperature range, in cold-plate applications, the valve may start with a completely defrosted plate at, say, 80°F, and have to regulate the flow of refrigerant to temperatures as low as −40°F.

The cold plate of a properly sized boat refrigeration unit in regular use should not quite thaw out before it is pulled down again, and the compressor should not pull into a vacuum, even in freezer applications (i.e., the evaporator coil temperature should not go below −20°F). This considerably narrows the normal operating range of an expansion valve from approximately +30°F to 0°F in refrigerator use; +10°F to −20°F in freezer use. Having an expansion valve that can operate at least 20°F lower than these temperatures to handle abnormal conditions at the lower end of a cycle (−20°F in refrigerator use, −40°F in freezer use) is a good idea.

Table 7-3 indicates the operating range of various power element charges in ALCO valves (the F denotes that the valve is for R-12). The FC charge (+50°F to −20°F) will work in our applications, but the FWZ would be better, especially in a freezer, since it gives control to lower temperatures (+20°F to −50°F).

Miscellaneous Sizing Considerations.

Valves come with a certain length of capillary tubing for

Table 7-3. *Operating Ranges of Power Element Charges For R-12*

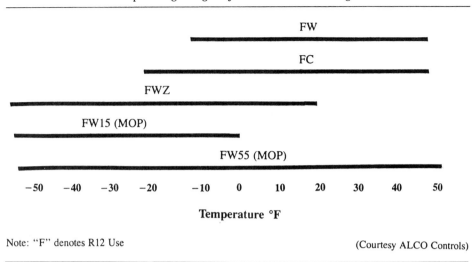

Note: "F" denotes R12 Use   (Courtesy ALCO Controls)

remote positioning of the sensing bulb. You will rarely need more than three feet in boat refrigeration. The valves also come with a pre-set factory superheat setting of 6°F or 10°F. Either will do since we probably will have to adjust it anyway. *Just be certain to buy a valve with an external superheat adjusting screw.* On some valves, the screw is in the outlet port and the valve must be removed from the unit to make an adjustment—a major undertaking and extremely aggravating.

All that remains is to specify the size of the connections on the inlet and outlet flanges of the valve. In most instances we will have $3/8$-inch refrigerant tubing for the liquid line (maybe $1/4$-inch on some smaller capacity units), and $1/2$-inch or $5/8$-inch evap-orator tubing (see Chapter 4). Line sizes are also covered in the next chapter.

Specifying an Expansion Valve.
We now have all the information needed to specify an expansion valve:

1. HC or RC series.
2. For our sample system, $1/4$-ton in water-cooled refrigeration use; 1-ton in freezer use.
3. For R-12.
4. Internally equalized.
5. FWZ power element charge.
6. Inlet and outlet ports of $1/4$ inch or $3/8$ inch by $1/2$ inch or $5/8$ inch .

Chapter 8

Putting Things Together: Avoiding Liquid Slugging, Flash Gas, Pressure Drop, Seizure, and Other Diseases of the Circulation

Receivers, Filters, and Driers

Liquid Receiver. All systems need some kind of a receiver between the condenser and the evaporator. The receiver holds a reserve of liquid refrigerant to feed to the expansion valve. It should be large enough to hold the system's entire refrigerant charge and be fitted with inlet and discharge valves so that the refrigerant can be pumped into it and retained during servicing on the rest of the unit. In order to do this, run a unit with the receiver discharge valve closed. The compressor will pull down the low side of the system and pump most of the refrigerant into the receiver. When the compressor pulls its maximum vacuum, the receiver's suction valve is closed and the unit is shut down. Now you can open the system and repair or replace various components without losing the refrigerant.

Because R-12 is cheap and valved receivers moderately expensive, few boat refrigeration units have such valves. This is the height of irresponsibility. R-12 is a fluorocarbon, and when it is vented into the atmosphere, it attacks the earth's ozone layer. Pending the banning of fluorocarbons altogether, unvalved receivers would be made illegal by any ecologically responsible government. I hope that readers of this book will do their part to reduce unnecessary emissions.

Filter/Drier. A filter/drier is a vessel containing a fine screen and a supply of dessicant—a moisture-absorbing substance. It filters out trash and removes moisture from the system. It is placed before the expansion valve in order to protect the tiny orifice in the valve from plugging.

Sight Glass. A sight glass is generally placed in the liquid line after the condenser and receiver. It is a very useful troubleshooting tool (see Chapter 11).

Accumulators and Heat Exchangers

Because of the intermittent use of cold-plate refrigeration units, interspersed with long periods of shutdown, pockets of liquid refrigerant and oil tend to puddle out at the low points in the system. On initial start-up, the expansion valve is likely to be wide open until normal operating temperatures and pressures have been established, and this may cause slugs of liquid to hit the compressor, which will damage it. An accumulator prevents this from happening.

Accumulators. An accumulator is nothing more than a tank with internal baffles (see Figure 8-1). This is installed in a compressor suction line. The refrigerant from the evaporator coil enters at the bottom and exits from the top on its way back to the compressor. Fluid in the suction vapor falls harmlessly to the bottom of the tank, where it evaporates over time once the unit is operating normally. Accumulators are relatively inexpensive and represent a good investment in compressor security. (Note that in the accumulator illustrated, due to the configuration of its internal piping, the refrigerant goes in at the top and comes out at the bottom.)

Heat Exchangers. When the liquid refrigerant boils off in an evaporator coil, a certain proportion of the latent heat of evaporation absorbed by the refrigerant cools the incoming liquid to the temperature of the vapor in the coil. This is all heat lost to the refrigeration process. (Refer back to Chapter 1 and the explanation of net refrigerating effect).

Once a system has stabilized, the liquid refrigerant exiting a condenser is normally still warm, whereas the suction gas exiting the evaporator coil is cool. If the liquid refrigerant can be cooled before it reaches the expansion valve, it will reduce the heat losses in the evaporation process. This is the function of a

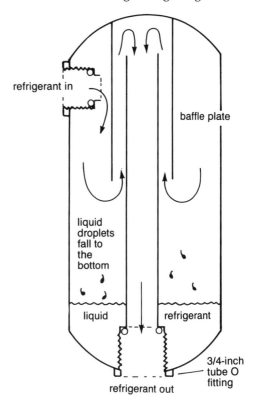

Figure 8-1. *A cutaway view of an accumulator tank.*

refrigerant heat exchanger. The warm liquid coming from the condenser passes through a coil in a cylinder in one direction, while the cold suction gas coming from the evaporator coil travels through the cylinder and around the coil in the other direction. The cold vapor on its way back to the compressor cools the warm liquid on its way to the expansion valve. (This is similar to a shell-type condenser described in Chapter 6.)

A heat exchanger (Figure 8-2) serves the same function as an accumulator because it acts as a receiver for liquid in the suction line and helps to boil off such liquid by warming the suction vapor. It also has another distinct use. Sometimes, especially where there are long liquid lines from a condenser to an expansion valve in a hot environment, the liquid will warm up to the point at which pockets of refrigerant begin to boil off in the liquid line, forming *flash gas*. This interferes with the proper operation of an expansion valve and reduces the efficiency of the system. A

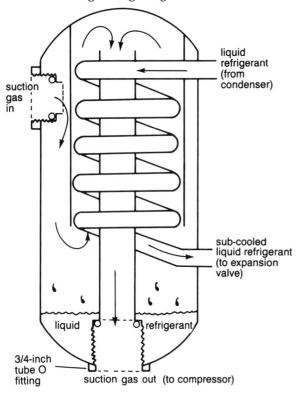

suction
gas
in

liquid
refrigerant
(from
condenser)

sub-cooled
liquid refrigerant
(to expansion
valve)

liquid   refrigerant

3/4-inch
tube O
fitting   suction gas out (to compressor)

Figure 8-2. *A cutaway view of a heat exchanger.*

heat exchanger cools the liquid refrigerant after it comes out of the condenser and, in so doing, it pulls the temperature of the liquid below its condensation temperature at the given compressor head pressure. This is known as *sub-cooling.*

An example: We have a compressor head pressure of 126.6 psi. The condensation temperature of R-12 at this pressure is 105°F (see Table 1-1 in Chapter 1). Let us say that the condenser liquefies the refrigerant and lowers its temperature to 100°F. It is now 5°F below its condensation temperature—it has 5°F of sub-cooling. However, we have a long liquid refrigerant line in a hot engine room. The line introduces a 4-psi pressure drop so that by the time the liquid reaches the expansion valve, it is at a pressure of 122.6 psi. Its evaporation temperature at this pressure is around 103°F—we now only have 2°F of sub-cooling. At the same time, the hot engine room raises the temperature of the liquid by 2°F so that it is now at its evaporation temperature. Pockets of flash gas will form. To solve

this problem, we introduce a heat exchanger, which drops the temperature of the liquid by another 5°F. Now, even at our lowest pressure (122.6 psi) and highest temperature we will still have 5°F of sub-cooling, and no flash gas will form.

Heat exchangers are fairly expensive, but you can achieve a similar effect at almost no cost by designing the tubing runs so that the liquid line from the condenser and the suction line to the compressor can be strapped together with copper wire for a few feet and enclosed in pipe insulation.

Hook Up

Undersized tubing, long tubing runs, and multiple bends increase friction and introduce *pressure drops* in a system. Since the efficiency of a refrigeration system is totally dependent on creating a pressure differential from the high side to the low side, anything that generates a pressure drop will have an impact on performance. Undersized suction lines, in particular, are a common problem in boat refrigeration—they cause resistance in the line. Although the compressor may be pulling a suction pressure of 0 psi, or even a vacuum, giving a theoretical evaporator temperature of −20°F or lower, this resistance causes the actual pressure at the evaporator coil to be as much as 10 psi higher. The higher pressure gives an evaporation temperature of just 0°F. This is not cold enough to pull down most freezer plates.

Tubing Sizes. All bends, Tees, elbows, and fittings create resistance to flow, so you should use as many straight tubing runs as you can. You should also place the evaporation and condensing units as close to each other as possible. Table 8-1 gives correct tubing sizes for various parts of a system, and for units of differing capacity. Note in particular the large suction lines needed in freezer applications. Since the largest service valve available for an automobile compressor is 5/8 inch, engine-driven systems using automotive compressors are restricted to 5/8-inch suction lines. The normal automotive compressor discharge fitting is 1/2 inch.

If you cannot avoid a number of bends, go to a larger size of tubing than that shown. Note also that low spots tend to accumulate oil, which will block a line and cause a pressure differential as the oil is

Table 8-1. *Piping Sizes For R-12: Type-L Tubing (OD)*

System capacity Btus/hr	Discharge gas line		Liquid line		Suction lines					
					20°F suct. temp.		0°F suct. temp.		−20°F suct. temp.	
	up to 25'	50'	up to 25'	50'	up to 25'	50'	up to 25'	50'	up to 25'	50'
3,000	3/8"	3/8"	1/4"	1/4"	1/2"	1/2"	5/8"	5/8"	5/8"	3/4"
4,500	3/8"	1/2"	1/4"	1/4"	1/2"	1/2"	5/8"	3/4"	3/4"	7/8"
6,500	1/2"	1/2"	1/4"	3/8"	1/2"	5/8"	3/4"	7/8"	7/8"	1 1/8"
8,500	1/2"	1/2"	3/8"	3/8"	5/8"	3/4"	7/8"	1 1/8"	1 1/8"	1 1/8"
12,000	1/2"	5/8"	3/8"	3/8"	3/4"	3/4"	7/8"	1 1/8"	1 1/8"	1 1/8"
18,000	5/8"	3/4"	3/8"	1/2"	3/4"	7/8"	1 1/8"	1 1/8"	1 1/8"	1 3/8"

sucked out. All suction lines should slope gently down to a compressor, but this may be impossible.

Flexible Connections. The lines to and from a belt-driven compressor need to be flexible to absorb vibration and allow for adjustment of the belt tension. The correct hose and fittings are available from automotive parts stores. *You must use proper refrigeration hose.* Even some heavy-duty hydraulic hoses (recommended in the first edition of this book) are minutely porous to R-12 and will allow a very slow, almost undetectable leak. Refrigeration hose comes in the sizes illustrated in Figure 8-3, and with a wide variety of end fittings and adaptors.

Service Valves. Service valves must be added to compressor suction and discharge ports before any other connections are made. A service valve incorporates a fitting that enables a set of refrigeration gauges to be hooked into the system for charging, monitoring performance, and so on. Compressors have different types of flanges on their ports, the most common being illustrated in Figure 8-4. You must match a service valve to the type of flange fitting on the compressor.

The most common type of service valve is a Schrader valve. These are the same as the spring-loaded air valves found on car tires. Avoid them because they are prone to leaking. Stem-type valves are much better. These have a squared-off stem that you screw in and out to open and close the valve (see Figure 8-5). Be sure to buy a proper square ratchet wrench to fit the stem because the use of Vise-Grips or pliers will soon mess up the valve.

refrigerant hose
(double braid rubber, max.
350 working psi, min.
burst 1,750 psi)

Description	Hose size	Hose ID
3/8" double braid	6	5/16"
1/2" double braid	8	13/32"
5/8" double braid	10	1/2"
3/4" double braid	12	5/8"

Hose clamps (use with hose)

Size	ID	Type
10-12	1/2"-5/8"	Rubber
All	All	Nylon
6-8	5/16"-13/32"	Rubber

Hose protector
(covers and protects hose from heat and abrasion)

Hose size	Hose ID
6 and 8	5/16" and 13/32"
10 and 12	1/2" and 5/8"

Figure 8-3. *Refrigeration hose sizes and fittings. Note that hose clamps should be tightened to 40 in/lb for all sizes.* FOUR SEASONS

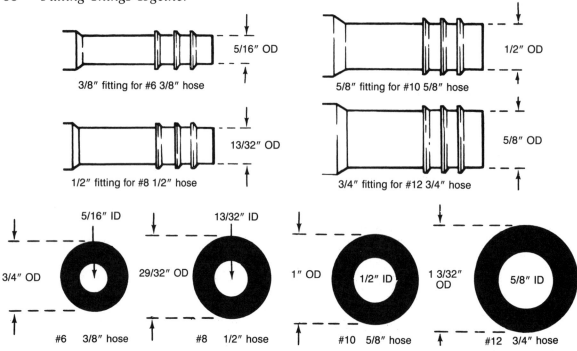

Figure 8-3 continued. *Refrigeration hose sizes.*

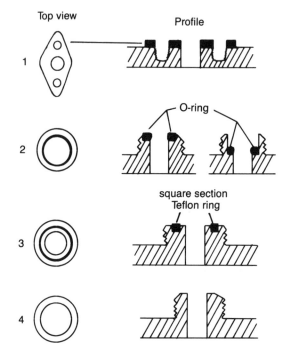

Figure 8-4. *Compressor port fittings for (1) flange type, (2) tube O, (3) rotolock, and (4) flare. You must match the service valve to the type of flange fitting on the compressor.*

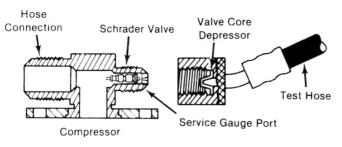

Figure 8-5A. *Schrader-type valves (compressor location shown) with two types of Schrader fittings. Schrader valves are the same as those used in the air valves of your car's tires. They sometimes leak; stem-type valves (see Figure 8-5B) open and close more securely, therefore do not leak.*

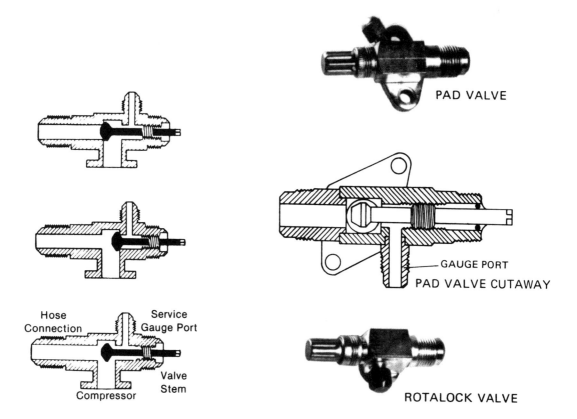

Figure 8-5B. *Stem-type valve operation:* **(Top)** *Valve is closed to system but open to gauge set, for compressor removal, etc.* **(Middle)** *Valve is closed to gauge set but open to system, for normal operation.* **(Bottom)** *Valve is open to both system and gauge set, for monitoring performance, etc. There are two types of stem valves—pad valves* **(right, top)** *and roto-lock valves* **(right, bottom)**.

Tubing Connections

Some people, myself included, like to use soldered joints wherever possible to eliminate leaks, but others like to use quick connects and flare fittings to make a system easier to assemble and tear down. In any event, the fewer the connections the better—every one is a potential leak, and leaks are the bane of refrigeration.

Table 8-2. Some Common Solders

Solder	Melting point (°F)	Flowing point (°F)	Shear strength (psi)
50/50 tin/lead	358	414	83.4
50/50 tin/antimony	450	465	327.0
Silver solder	1,120	1,145	8,340

Soldering and Brazing. Because of the extreme temperatures in boat refrigeration, soft solders (the variety normally sold in hardware stores) are not recommended. Soft solders contain a high percentage of lead and have a correspondingly low melting point, a small propane torch being more than adequate for their use. Hard solders have a higher percentage of tin, silver, and other metals, which require increasingly high temperatures for their use. Some of the low-content silver solders (e.g., StayBrite) can be applied using a propane torch, and are satisfactory for refrigeration work. When it comes to solders of high silver content and brazing rods, you will need an oxyacetylene rig.

The same principles apply to all soldering and brazing (see Figure 8-6):

1. The surfaces to be joined must be scrupulously cleaned. Emery cloth cannot be used because oils in the cloth backing mess up the soldering.
2. The surfaces must make a good fit.

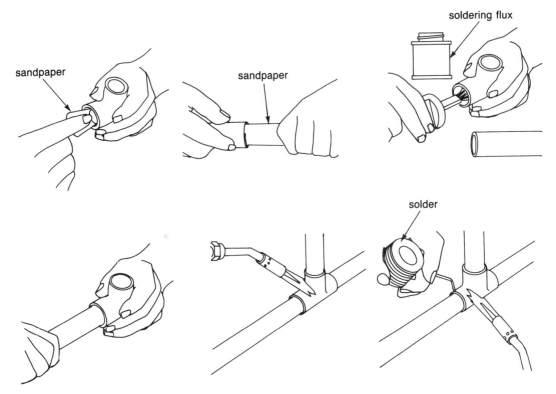

Figure 8-6. *Soldering. Refer to the text for an explanation of this process.*

3. The joint must be well fluxed with an appropriate flux for the solder being used. The flux is there to keep out oxygen and contaminants *once the joint is clean*. Apply the flux to the *male* fitting so that it is not pushed into the tubing.

4. The joint must be heated evenly until it is hot enough to melt the solder when you touch it to the metal. The solder is not heated and melted by the torch. If the metal in the joint is not hot enough to melt the solder, the solder will not flow into the joint correctly.

5. The joint must be well cleaned after soldering because many fluxes leave corrosive residues.

Soldering and brazing take some practice to do right. You would be wise not to experiment on the refrigeration unit itself!

Flaring Tubing. Tubing flares are made with a special tool. There are a number of relatively inexpensive flaring kits on the market, and one or two real Cadillacs for around $80. The cheaper kits consist of a beveled clamp that goes around the tube to be flared. A horseshoe-shaped bracket, with a threaded bolt in

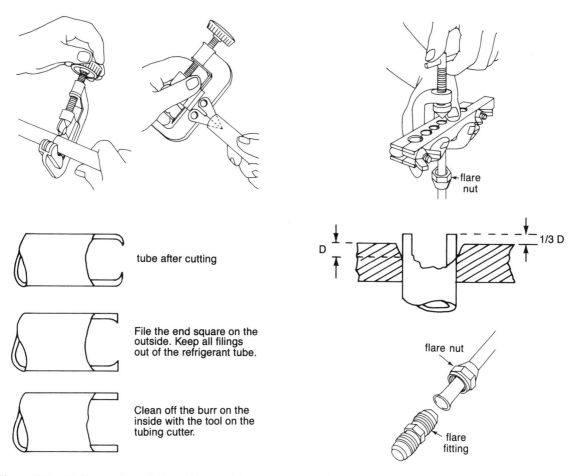

Figure 8-7. *Making a flare fitting. Use a tubing cutter to make a straight, even cut on the tubing. Then clean off the burrs inside and out using a crosscut file and the fitting on the tubing cutters. Put the flare nut on the tubing and then use the flaring kit—clamping the tube, fitting the bracket, and screwing down the spinner. Finally slide the flare nut to the now flared end of the tube and tighten the nut to the flare fitting.*

its center, fits over this. On the base of this bolt is a spinner—a block of metal cut to the same bevel as the recess in the clamp. Screwing the spinner into the mouth of the tubing forms the flare. Here are some tips on the use of a flaring tool (see Figure 8-7):

1. PUT THE NUT ON THE LINE BEFORE MAKING THE FLARE! *Long-nosed* flare nuts should be used instead of short-nosed nuts because the former support the tubing better.

2. The end of the tube must be cut square and cleaned of all burrs inside and out before you attempt to flare it. You should use a pair of tubing cutters, even though these bend in the end of the tube and leave a small burr. After you cut the tube, square it on the outside edge with a file, then clean any remaining burr from the inside with the diamond-shaped tool on the back of the tubing cutters.

3. At no time can you allow dirt or metal filings into the refrigerant tubing—it is sure to come back to haunt the system later on. Keep all refrigerant tubing capped and scrupulously clean.

4. The tubing should protrude above the clamp's face by one third to one half the depth of the recess. If you set it flush with the face of the clamp, the resulting flare will be skimpy and prone to leaking.

5. Oil the spinner with refrigeration oil.

6. Screw the spinner down one-half turn forward, one-quarter turn backward, and so on. Do not screw it down too tightly—it will work-harden the copper and weaken the flare. You do not have to force the tubing all the way against the sides of the recess in the clamp. When you have finished the joint, the flare nut will snug up the flare.

7. If the flare looks uneven or in any other way unsatisfactory, cut it off and remake it. It will be a lot easier now than later.

Sometimes tubing becomes brittle for one reason or another and prone to cracking. (You can soften it by heating it to a cherry red color, then cooling it rapidly by plunging it into cold water. This is called *annealing*.) In cold weather, warm the tubing before you make flares.

Oil

Compressors generally come pre-charged with enough oil for a normal system, but the addition of cold plates, accumulators, and other items, plus long tubing runs and low temperatures can lead to oil starvation and burnout, especially with swash-plate compressors. On hook up, add extra oil to a system in the following amounts: receiver/filter/drier—1 ounce; each cold plate—2 ounces; swash-plate compressors—add a couple of ounces to the system for insurance.

Only low-temperature refrigeration oil should be used (available from automotive parts stores). Engine oil will wreck a system. If any parts of a system are changed at any time, be sure to measure both any oil vented when you bleed off refrigerant and any oil left in the part, and replace it. If you install a used compressor, be sure it has the correct amount of oil. If any refrigerant leaks develop, look also for signs of oil loss. If you do any serious maintenance or overhaul on your system, get a manual from the manufacturer of your compressor and find out how much oil should be in it and how to check the oil level. Automotive parts stores stock oil for R-12 systems. It comes in pressurized cans, and you can add it to a system that is already charged.

Chapter 9

System Controls

We have now assembled all the components for a functioning refrigeration system. All that remains is to wire it and control it.

The Basic Circuit

A basic circuit, applicable to all refrigeration units, is illustrated in Figure 9-1. The power supply (AC or DC) feeds through a fuse or breaker to an on/off switch. From here, the current runs through an indicator lamp and a high-pressure switch on its way to the compressor motor or magnetic clutch (in the case of automotive compressors). Last, we have a condenser cooling pump or fan, which may or may not be individually fused. The primary fuse or breaker must be rated for the full system load, including the start-up surge of any electric motors (at least twice the running load, and sometimes momentarily as much as six times higher). Fuses for individual pieces of equipment are rated for that piece only.

High-Pressure Switch. A high-pressure switch is an essential safety device. Any time a condenser malfunctions, the compressor responds by driving up the head pressure (see Chapter 6). Most compressors are capable of generating enough pressure to blow up a system. A high-pressure cut-out switch disables the compressor before this happens.

Some compressors come with built-in high-pressure switches or bypass valves (which recirculate

vapor from the high side to the low side), but in many instances a switch must be added. It will be either Teed into the hot gas line from the compressor or fitted to the gauge fitting on the discharge-side service valve, in which case the high-pressure switch will have to be removed when a gauge set is hooked up.

Switches Teed into the system generally come with adjustable cut-out and cut-in points. We want a switch with an operating range of around 100 psi to 300 psi (most actually go up to 400 psi). The cut-out point must be set a little higher than maximum normal operating pressure. In boat refrigeration with a water-cooled condenser, 200 psi is generally more than high enough. Some air-cooled condensing units may need to be set as high as 250 psi. The cut-in point needs to be set considerably lower (a 50-to-100-psi differential works well) so that in the event of a malfunction, the compressor does not cycle on and off at short intervals.

Inexpensive, non-adjustable, 12-volt high-pressure switches are available from automotive parts stores. These screw onto the compressor discharge service valve and are generally set to open somewhere around 350 psi to 375 psi. This is too high for any boat refrigeration system, but it will still provide ultimate system protection. Note that if a high-pressure switch is mounted on a stem-type service valve, when the valve is fully back-seated (Figure 8-5B), the pressure switch will be inoperative. A unit should never be run like this.

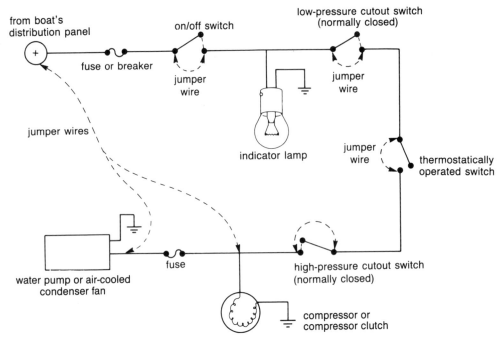

Figure 9-1. *Schematic of a simple refrigeration system. To operate, all switches and breakers must be closed and any fuses intact. To troubleshoot the compressor, clutch, or water pump first check the ground connection, then connect a jumper wire from the positive terminal as shown. If the unit now works, there is a problem in the circuit. Jump out individual switches to isolate the problem as shown here, starting from the positive supply end of the circuit.*

Temperature Controls

We want a unit to shut down when it is cold. As we have seen, the temperature in an evaporator coil is tied to the suction pressure pulled by its compressor (Chapter 1)—as the pressure declines the temperature falls. A cold plate with a eutectic solution will pull down to the freeze-up point of the solution and will then hold a relatively stable evaporator temperature and pressure while the solution freezes. Once frozen, the refrigerant begins to pull down the temperature some more, and the compressor suction pressure will decline further.

A cold plate with an antifreeze solution behaves a little differently since the plate has no constant-temperature freeze-up point. As the plate progressively freezes, the refrigerant produces ever lower temperatures and the pressure declines accordingly.

Whatever the system, at a certain evaporator temperature and pressure, we want the unit to shut down. With cold plates, the time it takes to reach this point can be determined by experience, and a simple timer can be set in the circuit to switch off the unit. For more sensitive control, wire in a switch that measures either the evaporator coil temperature, or its pressure, and breaks the circuit at a pre-set point.

A temperature-sensitive switch is called a *thermostat* and has a sensing bulb strapped to the cold plate or the exit line from the evaporator coil. A pressure-sensitive switch has a capillary tube Teed into the suction line to the compressor. This capillary tube connects to a diaphragm within the switch in a way that causes changes in pressure to trigger the switch. A low-pressure switch will have cut-out and cut-in points just as a high-pressure switch does, and our switch needs to be adjustable to cut out in the range of

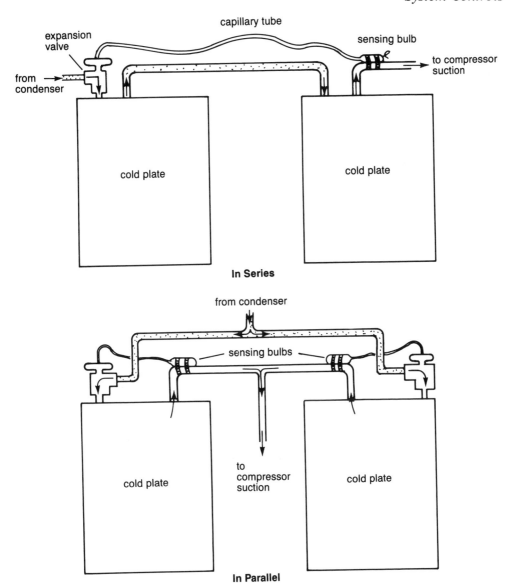

Figure 9-2. *Cold plates in series and in parallel.*

+20 psi to −20″ Hg, with an adjustable differential of up to 35 psi. Except on constant-cycling units, the differential should be set fairly high to stop the unit from cycling on and off at short intervals.

Cold Plates in Parallel

Where cold plates are installed in parallel (see Figure 9-2), being able to close off the flow of refrigerant to a

circuit is sometimes desirable. For example, we have a refrigerator icebox (or section of an icebox) with a couple of refrigerator cold plates. These are plumbed in parallel with a couple of cold plates in a freezer box. Freezer plates invariably take longer to pull down; therefore, if the refrigerant continues to flow through the refrigerator plates after they are frozen, the temperature in the refrigerator box will be pulled way down, freezing sensitive produce. We need to cut

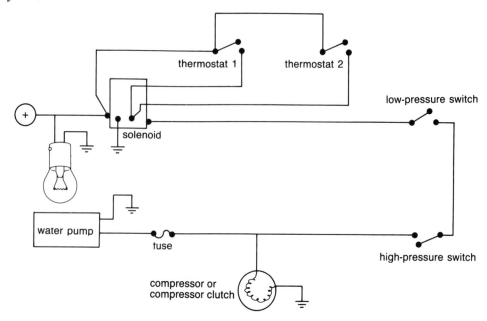

Figure 9-3. *A schematic for a unit with dual cold plates and thermostats. The thermostats supply power to close a solenoid, which then supplies power to the compressor or compressor clutch and water-pump circuit. With either thermostatic switch closed, power is supplied to close the solenoid; when both are open, the circuit is broken.*

off the flow of refrigerant to the refrigerator plates when they are frozen, but still allow the unit to run until the freezer plates are pulled down.

A solenoid valve placed in the liquid refrigerant line running to the refrigerator plates permits us to close off the flow to these plates. A solenoid is a valve that normally is held in a closed position by a spring. It is operated by an electromagnet, which, when energized, opens the valve against the spring's pressure. The electrical side of the valve is wired to a thermostat, which has its sensing bulb strapped to the exit line from the refrigerator cold plates. When the plates are pulled down, the thermostat breaks the circuit to the solenoid valve, and the internal spring closes the valve. A second thermostat wired to the exit line from the freezer cold plates shuts down the unit when these plates are finally frozen. This circuit is illustrated in Figure 9-3.

A more complex variation of the same circuit is shown in Figure 9-4. In this case, both sets of plates have individual solenoid valves so that the refrigerant

flow can be closed off to either one but still leave the unit running until the other set is pulled down. Note the diodes in the electrical circuit. These prevent the two thermostat circuits from paralleling one another, therefore negating the purpose of the circuit.

Any circuit that shuts down one set of plates concentrates the full compressor output on the remaining plates. This frequently results in considerable vacuum, especially at the bottom end of a cycle. If such a system utilizes a hermetic or swash-plate compressor, it must be engineered to avoid sustained deep vacuums or compressor damage is likely.

Electrical Considerations

Stranded copper cable, rather than solid core, should always be used in boat electrical circuits. It is less likely to fracture from vibration.

Wire Sizes. The heavier the amp draw of a refrigeration circuit, the heavier its electrical cables must be.

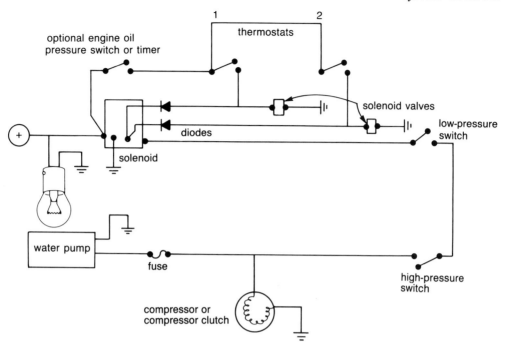

Figure 9-4. *This schematic is of a more complex system, with dual cold plates and thermostats and individual shut-down solenoids on each cold plate to close off the flow of refrigerant to that plate. The thermostats supply power to close the main solenoid, and also open individual solenoid valves on the liquid lines to each expansion valve. When a thermostat opens (i.e., breaks the circuit), its liquid line solenoid closes and shuts down its cold plate. The diodes prevent power from one thermostat feeding back via the common connection on the main solenoid to the other thermostat's liquid line solenoid valve, which would keep the solenoid valve open when it should be closed. When both thermostatic switches open, the circuit is broken and the unit shuts down.*

Some intermediate and large DC units need surprisingly heavy cables. The failure to provide adequate wiring leads to voltage drop in the lines, overheating, and burned-out motors.

Two tables for wire sizes are commonly given in boat use—one assumes a 10-percent voltage drop through the wire; the other assumes a 3-percent voltage drop. I always use the latter—the marine environment is tough enough on electrical circuits without trying to shave things as fine as possible in the first place. Table 9-1 shows the wire size required to carry any particular current over any particular distance, for 12-volt DC circuits, assuming a voltage drop of 3 percent. Note that small 12-volt hermetic units generally

pull up to 7 amps, with start-up (surge) loads to 15 amps. Intermediate 12-volt DC units (1/2 h.p.) will pull up to 40 amps; and 3/4 h.p. to 1 h.p. 12-volt DC units from 60 to 80 amps. Remember that the return (negative) lead to a battery is a full current-carrying wire and needs to be the same size as the positive cable. Table 9-2 shows wire sizes for 24-volt systems.

Relays. Heavier amperages with long cable runs between control devices and the main refrigeration unit commonly require *relays*. A relay is an electrically operated switch. Inside is a small electromagnet. Passing a current through this magnet pulls down a plunger, which either makes or breaks two contacts in

Table 9-1. *Conductor Wire Sizes For 12-Volt DC Circuits With 3-Percent Drop in Voltage*

American wire gauge

Total current on circuit in amps	Length of conductor from source of current to device and back to source—feet																		
	10	15	20	25	30	40	50	60	70	80	90	100	110	120	130	140	150	160	170
5	18	16	14	12	12	10	10	10	8	8	8	6	6	6	6	6	6	6	6
10	14	12	10	10	10	8	6	6	6	6	4	4	4	4	2	2	2	2	2
15	12	10	10	8	8	6	6	6	4	4	2	2	2	2	2	1	1	1	1
20	10	10	8	6	6	6	4	4	2	2	2	2	1	1	0	0	0	0	2/0
25	10	8	6	6	6	4	4	2	2	2	1	0	0	0	0	2/0	2/0	2/0	3/0
30	10	8	6	6	4	4	2	2	1	1	0	0	0	2/0	2/0	3/0	3/0	3/0	3/0
40	8	6	6	4	4	2	2	1	0	0	2/0	2/0	3/0	3/0	3/0	4/0	4/0	4/0	4/0
50	6	6	4	4	2	2	1	0	2/0	2/0	3/0	3/0	4/0	4/0	4/0				
60	6	6	4	2	2	1	0	2/0	3/0	3/0	4/0	4/0	4/0						
70	6	4	4	2	1	0	2/0	3/0	3/0	4/0	4/0								
80	6	4	2	2	0	0	3/0	3/0	4/0	4/0									
90	4	2	2	1	0	2/0	3/0	4/0	4/0										
100	4	2	2	1	0	2/0	3/0	4/0	4/0										

(Courtesy ABYC)

Table 9-2. *Conductor Wire Sizes For 24-Volt DC Circuits With 3-Percent Drop in Voltage*

American wire gauge

Total current on circuit in amps	Length of conductor from source of current to device and back to source—feet																		
	10	15	20	25	30	40	50	60	70	80	90	100	110	120	130	140	150	160	170
5	18	18	18	16	16	14	12	12	10	10	10	10	10	10	8	8	8	8	8
10	18	16	14	12	12	10	10	10	8	8	8	6	6	6	6	6	6	6	6
15	16	14	12	12	10	10	8	8	6	6	6	6	4	4	4	4	4	4	2
20	14	12	10	10	10	8	6	6	6	6	4	4	4	4	2	2	2	2	2
25	12	12	10	10	8	8	6	6	4	4	4	2	2	2	2	2	2	2	1
30	12	10	10	8	8	6	6	6	4	4	2	2	2	2	2	1	1	1	1
40	10	10	8	6	6	6	4	4	2	2	2	1	1	1	0	0	0	0	0
50	10	8	6	6	6	4	4	2	2	2	1	0	0	0	2/0	2/0	2/0	2/0	2/0
60	10	8	6	6	4	4	2	2	1	1	0	0	2/0	2/0	3/0	3/0	3/0	3/0	3/0
70	8	6	6	4	4	2	2	1	1	0	2/0	2/0	3/0	3/0	3/0	4/0	4/0	4/0	4/0
80	8	6	4	4	2	2	1	0	0	2/0	2/0	3/0	3/0	4/0	4/0				
90	8	6	4	4	2	2	1	0	2/0	2/0	3/0	3/0	4/0	4/0					
100	6	6	4	4	2	2	0	2/0	2/0	3/0	3/0	4/0	4/0						

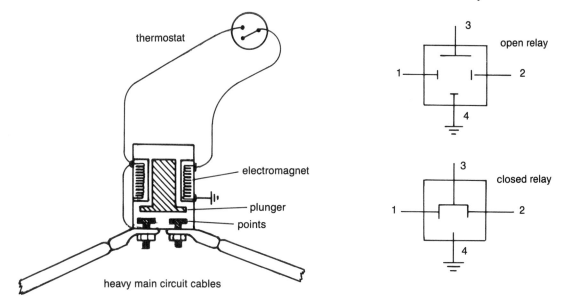

Figure 9-5. **(Above)** *A solenoid.* **(Right)** *Operation of a relay. Current supplied to the relay energizes a small electromagnet, which pulls down a contact (3). This in turn completes a circuit across the two points (1 and 2).*

a much heavier circuit. A relay can be installed in the main wiring harness to a refrigeration compressor, with a remote control (e.g., a thermostat) wired to the electromagnet. Since the electromagnet requires little current to operate, the wiring to and from the thermostat can be quite small. The heavy main wiring harness does not have to be run to the thermostat (see Figure 9-5).

Wiring Connections and Insulation. Wiring connections in the marine environment are best soldered, although these days almost all are crimped, using a variety of splices and terminals. Be sure to use proper marine terminals (plated copper as opposed to steel) and preferably ring or captured-fork terminals (see Figure 9-6) since these will not pull off loose terminal screws. Terminals need to be insulated—heat-shrink tubing (spaghetti tubing, available from Radio Shack stores) works much better than insulating tape. Pick a size of heat-shrink tubing that will just fit over a connection or splice, cut it 50 percent longer than the exposed wire, then heat it gently with a hair dryer

(or even a cigarette lighter, but keep the flame moving). It will shrink around the wire to form a tight seal.

Loose cables will flex with the motion of a boat, and sooner or later the conductor will break inside the insulation. Such breaks are difficult and frustrating to track down. Support all cable runs at least every 18 inches with suitable cable ties.

DC Hermetic Compressors. Electric motors inside hermetic units cannot use brushes because carbon from the brushes would contaminate the oil in the system. As a result, the motors inside hermetic compressors in DC systems must be electronically commutated. Electronic commutation depends on sending current back to the battery for short pulses during each motor revolution, and anything that prevents this return current flow will damage the electronic unit. *To ensure the proper current flow, 12-volt hermetic compressors generally have to be wired directly to a battery. Pay close attention to the manufacturer's installation bulletin.*

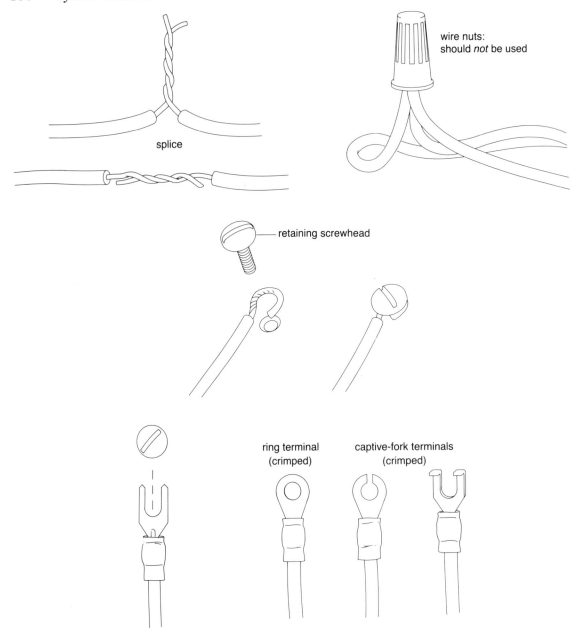

splice

wire nuts:
should *not* be used

retaining screwhead

ring terminal
(crimped)

captive-fork terminals
(crimped)

Figure 9-6. *Wiring installation tips. Several acceptable connections are shown. The wire nuts frequently used as insulators over twisted or spliced connections in household circuits are not recommended for marine use. If you do use them, be sure the ends point down. Note that an oversized hole in a terminal block invites a poor connection; the wire ends will shift and slide when the retaining screw is tightened. Incorporate drip loops around all connections to keep water from the wire ends.*

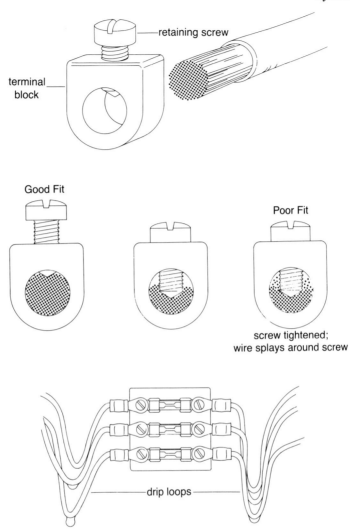

Figure 9-6 continued. *Wiring installation tips.*

Chapter 10

Charging, Testing, Fine Tuning, and Performance Analysis

R-12 and Safety

Most automotive parts stores sell R-12 in 1-pound cans, the actual contents of which is 14 fluid ounces. You will need more than one can to charge even the smallest unit. On my boat, I carry a 15-pound or 30-pound can. These are also available at automotive parts stores, and the cost should be between $1 and $2 a pound. Even if you never need all this refrigerant, someone you meet along the way will be eternally grateful for a topping up from your can! A gauge set is used to put the refrigerant in the system (see this chapter's section, "Refrigeration Gauges").

R-12 is basically safe (discounting destruction of the ozone layer) but you need to observe a few precautions in its handling.

1. Evaporating refrigerant is extremely cold. It can cause frostbite and permanent damage to the eyes. Always bleed a system right down with a gauge set (see "Refrigeration Gauges") before opening it up, and keep fingers away from the venting refrigerant. Wear safety glasses.

2. R-12 is heavier than air and in large quantities will displace the oxygen you need to breathe. In the small enclosed space of a boat, leaks will sink to the bilges and gradually displace the air in the cabin. Any serious leaks need to be dispersed with a good air flow through the cabin.

3. Brazing or soldering on a system that contains R-12 is not safe. At high temperatures, R-12 produces a gas similar to phosgene, which was used in the trenches in World War I. Therefore, if a unit is built with soldered connections, pressure test it with nitrogen or carbon dioxide before charging it with R-12. Otherwise fixing any leaks that show up later will require bleeding the system and blowing nitrogen or carbon dioxide through it. *Never blow oxygen or acetylene through a unit and never pressure test a unit with these gases. Oxygen and acetylene may explode when mixed with refrigeration oil.*

4. *Never add R-12 to the high side of a compressor when it is running*—the high pressures can blow up a can of refrigerant.

5. Do not leave R-12 containers in direct sunlight and do not heat them—they are unsafe at temperatures above 125°F.

6. Always keep a can of refrigerant upright when charging a system. If you invert it, liquid, not vapor, comes out. Professionals frequently rapidly charge a system with liquid refrigerant, but amateurs should never attempt this.

LOW SIDE
(EVAP. PRESSURE)

HIGH SIDE
(DISCH. PRESSURE)

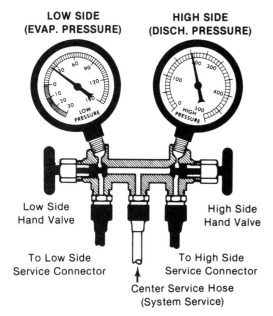

Low Side
Hand Valve

High Side
Hand Valve

To Low Side
Service Connector

To High Side
Service Connector

Center Service Hose
(System Service)

Figure 10-1. *A gauge set includes one red and one blue gauge screwed into a manifold. Below each gauge is a hose. The service hose is located between the gauge hoses.* FOUR SEASONS

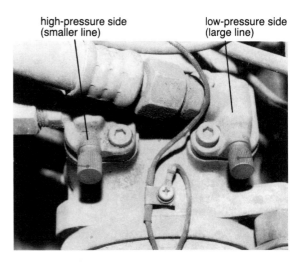

high-pressure side
(smaller line)

low-pressure side
(large line)

Figure 10-2. *The suction and discharge lines may not be labeled on compressors, but the suction line is always larger than the discharge one.*

Refrigeration Gauges

All servicing of completed refrigeration units is done via a set of refrigeration gauges. A gauge set is not expensive ($20 to $50—shop around) and is an essential troubleshooting tool (see Figure 10-1).

A gauge set includes one red and one blue gauge screwed into a manifold, and below each gauge is a hose. On either side of the manifold is a valve. A third hose, the service hose, is located between the two gauge hoses. When the gauge valves are closed, the gauges will register the pressure in their respective hoses. When either valve is opened, its hose is connected with the service hose. When both valves are opened at the same time, all three hoses equalize with each other.

The blue side of a gauge set always connects to the suction (low-pressure) side of a compressor, the red side to the discharge (high-pressure) side. Suction and discharge connections will be found on the suction and discharge service fittings on a compressor. Belt-driven compressors generally have SUCT and DISCH

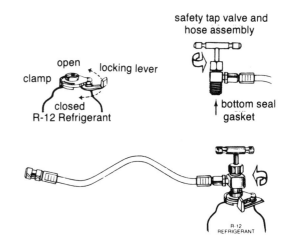

safety tap valve and
hose assembly

open
clamp
locking lever

closed
R-12 Refrigerant

bottom seal
gasket

R-12
REFRIGERANT

Figure 10-3. *The special adapter needed to connect the service hose to a 1-pound can of refrigerant.*

stamped on the cylinder head. Hermetic compressors may not be labeled, but their suction line is always larger than the discharge line (see Figure 10-2).

The service hose is connected to a can of refrigerant or a vacuum pump (see "Vacuuming a Unit"). Note that the 1-pound cans of refrigerant need a special adapter (see Figure 10-3). These adapters are readily available from automotive parts stores.

Never let dirt enter a system. Before making any connections, make sure that everything is spotlessly clean. Tighten the hose fittings by hand only—excessive force will damage internal sealing rings.

One end of each hose on a gauge set has a metal piece built into it. If a compressor has Schrader service valves (see Chapter 8), this metal piece must go onto the compressor end of the hose. It is used to depress the pin, which opens the Schrader valve. If the compressor has stem-type service valves, the position of the metal piece is immaterial, but the valve will have to be opened a turn (clockwise) to connect the system to the gauge hose.

Vacuuming (Evacuating) a Unit

During assembly of a unit or when components are replaced, various contaminants and moisture may find their way into refrigerant lines. Moisture is a special problem. Water droplets freeze instantly as they emerge from an expansion valve, plugging up the orifice. Water also reacts with the refrigerant to form corrosive acids. A filter/drier can eliminate some contaminants, but a unit must be basically clean before charging. It also must be void of all air because the gases in air do not liquefy at the temperatures and pressures found in a refrigeration system. They end up in the condenser, occupying space that would otherwise be taken by the refrigerant. The result is a reduction of the condenser's efficiency.

Professionals clean out a unit with a vacuum pump, a highly specialized piece of equipment that only a refrigeration specialist is likely to have. A gauge set is connected to the service fittings on a compressor and a vacuum pump is hooked to the service hose on the gauge set. Both gauge valves and any stem-type valves are opened, and the pump is turned on. The pump sucks all the air out of the system, down to an almost complete vacuum ($-29.2''$ Hg). As the pressure falls (the vacuum increases) so too does the evaporation temperature of water (see Chapter 1). At a vacuum of $29''$ Hg, water boils at below 70°F. If a unit is vacuumed down on any day that the temperature is above 70°F, moisture in the system will boil off and be drawn out by the pump. *A cold system must be allowed to warm up to the ambient temperature before vacuuming.* Once the pump is pulling a

complete vacuum, it should be left on for *at least 30 minutes*, preferably for an hour or two.

At some point the gauge valves should be closed while a unit is at full vacuum and the vacuum pump turned off. If you observe the pressure (vacuum) for five minutes or so, you will soon discover whether the system has any leaks. If the vacuum declines, there is a leak. In this case the unit will have to be pressured up, and leak tested (see "Charging a System").

If you do not have a vacuum pump, you can evacuate a system using the compressor (see Figure 10-4), but do not use this procedure if you have any other choice. It is not as effective as a vacuum pump and carries the risk of damaging the compressor (especially a hermetic or swash-plate compressor).

1. Connect the gauge set to the compressor. Close the gauge valves. Loosen the discharge hose at the gauge set. Open stem-type valves (if fitted) one turn. Connect a can of refrigerant to the service hose. Open wide the can's valve and then the suction gauge valve. Refrigerant will blow around the system and out through the discharge hose at the loose connection on the gauge manifold. Let it blow for a few seconds, then close the valve on the can of refrigerant, tighten the discharge hose while it is still venting, and close the suction-side gauge valve. Both valves are now closed. Disconnect the service hose at the can of refrigerant. At this point most of the moisture and air will have been blown out of the system.

2. Put an inch or two of clean refrigeration oil in a jam jar. Start the unit and turn on the compressor. Keep the compressor speed down if at all possible (for example, idle the engine on an engine-driven unit). Open the discharge-side gauge valve—the compressor will pump down the system through the open service hose. When the gas flow from the service hose slows (this won't take long), dip the hose into the jar of refrigeration oil so that no air can be sucked back in. Watch the suction gauge.

3. The service hose in the oil will stop bubbling and the suction gauge will go into a vacuum quite quickly (within a minute or two). If it doesn't, you have either a bad leak on the system (in which case the service hose will continue to bubble) or a defective compressor.

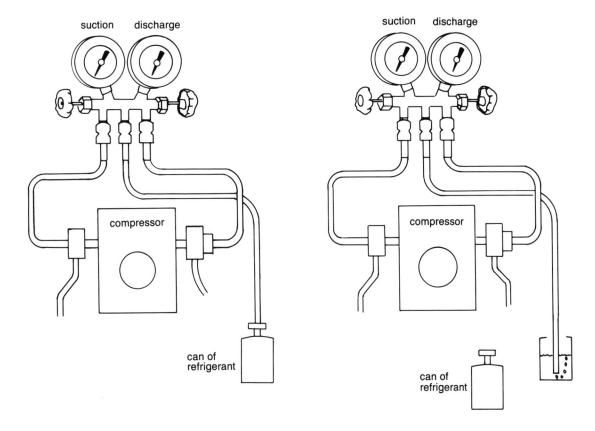

Figure 10-4. *Using the compressor to evacuate the unit. See the text for a full explanation.*

Engine-driven and other powerful compressors should pull a vacuum of up to $-28''$ Hg; smaller units a little less. Once the system is at its deepest vacuum, close the discharge gauge valve and *shut down the compressor.* The unit is now evacuated.

4. Reconnect the can of refrigerant. Loosen the service hose at the gauge manifold. Then open the valve on the can of refrigerant and purge the service hose, i.e., blow off refrigerant for a second or two at the loosened connection on the manifold and snug up the hose connection. Open the suction-side valve and fill the unit with refrigerant. Loosen the discharge hose at the gauge manifold and blow off refrigerant again—we are back at step 1. Close the valve on the can of refrigerant, tighten the discharge

hose while it is still venting, and close the suction-side gauge valve. Both valves are now closed. Disconnect the can of refrigerant.

5. Repeat steps 2 and 3.
6. Reconnect the can of refrigerant, purge the service hose as in step 4, and charge the unit. *On no account remove the gauge set until enough refrigerant has been put into the system to give a positive pressure, or you will have wasted your efforts!*

Purging a Gauge Set

Once a refrigeration unit has been charged, you must never allow air to enter the system. What this means in practice is that anytime you hook a gauge set into

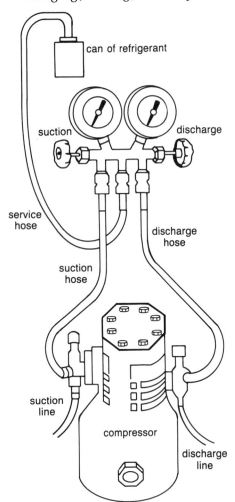

Figure 10-5. *Purging a gauge set using a can of refrigerant. Use this method when the system has been vacuumed down and has no refrigerant in it.*

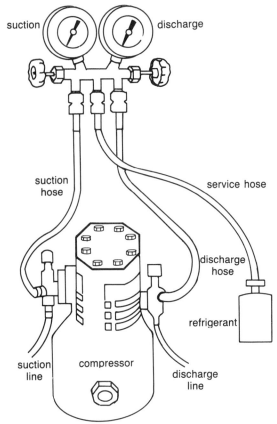

Note: suction line is larger than discharge line

Figure 10-6. *Purging a gauge set using refrigerant already in the system, when the system has at least a partial charge.*

the system, you must purge all air from the hoses and replace it with refrigerant before you make the final connections. Shut down the unit and follow one of these two methods:

1. Using a can of refrigerant—for systems that have been vacuumed down and have no refrigerant in them (see Figure 10-5). Close the valve on the can, then connect the can to the gauge manifold with the service hose and tighten both connections. Tighten the other two hoses at the manifold and connect them *loosely* at the compressor. We do not want to

open a Schrader valve at this stage. Close both gauge valves and open the valve on the can of refrigerant. Crack each gauge valve in turn, blowing refrigerant out of the loose hose connection at the compressor before you tighten the connection. Close the gauge valves so that you do not add refrigerant to a system that has Schrader valves. If the unit has Schrader valves, the gauges are always open to the system after the hoses have been tightened. If stem-type valves are fitted, the valves must be opened one-half to one turn clockwise.

2. Using refrigerant already in the system, presupposing it has at least a partial charge (see Figure 10-6). Close both gauge valves, loosen

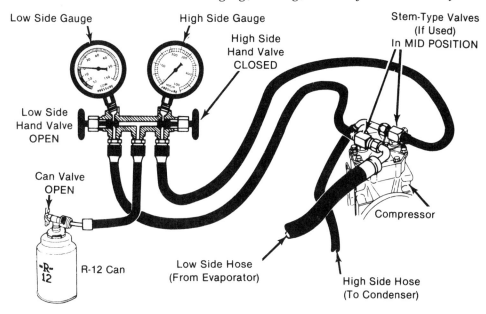

Figure 10-7. *Connections for adding refrigerant.* FOUR SEASONS

the hoses below the gauges, and prepare to screw the hoses onto their compressor connections.

If the compressor has Schrader valves, as each hose is done up, it will open the valve and refrigerant vapor will blow out of the loosened connection at the gauge manifold. Allow the hose to vent for a second or two, then snug it up. This hose is purged.

If the compressor has stem-type valves, turn the valves fully counterclockwise before you make any connections. Close the gauge valves. Attach the hoses at the compressor and snug up, but leave the hose connections loose at the gauge manifold. Turn the stem-type valves clockwise one-half to one turn. Refrigerant will blow out of the loosened connections at the gauge manifold. Now snug up these connections. The hoses are purged.

Connect a can of refrigerant to the service hose (metal piece to the can), leaving the hose loose at the can. Crack open either one of the gauge valves—refrigerant will blow out of the loose connection at the can. Snug up the connection. Purging is complete.

Charging a System

Before you charge any system, check its oil level.

Purge the hoses. If the unit has just been vacuumed down, merely purge the hose from the can of refrigerant to the gauge manifold. Do this by blowing off a little refrigerant from the can at the service hose connection on the manifold. Check to see that both gauge valves are closed and the stem-type valves on the compressor (if fitted) are open one turn (see Figure 10-7). *Make sure the can of refrigerant is upright, then open its valve.* Open the suction-side gauge valve. Refrigerant will enter the system. Wait until the pressure in the system has settled down—probably at around 60 psi to 70 psi, but this will depend on the ambient temperature. If you are using a small can of refrigerant and the can runs out, close the gauge valve, put on a new can, purge the service hose, and continue. When the pressure in the system has stabilized, close the suction valve on the gauge set. If the unit needs leak-testing, now is the time to do this (see "Leak Testing").

Locate the sight glass on the system—it will be between the receiver and the expansion valve. It will be clear (all vapor). Now start the unit, crack the valve on the can of refrigerant so that the compressor suction pressure holds at between 15 psi and 30 psi, *but no higher,* and watch the sight glass closely. Fairly soon, foamy, fast-moving bubbles will appear as the first liquid refrigerant comes out of the condenser mixed with gas bubbles. *Close the valve on the can of refrigerant!* The bubbles should steadily decrease. In a fully charged, fully cold system, they will disappear altogether, leaving the sight glass completely clear, but this time filled with liquid.

This initial charge of refrigerant is not going to be enough to clear the sight glass. The problem is to determine how much more to put in—too much will damage the compressor. *The final charge can only be determined when a unit is cold.* In the case of a constant-cycling unit, this takes only five minutes or so; if cold plates are fitted, it is likely to take 20 minutes to an hour.

Monitor the sight glass continually. If the stream of bubbles is still pretty steady once the unit has cooled off, open the suction-side gauge valve to let in more refrigerant. The bubbles will start to decrease. After a while just one big bubble may hover in the top of the sight glass. Close the gauge valve and let the unit stabilize for several minutes. If more bubbles appear, add more refrigerant. Let the unit get really cold—don't rush things—before doing the final topping off. Eventually the sight glass should be completely clear (all liquid). Don't add any more refrigerant. If compressor discharge pressures become excessively high (much over 200 psi), and/or the suction line starts to frost up heavily all the way back to the compressor and down the compressor side, the system is almost certainly overcharged. If the compressor starts to knock and bog down (stall out its driving motor or engine), it is dangerously overcharged and about to suffer serious damage: *shut it down* and bleed off some refrigerant.

Removing a Gauge Set

Shut down the unit. Close off the can of refrigerant but leave its hose connections tight. Open both gauge valves until the system equalizes—both gauges reading the same pressure. Close both gauge valves. Loosen the hose connection at the can of refrigerant, allow the hose pressure to bleed off, and remove it.

For Schrader Valves. Remove each hose in turn at the compressor as quickly as possible. Refrigerant will vent as long as the valve stem is depressed, which is why the hoses must be undone quickly.

For Stem-Type Valves. Backseat the valves counterclockwise. Crack one of the gauge valves and bleed off its hose through the service hose. Close the valve and observe the pressure. If it climbs back up, the valve is not properly seated. The high-pressure side may show a slight rise initially but then should stabilize. When the valve is holding, bleed off and remove its hose.

Cap all valves and hose ends to make sure that no dirt can enter the system.

Leak-Testing

To leak test a unit, put in a small charge of refrigerant—enough to bring the pressure up to 50 psi or so. A 50/50 solution of dishwashing liquid and water should be brushed on all tubing and hose connections. Any kind of a serious leak will cause a mass of small bubbles to form.

If this fails to detect a suspected leak, you can use a Halide leak detector. This is a catalytic fitting that sells for around $25. To use it, screw the detector onto a standard propane torch, which you then light. Hold the hose, which is attached to the fitting, close to all connections in the refrigeration system. Air is sucked up the hose and into the burner. If any refrigerant is present in the air, the flame in the burner changes color: pale blue for no leak; pale green for a slight leak; brilliant green for a medium leak; brilliant peacock blue for a large leak.

If you are plagued with hard-to-find leaks, the ultimate sniffing device is an electronic leak detector. These are incredibly sensitive—a little too much so in many circumstances. Before using one, thoroughly vent the refrigeration unit compartment because the leak detector may pick up refrigerant previously discharged during servicing operations and give you a false reading. Note also that all belt-driven compressors tend to have a minute leak from the area of the compressor drive shaft. The electronic detector may pick up that leak, but this is no cause for alarm. There should be no other leaks anywhere in the system.

Initial Tuning

By now we should have an operating unit. It is almost impossible to be very specific about what pressures to expect in the system. There are just too many variables: compressor size, motor or engine speed, tubing and line sizes, expansion valve size, condenser and evaporator coil sizes, ambient air and water temperatures, cooling water flow, and so on. On initial start-up, when everything is warm, discharge pressures may go as high as 170 psi to 200 psi, particularly on air-cooled units. In the tropics the discharge pressure may stay this high. Suction pressures on warm systems and defrosted cold plates are likely to start out as high as 30 psi, but should pull down steadily.

The discharge pressure on a unit with a water-cooled condenser should peak out within two minutes and begin to pull below 150 psi. If pressures remain steady at much above this, suspect overcharging or a malfunctioning condenser (see Chapter 11). After a few minutes, the discharge pressure should be down to below 120 psi; it may work down to 100 psi. Suction pressures should fall steadily to around 10 psi on refrigeration units and 0 psi on freezer units. As a unit gets colder and cold plates freeze up, the suction pressure will decline further. Some systems will eventually pull into a deep vacuum of $-10''$ Hg or more (though this is undesirable for a number of reasons already outlined).

When a unit first kicks on, the suction line to the compressor may frost up immediately as pockets of liquid refrigerant in the evaporator coil come through and boil off. If heavy or persistent frosting continues on the suction line *at the compressor*, this indicates either an overcharged system or an expansion valve with too low a superheat setting—it is allowing too much refrigerant into the evaporator coil and not all of it is boiling off. In either case, there is a danger of liquid slugging at the compressor and of compressor damage. This danger increases as a unit gets colder. Note that some frosting of the suction line where it exits the evaporator coil is acceptable and desirable.

If there is too much frosting, but you believe that the unit is not overcharged, the expansion valve needs to be choked down some. The valve operation is controlled by the sensing bulb strapped to the exit line of the evaporator coil. Simply tightening the bulb clamps or insulating the bulb and line it is attached to may get sufficient response to solve the problem. If this is inadequate, you will need to increase the valve superheat setting (see Chapter 7 for a description of superheat). Take off the cap that protects the superheat adjusting screw and back out the screw, which may have either a screwdriver slot or a squared off stem. (The procedure for adjusting an expansion valve usually is included in the instructions that came with the valve.) Never adjust the superheat screw by more than one-half turn at a time, preferably only a quarter turn, and always give the unit plenty of time to stabilize after each adjustment (cold-plate units may take up to 20 minutes).

Once a unit begins to get cold, if the suction line does not sweat at all near the compressor, there is either too little refrigerant in the system or the expansion valve needs to be opened some. Warm the expansion valve's sensing bulb with your hand—this should have opened the valve wide. If this produces the desired sweating, it is a pretty fair indication that the superheat setting needs lowering. The warming may produce immediate frosting, in which case you should not do it for prolonged periods of time or you may damage the compressor. To lower the superheat setting, screw in the adjusting screw. Make no adjustments of more than one-half turn at a time and allow the unit to stabilize between adjustments.

Cold-plate units with multiple plates in series should be adjusted to permit frosting of the suction line where it exits the last plate. Where cold plates are in parallel, the exit line from each set of plates should frost. Be sure to make any adjustments when the unit is cold but before any solenoid valve has closed off the supply of refrigerant to the plate circuit.

Fine-Tuning

By now the unit should be operating fairly well, and any further tuning is done by tinkering with the superheat setting.

By maintaining a few degrees of superheat on the suction side of a system, we protect the compressor against liquid slugging. Too high a superheat setting, however, represents a loss of efficiency; less refrigerant circulates than the system can handle, which results in a system pull-down time that is longer than it need be. A superheat setting of 6°F to 10°F is correct for most refrigeration applications.

Until the unit is cold, especially one with cold plates, it can most likely handle all the refrigerant that the system is capable of pumping through the evaporator. In other words, even with the expansion valve wide open, there will still most likely be a high superheat. If you attempt adjustments at this stage, the expansion valve superheat setting will likely drop far too low in a vain attempt to circulate more refrigerant. Then, when things begin to cool off and it becomes necessary to choke the flow of refrigerant some, the expansion valve will still be going at full bore and liquid slugging will result at the compressor.

Expansion valve superheat adjustments must be made only when the unit is already cold (after 15 to 20 minutes minimum on a cold-plate system).

To calculate superheat we need to know: the temperature of the R-12 exiting the evaporator coil; the pressure of the R-12 exiting the evaporator coil, and the saturation temperature of R-12 at this pressure (found from Table 1-1 in Chapter 1).

Example 1: Temperature of the R-12 exiting the evaporator coil is 25°F. Pressure of the R-12 exiting the evaporator coil is 14.64 psi. The saturation temperature of R-12 at 14.64 psi is 10°F (Table 1-1). We have 15°F of superheat and the expansion valve needs to be opened up some.

Example 2: Temperature of the R-12 exiting the evaporator coil is −10°F. Pressure of the R-12 exiting the evaporator coil is 2.45 psi. The saturation temperature of R-12 at 2.45 psi is −15°F (Table 1-1). We have 5°F of superheat and the expansion valve could probably stand being choked down a hair (about a quarter turn on the screw).

Example 3: Temperature of the R-12 exiting the evaporator coil is 5°F. Pressure of the R-12 exiting the evaporator coil is 11.79 psi. The saturation temperature of R-12 at 11.79 psi is 5°F (Table 1-1). We have 0°F of superheat and almost certainly have liquid slugging at the compressor. The suction line is probably heavily frosted. Choke down the expansion valve immediately.

The biggest problem is obtaining accurate temperature and pressure measurements of the R-12 exiting the evaporator coil. The temperature is the easiest if you don't mind spending a little money. Refrigeration supply houses have very accurate digital thermometers especially for refrigeration work. The probe must be pushed firmly against the evaporator tubing and the thermometer allowed to stabilize at its lowest reading. A misreading of only a few degrees will lead you to assume a much higher superheat setting than is actually present and cause you to open up the expansion valve too wide.

Pressure measurements are the real problem. The suction-side gauge on a gauge set is normally hooked onto the compressor's suction service valve, and it accurately reads the pressure at this point. However, the evaporator coil is frequently some distance away, creating substantial friction losses in the line. Having a suction-side pressure drop of up to 10 psi between the evaporator coil and the compressor is not unusual, but it is highly undesirable (see Chapter 11). Such a pressure drop falsifies all superheat calculations.

If the system includes an accumulator or refrigerant heat exchanger, it may have a service fitting on the suction side. If the suction gauge hose is hooked up here (properly purged, of course), it will give a reading closer to that in the evaporator coil but still with some pressure difference. *A gauge hose should not be connected to a Schrader valve if the suction side of the system is under a vacuum because the unit will suck in air as the hose is tightened.*

There are tables for calculating the pressure drop in refrigeration lines, but this becomes fairly involved. The simplest way to get a pretty good approximation of the pressure drop is to switch off the compressor while watching the suction gauge. The pressure will almost immediately jump up, and then proceed to rise slowly. This initial jump is the pressure equalizing in the suction line, and the slow rise thereafter is the high-side and low-side pressures on the system equalizing. The pressure indicated after the first jump will be fairly close to the actual suction pressure at the evaporator coil when the unit is running. This is the pressure we need for superheat calculations.

If no amount of adjustment of the expansion valve superheat setting will provide satisfactory performance and everything else is set up right, you may have to change the valve capacity. This is where an ALCO RC series valve comes into its own as it is possible to use the same valve but with a different nozzle (cage). Before changing the cage, make sure that an excessive pressure drop in the evaporator coil itself is not messing up valve operation—an externally equalized valve may be needed (see Chapter 7).

Performance Analysis

Previously I extolled the virtues of keeping the water circuit of a water-cooled condenser separate from the water that cools the engine. One of the advantages is that you gain a pretty fair idea of the overall system performance, using the following method:

1. Place a gallon milk jug under the overboard discharge from the condenser cooling pump and time how long it takes to fill the jug. From this calculate the flow rate in gallons per minute (e.g., one gallon in 15 seconds equals four gallons per minute).

2. Measure the ambient temperature of the sea-water and the temperature of the water as it exits the condenser discharge. Then calculate the differential (e.g., an ambient of 76°F with an overboard discharge of 79°F gives a differential of 3°F).

We have, in this example, 4 gallons per minute with a differential of 3°F. Since one (US) gallon weighs 8.3 pounds we have 33.2 (4 × 8.3 = 33.2) pounds of water per minute. The specific heat of water is 1.00 (by definition); saltwater is about 0.8. It takes 1 Btu to raise one pound of water by 1°F (by definition); therefore, the condenser cooling water is absorbing:

$$33.2 \times 0.8 \times 3 = 79.68 \text{ Btus per minute}$$
$$= 4,781 \text{ Btus per hour.}$$

This figure includes mechanical heat absorbed from the compressor, the cooling pump, the engine room, etc. If we assume 25 percent for these and other extraneous heat sources, the condenser is pulling 3,825 Btus per hour out of the evaporator.

For example, Table 10-1 shows some temperatures and pressures measured on a real-life unit. It has a single cold plate and is used as a refrigerator in a 4-cubic-foot, well-insulated icebox. The following readings were taken at five-minute intervals: the suction pressure, the temperature of the evaporator coil exit line, and the temperature of the condenser overboard discharge. The compressor was momentarily switched off when the suction pressure was at −11″ Hg: the pressure jumped up to 1 to 2 psi, indicating a pressure drop in the suction line of 6 to 7 psi. The following factors were constant:

- Compressor speed: 2,600 rpm;
- Ambient water temperature (i.e., condenser intake): 70°F;
- Water flow through the condenser: 4 gallons per minute;
- The boat is in fresh water with a specific heat of 1.0;
- The compressor head pressure (discharge pressure) was not measured (it should have been)—for the purposes of the following calculations, it is assumed to be 117 psi.

Table 10-1. *Performance Data for a Refrigeration Unit*

1	2	3	4	5	6
Time (mins.)	Evaporator coil outlet temperature (°F)	Compressor suction pressure	Condenser water discharge (°F)	Condenser water differential	Heat absorbed by condenser (Btus)
0	68°	15 psi	75°	5°	
5	18°	1 psi	74°	4°	825
10	3°	−4″Hg	73 1/2 °	3 1/2 °	660
15	3°	−7″	73°	3°	577
20	−6°	−9″	72 3/4 °	2 3/4 °	495
25	−7°	−10″	72 1/2 °	2 1/2 °	454
30	−8°	−11″	72 1/4 °	2 1/4 °	412
35	−9°	−11 1/2 ″	72°	2°	371
40	−10°	−12″	72°	2°	330
45	−10°	−12″	72°	2°	330
					4,454

The conclusions we can draw from just this little information are instructive.

Column 5 was calculated by subtracting the temperature of the condenser cooling water outlet from the inlet temperature (70°F). Column 6 is the heat absorbed by the condenser in each five-minute period, calculated by taking the volume of water (4 gals/min = 33 pounds), its specific heat (1.0), and the temperature differential during that 5 minutes (column 5).

The cold plate was totally defrosted at the start of the cycle. Note:

1. The very rapid fall in temperature and pressure in the first 10 minutes as the plate was pulled down to its eutectic freeze-up point (18°F on this plate), and the slow decline during freeze-up as the latent heat of fusion was removed and the evaporator coil gradually iced up and became insulated.
2. The rate of cooling (column 6) decreased markedly as the temperature and pressure in the system declined and the evaporator coil iced up.

Compressor Volumetric Efficiency.

The system is using a York 210 compressor with a swept volume of 10 cubic inches. At 2600 rpm its nominal compressing capacity in five minutes is:

$$2600 \times 10 \times 5 = 130000 \text{ cu.in.} = 75 \text{ cu.ft.}$$

In the period from 10 to 15 minutes, the average suction pressure was −5.5″ Hg. At this pressure, R-12 has a vapor volume of 3.06 cubic feet per pound (Table 1-1, Chapter 1)—the compressor was nominally circulating 24.5 ($75 \div 3.06 = 24.5$) pounds of R-12 every five minutes.

Given a net refrigerating effect of 45 Btus (see Chapter 5—this may be a little high in this situation), the compressor has a nominal output of 1,102 (24.5 × 45 = 1,102) Btus in this five-minute period.

The actual heat absorbed by the condenser during these five minutes, as measured by its cooling water, was 577 Btus. The compressor volumetric efficiency was therefore:

$$(577 \div 1102) \times 100 = 52 \text{ percent.}$$

Later on in the cycle it got worse!

Compression Ratio.

Assuming a compressor discharge pressure of 117 psi (it would have been nice to have some actual readings!), after 10 minutes, the suction pressure was −4″ Hg, which is approximately −2 psi, which is an absolute pressure of 12.7 (−2 + 14.7) psi. The absolute discharge pressure was 131.7 (117 + 14.7) psi. The compression ratio was:

$$131.7 \div 12.7 = 10:1$$

Later on in the cycle it got even higher!

Condenser Calculations.

The condenser has a ⁵/₈-inch, type-L water tube with an internal volume of 2.88 cubic inches per foot of length (Chapter 6). The measured water flow was 4 gallons per minute, or:

$$4 \div 7.5 = 0.53 \text{ cu.ft./min} = 922 \text{ cu.in./min.}$$

The water speed is therefore 922 ÷ 2.88, which equals 320 feet per minute. This is faster than the highest water speed for which I have information (Chapter 6), so I assume the highest rate of cooling, which is 330 Btus per square foot of water tube area, per 1°F temperature differential between the refrigerant and the cooling water, per hour. This comes to 27.5 (330 ÷ 12 = 27.5) Btus per five minutes.

The formula for condenser capacity is:

$$\text{Btus} = K \times A \times L \times (t_1 - t_2),$$

where:

K is as defined above (27.5);
A is the surface area of the condenser water tube per foot of length (0.16 sq.ft. with ⁵/₈-inch tubing);
L is the length of the condenser, 11 feet in this case;
$(t_1 - t_2)$ is the temperature differential between the refrigerant and the average water temperature. At an assumed compressor head pressure of 117 psi, the condensing temperature (CT) is 100°F, while the average water temperature (AWT) in the first five minutes of operation was 72.5°F, giving a differential of 27.5°F.

During the first five minutes of operation the nominal condenser capacity was therefore:

$$27.5 \times 0.16 \times 11 \times 27.5 = 1,331 \text{ Btus/5 min.}$$

The measured heat absorption was 825 Btus in this period, indicating that the condenser was operating at $(825 \div 1331) \times 100 = 62$ percent of efficiency. Note that the ambient water temperature was only 70°F. In the tropics, it would be considerably higher. In order to sustain this rate of heat removal, the compressor would probably drive up the head pressure on the system during the first few minutes of operation. This would maintain the temperature differential between the hot gas discharge and the cooling water in spite of the rise in the temperature of the water.

In the last five minutes of operation, the condenser absorbed 330 Btus, so it would appear to be operating at 25% efficiency.* However, in all likelihood, as the unit cooled down, the pressure in the system decreased, lowering the condensing temperature and therefore reducing the temperature differential between the refrigerant and the average water temperature. Without accurate head pressure measurements we cannot accurately gauge condenser performance.

*$(330 \div 1331) \times 100 = 25\%$ efficiency.

Cold-Plate Capacity.

The plate is 11 inches by 24 inches by 3 inches, which equals 792 cubic inches. Assuming 30 percent of this volume is taken up with the evaporator coil and vacuum (see Chapter 4), the solution in the cold plate is:

$$792 \times 0.7 = 554 \text{ cu.in.} = 0.32 \text{ cu.ft.}$$

Since there are 7.5 gallons in a cubic foot, there are 2.4 $(0.32 \times 7.5 = 2.4)$ gallons of solution. Assuming a latent heat of 1,000 Btus per gallon (Chapter 4), this plate has a capacity of 2,400 Btus.

The total number of Btus absorbed by the condenser in the 45-minute running period was 4,454, which is 2,054 more than the cold-plate capacity! The extra Btus are accounted for as follows:

1. There is extra heat—mechanical heat—generated during the refrigeration process, which the condenser must get rid of. Assuming 25 percent, this amounts to 890 Btus.
2. The cold plate was pulled down from 70°F to 18°F before freeze-up started. This is a temperature drop of 52°F on approximately 24 pounds of solution with a specific heat of around 0.8; therefore, the heat absorbed is:

$$52 \times 24 \times 0.8 = 998.4 \text{ Btus.}$$

3. Not only was the cold plate pulled down, but

the box and its contents were cooled off, including 1.5 gallons of water, which was at 70°F at the start of the cycle.

4. Some of the frozen solution, especially that close to the evaporator coil, was pulled well below its freeze-up point.
5. The figures themselves are not that accurate. The thermometer used to measure the temperatures was not particularly sensitive. This whole experiment is intended to show what can be done in the way of analysis with even quite crude information and cheap sensing devices.

Cold-Plate Pull-Down Rate.

The cold plate has a $^1/2$-inch evaporator coil with a length of approximately 25 feet (25 × 12 inches). Its surface area is therefore:

$$\pi \times D \times L = 3.14 \times 0.5 \times (25 \times 12)$$
$$= 471 \text{ sq.in.} = 3.27 \text{ sq.ft.}$$

During the plate freeze-up period (say from 20 to 45 minutes), the compressor suction pressure was fairly steady, averaging around −11″ Hg. As noted, however, when the compressor was momentarily switched off, the pressure jumped up to 1 to 2 psi, indicating a saturation temperature of around −18°F (Table 1-1, Chapter 1). The average temperature differential between the eutectic and the evaporator coil in this period, therefore, is going to be somewhere in the region of 18°F − (−18°F) = 36°F.

During this same period, the condenser absorbed 1,897 Btus. Allowing 25 percent for mechanical heat, this represents 1,518 Btus pulled out of the cold plate in a 25-minute period, which is:

$$(1518 \times 60) \div 25 = 3643 \text{ Btus/hr.}$$

The cold-plate K factor in these circumstances is therefore:

$$K = 3643 \div (3.27 \times 36) = 31.$$

This is well above the K factor assumed in Chapter 4, in spite of the high temperature differential (which should lower the K factor). Part of the explanation may lie in the crude data and assumptions. The rest of it is the result of having an extremely rapid refrigerant velocity, which will raise the K factor, and of having the refrigerant coil fastened to the cold-plate case. The case acts as a major heat-absorbing surface, in particular pulling heat out of the icebox.

Refrigerant Velocity.

Refrigerant Velocity. The normal compressing capacity of this compressor at this speed is:

$$2600 \times 10 = 26000 \text{ cu.in./min.}$$

At 50-percent volumetric efficiency, this is:

$$(26000 \times 50) \div 100 = 13000 \text{ cu.in./min.}$$

However, this figure includes a 25-percent allowance for mechanical heat. The actual flow rate through the evaporator coil will be:

$$(13,000 \div 5) \times 4 = 10,400 \text{ cu.in./min.}$$

The interior diameter of $1/2$-inch tubing with a wall thickness of 0.032 inch is:

$$0.50 - (2 \times 0.032) = 0.436 \text{ in.}$$

The internal volume of this tubing, per foot of length, is therefore:

$$\pi \times R \times R \times L = 3.14 \times 0.218 \times 0.218 \times 12$$
$$= 1.8 \text{ cu.in.}$$

The refrigerant velocity is therefore:

$$10400 \div 1.8 = 5778 \text{ ft./min.}$$

This is three times the refrigerant velocity recommended in Chapter 4.

Superheat. Superheat calculations are made only after a unit has cooled off. After 30 minutes, there is an evaporator coil exit temperature of $-8°F$ and a suction pressure of $-11''$ Hg. The saturation temperature of R-12 at $-11''$ Hg is $-40°F$, suggesting a grossly excessive superheat of $40 - 8 = 32°F$.

However, as noted, when the compressor was turned off, the suction pressure jumped up to 1 to 2 psi, which corresponds to a saturation temperature for R-12 of $-16°F$ to $-18°F$, giving a superheat setting of $8°F$ to $10°F$, which is just about right.

Conclusions. Just from the little information garnered in our test, we have been able to use most of the formulas in this book and can draw a number of conclusions about this system.

The compressor is quite clearly oversized for the cold plate. This is indicated by the excessive vacuums on the compressor suction; the excessive pressure drop in the suction line; the excessive speed of refrigerant flow through the evaporator coil, and the excessive compressor compression ratio as the unit pulls down. This situation is undesirable for several reasons.

1. The low suction pressures sharply increase the volume of vapor that has to be circulated per pound of refrigerant, thus dramatically reducing the compressor's refrigerating capacity (not too important in this situation).
2. The reduced weight of refrigerant circulated may result in a lack of lubrication at the compressor.
3. The excessively low pressures can sometimes cause a condition known as oil pumping, in which a compressor's reservoir of oil is sucked into circulation, potentially damaging the valves and burning out the compressor. Had we been using a hermetic or swash-plate compressor, damage would have been almost certain. As it is, the York reciprocal put up with these conditions for several years!
4. If any leaks develop on the suction side, moisture and air will be drawn into the system.

The performance of the system would be dramatically improved by adding a second cold plate with a $1/2$-inch evaporator coil in parallel with the first. This would raise the suction pressure, reduce the suction-side pressure drop, reduce the speed of refrigerant flow, and lower the compressor compression ratio. This example highlights clearly the limiting effect of a cold plate in many refrigeration situations. If no additional plate is put into the system, the compressor output needs to be held down by cutting its operating speed (probably to about half) with a different set of pulleys. The expansion valve would almost certainly benefit from being externally equalized.

Chapter 11

Troubleshooting

Troubleshooting starts long before a problem develops. Learn your way around your unit; identify all the components; get a feel for normal operating temperatures at different points. If you feel confident, hook up a gauge set and get an idea of normal operating pressures in a variety of conditions.

Find the sight glass and observe it during a number of starts—from a warm unit and from an already cold unit. See how quickly the stream of bubbles appears and then disappears as the condenser produces liquid. Check the sight glass at least monthly (see Figure 11-1). If the bubbles begin to take longer to clear or refuse to clear at all, the unit is losing refrigerant and the compressor, especially a swash-plate compressor, may be in danger of burning up.

If a water-cooled condenser has its own overboard discharge, measure the water flow. Get a thermometer and measure the ambient water temperature and the discharge water temperature to get an idea of typical differentials at various points in the cycle. All this information will be invaluable in helping to spot problems before they become serious.

Preliminary Checks

If the unit is performing unsatisfactorily, hook up a gauge set and check the following:

1. Low-side (suction) pressure. Once a unit is cool, this should vary from 20 psi on small hermetic units in refrigerator use only (evaporator temperature of around 20°F) to 10 psi on a typical hermetic unit with a small freezer compartment; to 0 psi on larger hermetic units with mid-size freezer capability or cold plates; all the way down to −10″ Hg on powerful cold-plate freezer systems at the bottom end of a cycle.

2. High-side (discharge or head) pressure. With an air-cooled condenser add 30°F to 35°F to the ambient air temperature in the condenser compartment and check Table 1-1 in Chapter 1 to see what the corresponding head pressure should be. With a water-cooled condenser, add 20°F to the ambient water temperature and check Table 1-1 to see what the corresponding head pressure should be. Note that these temperature differentials (30°F to 35°F and 20°F) are a fair average, but it would be much better to find out the normal operating differentials on your unit before it malfunctions and to use these figures as the benchmark for trouble-shooting.

3. Condenser temperature. The condenser temperature should correspond to the head pressure determined above. Check the in and out differential on a cooling water circuit. If it is above 10°F, the condenser is seriously undersized.

4. Sight glass. Turn off the unit and allow the high and low sides to equalize (10 to 15 minutes). Switch on the unit and watch the sight

115

glass. Liquid should come through in a few seconds to a minute, then all the bubbles should die out to leave the sight glass clear. If not, the unit is probably undercharged.

5. Check for signs of leaks (traces of oil) and if suspected, or if bubbles remain in the sight glass, test all connections.
6. Feel the various liquid and suction lines and compare their temperatures to normal. Look for any sudden temperature changes, indicating a constriction.
7. Is the unit running longer than normal? If so, see "No Cooling" and "Inadequate cooling."

Failure to Run

On all except hermetic compressors, see if the compressor is turning over. On an automotive compressor, look at the center of its magnetic clutch pulley, not its rim. If the compressor is turning over, go to "No Cooling" below. Otherwise continue with this section.

Electrical Circuits (All Compressors). Check for correct voltage at the compressor connections, with the compressor switched on. *Remember AC voltages can kill—use all appropriate precautions.* On an automotive compressor, check the voltage at its magnetic clutch.

1. Voltage present. Bypass any shut-downs mounted on a hermetic compressor or electric motor (high temperature; overload) and try again. On an automotive compressor, check the ground connection to the magnetic clutch. If the unit still fails to run, see below for further tests on hermetic compressors and electric motors. Replace a magnetic clutch on an automotive compressor (see Chapter 12).
2. Voltage not present. Methodically check the circuit, paying particular attention to fuses and breakers. If these are OK, the most likely culprit is one of the system controls correctly performing its function—e.g., low-pressure shut-down cutting the circuit due to a loss of refrigerant from the system. Bypass all controls one at a time to see which one is breaking the circuit, *then find out why.*

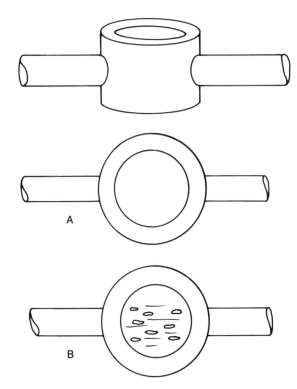

A

B

Figure 11-1. *Sight glass indications.* **(A)** *Clear sight glass—all liquid (fully charged and over-charged) or no refrigerant at all.* **(B)** *Bubbly sight glass—low on refrigerant, perhaps with air in the system. However, occasional bubbles may be normal.*

Hermetic Compressor Troubleshooting. If the compressor is hot, allow to cool down and try again. It may simply have tripped on overload or overtemperature. If so, find out why.

Turn on the compressor and give it a smart knock with a soft-faced mallet. It may simply be stuck. On a 115-volt AC compressor, try reversing the hot and neutral leads.

If an AC compressor hums but will not start, try replacing its capacitor (a cylindrical object generally under a cover on the side of the compressor). First, electrically disconnect the compressor, then discharge the capacitor by shorting out its terminals with a screwdriver blade or a piece of wire (see Figure 11-2). *This is important to avoid a shock.* Now remove the capacitor, replace it with an identical one,

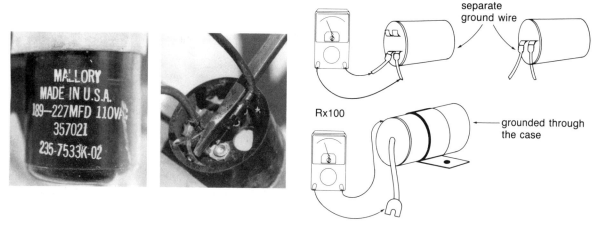

Figure 11-2. **(Left)** *Capacitors store electricity. Their capacity to do so is measured in microfarads (abbreviated MFD or μF). Because there often is sufficient electricity stored to administer a shock, discharge capacitors with a screwdriver as shown before working with them.* **(Right)** *Testing capacitors. Discharge first; then test across the capacitor terminals with an ohmmeter on R×100. The meter should jump to zero ohms and slowly return it to high. If it fails to go down, the capacitor is open-circuited. If it goes down and stays down (zero ohms), the capacitor is shorted. Testing from any terminal (or lead) to the case on R×100 must show infinity. If not, the capacitor is shorted.*

and try again. The capacitor rating in terms of type, voltage, and *microfarads* (μF) will be written on its side. Note: A capacitor can be tested after discharging by connecting an ohm meter set to the R×100 scale across the capacitor terminals. The meter should jump to zero ohms and then slowly return to a high ohms reading. If it fails to go down, the capacitor has an open circuit; if it goes down and stays down, the capacitor has a short circuit.

If you have fit a new capacitor and the compressor still fails to run, try the tests below. *For all these tests, the compressor (AC or DC systems) must be disconnected from its power source. If this is not done, the ohmmeter used in the tests will be damaged.*

An AC compressor generally has three terminals: one for a *start* winding; one for a *run* winding, and the *common*. Set the meter on the R×1 scale and test between each of these terminals in turn and the compressor case. Find a patch of bare metal or scratch around through the paint to make a good contact. The meter should read infinity on all three tests (needle all the way to the left on an analog meter). If not, a winding is shorted to the case, and the compressor needs

replacing. If the compressor passes these tests, set the meter on the R×100 scale and test between the start (S) terminal and the common (C) terminal; then between the run (R) terminal and the common terminal. Both tests should show a low ohms reading (needle all the way to the right on an analog meter indicating continuity). A reading of infinity indicates a burned-out winding; the compressor needs replacing.

Danfoss 12- and 24-volt DC compressors have the terminals shown in Figure 11-3. Test on R×1 from each terminal to the compressor case—the meter should read infinity on all four tests. Terminal 3 is the common terminal. Test on R×100 from 1 to 3, 2 to 3, and 4 to 3. All should show a very low resistance (see Table 11-1—most meters will not be sensitive enough to distinguish between these readings and zero). A reading of infinity indicates a burned-out coil.

Note that if a hermetic compressor burns out, the oil in the system is likely to form a powerful acid that will burn skin and clothing. Take care when bleeding down the unit and wear rubber gloves when opening it.

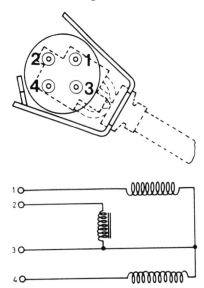

Figure 11-3. *Danfoss compressor terminals.*

Table 11-1. *Danfoss Compressor Resistances*

Terminals	Resistance values (ohms at 77°F)	
	12-volt models	24-volt models
Terminal 1 to 3	0.2	0.7
Terminal 4 to 3	0.2	0.7
Terminal 2 to 3	2.7 to 3.5	2.7 to 3.5

Notes: 1. A test between any terminal and the compressor housing should read infinity.
2. Do not try to 'run' the electronic module when the compressor is disconnected.

Electric Motor Troubleshooting

Mechanical problems—worn bearings, loose or out-of-alignment pulley, etc. If a motor is noisy in operation, remove its drive belt and spin it by hand in its normal direction of rotation. Any roughness indicates defective bearings. Hold the pulley and flex it up and down, from side to side, and attempt to push it in and pull it out. There should be only minimal movement (play) in all of these directions.

Electrical problems. Both AC and DC motors may have various overload and over-temperature cut-

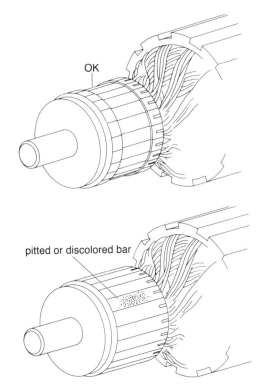

Figure 11-4. *Maintenance procedures for DC motors. Worn and grooved commutator is OK as long as the ring is shiny. A pitted or dark bar results from an open or short circuit in the armature winding.*

outs. If the motor is hot, allow it to cool down and try again. If this fails, bypass any such devices and try again to see if a defective switch is causing a problem. *Do not leave a switch bypassed since all electrical motors are air-cooled. If a motor is operated continuously in an excessively high ambient temperature without over-temperature protection, sooner or later it will overheat and burn out.*

AC motors are generally *capacitor-start induction motors.* If a motor hums but does not start, switch it on and spin it by hand. If it now runs, replace its capacitor (see "Hermetic Compressor Troubleshooting"). If this does not cure the problem, there is likely to be a centrifugal switch that is acting up. This will be found on one end of the motor shaft. Disassemble the motor (generally very straightforward), locate the switch, check its parts for free movement, and clean its points with 400- to 600-grit wet-or-dry sandpaper.

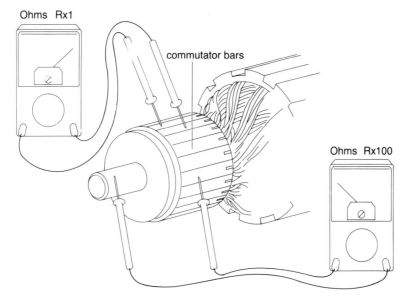

Figure 11-5. *Testing an armature. Testing between adjacent bars on the commutator should give a low ohms reading; all readings about the same. Testing from each commutator bar to the shaft should show infinity, indicating an open circuit.*

DC motors have *brushes* bearing against a *commutator* (segmented copper bars separated by mica insulation). Make sure the brushes are being held firmly against the commutator by their springs and that they are not excessively worn down. In the absence of other guidelines, brushes should be replaced when their length is less than their width.

A commutator should be inspected for signs of burning or pitting on any of its bars (see Figure 11-4). If such signs are present, the armature is likely to have a short- or open-circuited winding, and the motor will need rebuilding. To test, set an ohmmeter to R×1, touch one probe to one commutator segment, and the other probe to the adjacent segment (Figure 11-5). The ohms reading should be low. Test adjacent segments all around the commutator—all should read about the same. A high ohms reading indicates a burned-out winding. Next set the meter to R×100 and test from each segment to the armature shaft. A zero reading at any time indicates a shorted winding.

Commutator cleaning. A dirty commutator that checks out OK (not pitted, out of round, or excessively worn, and with no open or short circuits) can be cleaned by pulling a strip of fine sandpaper (400 or

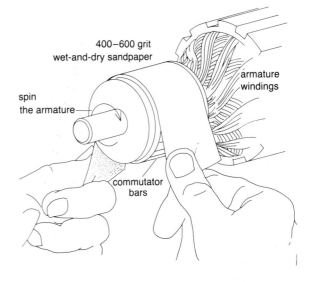

Figure 11-6. *Polishing a commutator.*

600 wet-or-dry) lightly to and fro until all the segments are uniformly shiny (see Figure 11-6). Cut back the insulation between each segment of the commutator to just below the level of the copper bars by drawing a knife, sharp screwdriver, or modified hacksaw blade across each strip of insulation, taking care

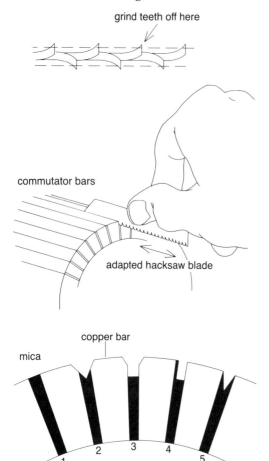

Figure 11-7. **(Top)** *Modify a hacksaw blade by grinding the teeth off as shown, then use the hacksaw to cut back the insulation on the commutator.* **(Bottom)** *At 1, the mica insulation is flush with the commutator bars. Cut back as 2 (good) or 3 (better). Avoid cutting back as in 4 and 5.*

not to scratch the copper or burr its edges (see Figure 11-7). Use a triangular file to bevel the edges of the copper bars. Always renew the brushes at this time.

Brush renewal. Pull out the old brushes and thoroughly clean away all traces of carbon from the commutator and motor housing, using a proprietary cleaner such as Electroclean or WD-40. Dry thoroughly. Slip in the new brushes. *These must slide in and out of their holders without binding.* Bed in the

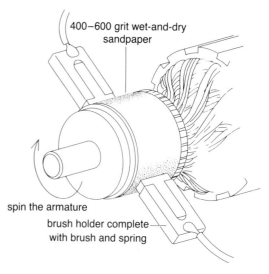

Figure 11-8. *Bedding in new brushes. Wrap a piece of 400 to 600 wet-or-dry sandpaper—not emery cloth—sanding surface out, around the commutator. Spin the armature until the sandpaper has bedded the brushes to the armature and the surface of each is almost shiny.*

commutator end of the new brushes. Wrap some fine sandpaper (400 or 600 wet-or-dry, but *not emery cloth*) around the commutator under the brushes (see Figure 11-8), with the sanding surface facing out. Spin the armature until the brushes are bedded to the commutator—they should be almost shiny over the whole of their contact surface. Remove the sandpaper and blow out the carbon dust.

No Cooling

The Compressor is Turning, but the Unit is Not Pulling Down. If it has been worked on recently, check to see that a stem-type service valve hasn't been inadvertently left in the closed position. Run up the unit and watch the sight glass closely. If it remains clear at all times—no liquid or bubbles—the unit is probably completely out of refrigerant. Put in a charge and do a leak test (Chapter 10). If necessary, vacuum the unit before recharging.

Where plates are fitted in parallel with separate shut-down controls, if one set of plates is cooling and the other is not, check the shut-down devices to the second set (jump them out, or apply power directly to a solenoid valve on a liquid line). If the second set of plates still fails to cool, suspect problems with the thermostatic expansion valve.

Expansion Valve Problems. A valve may be stuck shut, frozen shut, or plugged with trash. Make a close inspection of the capillary tube to the sensing bulb. If it is broken or kinked, the valve will have to be replaced. If the capillary tube is OK, try warming the bulb with your hand or warm water—this will sometimes force open a stuck valve.

Any moisture in the system will freeze in the expansion valve orifice (nozzle). If water is a problem, the unit will start to cool down and then stop cooling when the valve has frozen. Shut it down, allow the valve to warm up so that the ice melts, then restart it. With any luck the moisture will be picked up by the drier. If repeated stops and starts fail to cure the problem, the unit will have to be vacuumed down and recharged. Even if this does not prove necessary, *the drier should be replaced as soon as possible— moisture in the system will form harmful acids.*

A plugged expansion valve will produce symptoms that are similar to a frozen valve—e.g., an abnormally low suction pressure and no cooling—*but there will be no cooling on initial start-up.* Most valves have a filter on the liquid line inlet. The valve may sweat from this point on—in effect, the filter is now acting as the valve orifice.

Inadequate Cooling

Consider first whether there has been a marked increase in ambient temperatures, a change in the ice-box use (the WB factor—see Chapter 2), or a reduction in the compressor operating speed on engine-driven units.

Condenser Problems. Check the temperature of the condenser to see if it is hotter than normal, and check also the head pressure of the compressor to see if this is higher than normal. If so, before blaming the condenser, consider whether there has been a rise in the ambient air or water temperature.

Typical condensing temperatures and head pressures (as a function of ambient air and water temperatures) are given in Table 11-2. However, these are not necessarily the operating temperatures and pressures on your system. It is an excellent idea to establish the normal head pressure of your compressor in specific ambient temperatures. Using Table 1-1 in Chapter 1, you can then draw up your own table of ambient conditions, head pressures, and condensing temperatures. If the head pressure at any time deviates by more than 5 to 10 psi from this table, your system has a problem.

Air-cooled condenser problems. Check to see that the fan is working and that it is blowing in the right direction. Make sure the condensing unit has an adequate flow of cool air, with proper in and out ducting. Inspect the whole length of the ducting to make sure it is not obstructed or crushed. Check to see that the condenser fins are clean. If all else fails, install a larger fan—the faster the air flow, the more efficient the condenser.

Water-cooled condenser problems. Measure the water-flow rate by timing how long the discharge takes to fill a gallon jug, and compare this with system specifications (or normal flow). If low, check the raw-water filter for blockage; the seacock and water regulating valve (if fitted) to see that they are wide open; the pump to see if it is air-bound, and the water hoses to make sure they are not kinked or collapsed. If this reveals no problem, check the water pump impeller for wear. Finally, if all else fails, clean out the condenser. The water side of a manifold-type condenser can be opened and rodded out (use only soft bristle brushes or wooden dowels). Most tube-in-a-tube condensers are not this easy to clean—you will need a special brush with a long flexible handle.

Many times a condenser can be effectively descaled and cleaned by circulating through it a solution of muriatic acid. In this case the condenser will not have to be opened. You can buy the acid from hardware stores (it is used for cleaning brickwork) and marine chandlers. Wear rubber gloves and observe all safety precautions on the label. Flush the condenser well after running the acid through, and check zinc anodes because the acid will eat them up quite rapidly.

Check the inlet and outlet water temperatures on a condenser. If the differential is more than 10°F, the

Table 11-2. *Typical Condensing Temperatures and Head Pressures*

Condenser type	Air (water) temperature (°F)	Condensing temperature (°F)	Head pressure (psi)
Air-cooled, assuming a 30°F differential between the air and the condenser temperature	50	80	84
	55	85	92
	60	90	100
	65	95	108
	70	100	117
	75	105	127
	80	110	136
	85	115	147
	90	120	158
	95	125	169
	100	130	181
	105	135	193
	110	140	207
Water-cooled, assuming a 20°F differential between the condensing temperature and the entering water temperature	50	70	70
	55	75	77
	60	80	84
	65	85	92
	70	90	100
	75	95	108
	80	100	117
	85	105	127
	90	110	136
	95	115	147

Note: Low head pressures at low ambient water temperatures are sometimes undesirable. You may have to restrict the cooling water flow. This will increase the temperature differential within the condenser, therefore increase the compressor's head pressure.

condenser is seriously undersized in its present application, or the water flow rate through it is inadequate. Inadequate flow may be caused by a partially obstructed cooling circuit or a worn-out or too-small pump.

If the temperature differential is very low (1°F to 3°F), the condenser may just be oversized for its current operating conditions; it may be seriously scaled up, reducing the heat transfer from the refrigerant; air may have gathered in the condenser, which interferes with its operation; or the system may be overcharged with refrigerant. Overcharging causes the liquid to back up from the receiver into the condenser, reducing its overall effective length. If either air or over-

charging is the problem, the compressor head pressure will be higher than normal. The cure for both is the same—run the unit until it is cool, shut it down, and immediately vent vapor for a second or two from the compressor discharge service fitting. You may have to repeat this procedure two or three times.

Lack of Refrigerant. The sight glass will show a steady stream of bubbles, even when the unit is cold; pressures and temperatures throughout the system will be normal to low; and there will quite likely be a hissing at the expansion valve as vapor, rather than liquid, passes through the orifice. If the unit picks up with the addition of R-12, a lack of refrigerant is almost certain. Leak-test the system and *check that no oil has been lost* (especially if you have a swash-plate compressor). If you need to add oil to a system under pressure, use one of the special pressurized cans available from automotive parts stores. Instructions for putting the oil into the system are on the can. You will also need an adaptor.

Compressor Problems.

Compressors have three common problem areas: the shaft seal (not a problem on hermetic compressors); the valves or head gasket; and blow-by down the sides of the pistons. If the valves are defective or the pistons blowing by, the discharge (head) pressure will be lower than normal, the suction pressure will be higher than normal, and the compressor will run hot.

Compressors with stem-type service valves. Close the suction service valve (stem all the way in) and switch the unit on and off two or three times to eliminate any risk of oil pumping. Turn it on and run it until it pulls its maximum sustained vacuum, then shut it down.

1. Most compressors should be able to pull a vacuum of −28″ Hg. Any compressor that cannot pull at least −20″ Hg has defective suction valves.
2. If the compressor pulls a good vacuum but the vacuum fairly rapidly rises to 0 psi, the shaft seal is leaking and allowing the compressor to equalize with atmospheric pressure. (This does not apply to hermetic compressors.)
3. If the compressor pulls a good vacuum but the vacuum fairly rapidly rises to a positive pressure, the discharge valves are bad and allowing the system high pressure to leak back into the compressor.

Now leave the suction service valve closed, run the compressor until it pulls its maximum sustained vacuum, then close the discharge service valve while the compressor is still running. If the head pressure continues to increase, the shaft seal is leaking (does not apply to hermetic compressors). The compressor is sucking in air and using it to pump up the high side.

Shut down the compressor, open the suction service valve, and close the discharge service valve. Turn the compressor over *by hand* (this is important).

The discharge gauge should show a steady rise in pressure. If it fluctuates or falls back, the discharge valves are bad.

Compressors with Schrader-type service valves. Run the compressor normally for five minutes, then shut it down. If the suction and discharge pressures equalize in less than two minutes, the head gasket or valves are almost certainly bad.

As time goes by, general wear in a compressor will lead to lowered compression, leaking valves, piston blow-by, and worn bearings. There will be a steady decline in performance and an increase in noise and vibration. Discharge pressures will be lower, suction pressures higher, and the compressor will run hot. Lesser problems can frequently be overcome by changing the compressor valve plate, which is covered in the next chapter (except for hermetic compressors—on these the whole unit will have to be replaced), but more serious problems will require the compressor to be replaced. Extensive rebuilds should not be attempted by amateurs because the extraordinarily close tolerances in refrigeration compressors require specialized technicians and equipment.

Expansion Valve Problems.

The superheat setting may be too high, causing the unit to perform below capacity. In this case, the exit line from the evaporator coil is probably not frosting at all—it should frost here, but not all the way back to the compressor (see Chapter 10).

The effects of a plugged valve, or moisture in the system, have just been covered. If system performance has always been inadequate, the expansion valve orifice may simply be too small.

Restrictions.

On the liquid (high) side, any restriction in a line or across a fitting will act in much the same way that an expansion valve acts, causing a pressure drop across the restriction. If the restriction occurs in a liquid line, the pressure drop may lead to the evaporation of some of the refrigerant on the downstream side of the restriction, in which case the line, or fitting, will cool off at this point due to the absorption of latent heat of evaporation by the refrigerant. So, *any temperature change across a filter or at the inlet connection to an expansion valve, is a pretty sure sign of a plugged filter or filter screen.*

On the suction (low) side, a restriction or an undersized line will cause an excessive pressure drop through the evaporator coil and down the suction line to the compressor. This will greatly impair performance. Although the compressor may be pulling a pressure of, say, 0 psi, giving a nominal evaporator temperature of around $-20°F$, the actual suction pressure in the evaporator coil will be considerably higher (e.g., around 10 psi), giving a much higher evaporator temperature (around 0°F). This will greatly reduce the temperature differential between the evaporating refrigerant and an evaporator box or cold plate, which in turn will considerably slow the rate of heat removal.

Unless cold-plate coils are properly sized, the long tubing runs and many bends inside a plate are especially likely to cause excessive pressure drop. For proper performance, a cold plate needs a large-enough diameter evaporator coil or enough coils in parallel to achieve the refrigerant flow rates outlined in Chapter 4.

To check for pressure-drop problems, run the unit until it is cold; note the compressor suction pressure; then turn off the compressor while watching the suction-side gauge. The initial sudden pressure rise on the gauge is indicative of the suction-side pressure drop. If it is more than 2 psi, it is excessive. In this case the unit may need a larger suction line, another cold plate in parallel with the existing one, or a slowing down of its compressor. An externally equalized expansion valve may also be needed.

Other Problems. Standard refrigerator-type finned evaporators will sometimes freeze up, whereas cold plates will get a heavy layer of ice, especially if the icebox lid seals are leaking. In both situations, the ice acts as an insulator and the icebox will not be properly cooled. The evaporator or cold plate must be defrosted. Never try chipping ice off a finned evaporator. One tiny hole in the evaporator tubing will destroy the whole evaporator. Copper coils can be repaired with solder; aluminum can sometimes be patched with two-part epoxy.

A finned evaporator relies on a fan to circulate air over it, and a combined refrigerator/freezer with cold plates has some kind of a circulating fan or thermostatically operated spill-over device. Failure of the fan or spill-over unit will cause inadequate refrigeration.

Make sure your cold plates have enough surface area exposed in the icebox. In particular, a move to a warmer climate will increase the rate of heat loss from an icebox and call for a greater rate of heat absorption by the cold plate, which in turn will require a greater exposed surface area.

Excessive Frosting of a Suction Line and/or Compressor Knocks

Too much refrigerant is circulating through the evaporator coil. If the compressor is knocking, liquid refrigerant is finding its way back to the compressor and imminent damage is likely. Shut it down immediately.

Excessive refrigerant will be the result of either overcharging or expansion-valve problems. Overcharging is easily cured by venting some refrigerant. An expansion valve may have too low a superheat setting (see Chapter 10), but before you make any adjustments, check its sensing bulb and capillary tubing. The bulb may be making an imperfect contact with the evaporator coil exit line, or it may be in an area that is subject to warm air. The bulb should be clamped somewhere alongside the evaporator coil or on top of it, but not below it. The bulb needs to be in continuous contact with the evaporator coil along its whole length, and the bulb clamps need to be tight. The bulb and evaporator coil exit line may need insulating. The capillary tubing to the bulb must have no breaks or kinks—if either is present, the expansion valve will need replacing.

Occasionally an expansion valve will stick in the open position. Generally it must be replaced. If an expansion valve has only just been installed and excessive refrigerant is flowing through the system, the valve may simply have too large a capacity for the unit.

A Unit Operates Intermittently (Cycles On and Off)

Most likely a cut-out switch is performing its proper function, indicating a problem with the system. A hermetic compressor will cycle on and off on its overload protection if the supply voltage is low, or if the compressor head pressure is high. Check for voltage drop at the compressor while it is running and for poor condenser performance. If voltage drop is present on a DC compressor, inadequate wiring size is the probable cause (see Chapter 9).

All units will cycle on a high-pressure cut-out switch if the condenser malfunctions. The compressor responds by driving up the head pressure until the switch trips. Make all the condenser checks outlined above. Another cause of high pressure may be overcharging.

If a system with a low-pressure cut-out switch is low on refrigerant, it is likely to cycle off and on as it gets colder. Check the sight glass and the charge.

Cold Plates Fail to Hold Over

If this has always been the case, the icebox may have inadequate insulation, or the unit and cold plate may be too small for the demands being placed on them. Note in particular that many of the DC holding-plate units sold today are only designed for a holdover of 12 to 16 hours because it is assumed that the unit will be run twice a day. This may not be apparent to a buyer who does not read and understand the fine print on the unit's description. To get a 24-hour holdover, such a unit will have to be installed in a much smaller icebox than that given in the specifications, or the unit will have to be given much larger cold plates and a much longer once-a-day running time.

If the failure to hold-over is a new problem, check under the items covered in "Inadequate Cooling," Then:

1. Consider whether a recent change in operating conditions (such as a move to a warmer climate) is just now showing up a basic weakness in the system.
2. Consider whether the icebox usage has changed. For example, are some recently arrived heavy beer drinkers continually putting fresh cans of warm beer in the fridge?
3. Check the seal on the icebox lid and make sure the drains are plugged off.
4. Ask yourself if the icebox has the wrong insulation (e.g., EPS), and whether that insulation is becoming permeated with water vapor and losing its effectiveness.
5. Check the cold plates for heavy ice-up. If present, defrost.

Chapter 12

Compressor Overhaul

Hermetic Compressors

Aside from the tests and procedures outlined in Chapter 11, there is little you can do to repair a malfunctioning hermetic compressor except to replace the whole unit. A few have canisters that bolt together, but the vast majority have welded seams and cannot be opened up in the field.

Belt-Driven Compressors

Belt-driven compressors commonly have failed valves, leaking shaft seals, and burned up magnetic clutches on automotive compressors. Clutches and valves are quite easily replaced. Shaft seals are a little trickier to replace because of the very close tolerances involved. Such repairs should be left to a professional, or the compressor exchanged for a good one.

Valve Repairs. Note: valve replacement is illustrated with reference to York and Sanden (Sankyo) automotive compressors. A commercial reciprocal compressor will be similar to a York.

Before you begin, make sure you have the two gaskets required and a new valve-plate assembly. *Scrupulously clean off the external surfaces of the compressor and your work area.* Bleed the compressor of refrigerant. Remove the suction and discharge hoses, stem-type service valves (if fitted), and the compressor suction and discharge ports if they are *bolted* to the cylinder head (in which case the retaining bolts will also help to retain the cylinder head). Undo the cylinder head retaining bolts.

Beneath a cylinder head is a gasket, a thin metal plate (the valve plate), and another gasket, in that order. Pry off the head and then the valve plate. *Do not scratch any aluminum surfaces. Note which way around and which way up the various pieces go. Scrupulously clean all surfaces. Make sure no bits of dirt or old gasket fall in the cylinders.*

Clean everything once again. Lightly oil the cylinder block with refrigeration oil and set the new gasket in place. Do not use gasket cement of any kind. Lightly oil both faces of the valve plate and set it in place. Put on the new head gasket, lightly oil the cylinder head, and set it in place. Lightly oil the threads on the cylinder-head bolts and run the bolts in by hand. If they won't go in all the way, take them out and clean the threads. Check the lengths—some may be longer than others and must go in specific holes. Don't force them down—it is easy to crack or strip the threads from aluminum castings. When all fit easily by hand, torque to the manufacturer's specifications (or 20 ft.lbs. if in doubt). Torque in two stages (e.g., 15 ft.lbs. and then 20 ft.lbs.) and work from side to side (see Figure 12-2).

Magnetic Clutches. Engine-driven compressors employ an electromagnetic clutch. The drive pulley

Figure 12-1. *York and Tecumseh valve plate renewal.* **(Top)** *The service ports have been removed (only necessary if they are through-bolted) and the cylinder head bolts undone. The "S" cast into the right-hand side of the cylinder head denotes the suction side.* **(Left)** *The cylinder head has been tapped loose to reveal the valve plate. The two locating dowels ensure the valve assembly will be replaced correctly.* **(Right)** *The valve plate itself has now been tapped loose to reveal the pistons. The gasket material adhering to both faces will need to be scrupulously cleaned off. Take care not to scratch the soft aluminum surfaces or allow anything to fall into the compressor.*

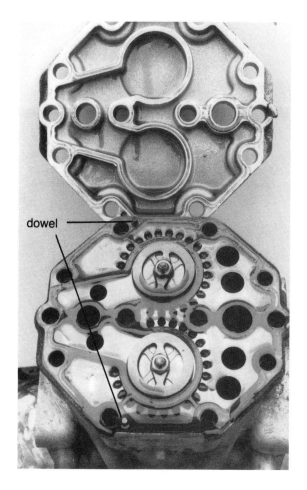

dowel

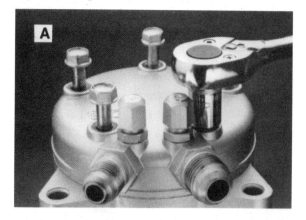

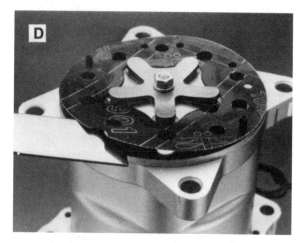

Figure 12-2. **(A)** *Remove the five cylinder head screws using a 13mm socket.* **(B)** *Tap the outer edge of the cylinder head with a small hammer and a gasket scraper until it is freed from the plate. Inspect for damage. (The cylinder head gasket normally sticks to the valve plate.)* **(C)** *Position gasket scraper between the outside edge of the valve plate and the cylinder block and lightly tap the valve plate loose. Inspect the reed valves and discharge retainer. Discard assembly if any portion is damaged.* **(D)** *If valve plate and/or cylinder head are to be reused, carefully remove gasket materials using the gasket scraper. Do not damage the cylinder block or valve plate surfaces.* **(E)** *Installing the valve plate and cylinder head: (1) Coat new valve plate with clean refrigerant oil. (2) Install valve plate gasket. Align valve plate gasket with locating pin holes and oil orifice in cylinder block (the gaskets have a notch at the bottom outside edge to aid alignment). (3) Install the valve plate. With the discharge valve, retainer, and nut pointing away from the cylin-* *der block, align the valve plate locating pins to the pin holes in the block and position valve plate.* **(F)** *Coat valve plate top with clean refrigerant oil. Position new gasket. Set cylinder head in place and torque it.* **(G)** *Torque cylinder head to 22 to 25 foot pounds (3.0— 3.4 kg.) using star configuration shown.* SANDEN

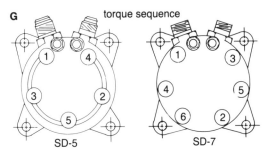

Figure 12-3. *York clutch renewal.* **(A)** *The proper clutch spanner (wrench) used to remove the clutch retaining bolt. (Continued on following page.)* CLIMATE CONTROL, INC.

freewheels around the clutch unit, which is keyed to the drive shaft. Energizing the clutch locks the unit and drives the compressor. When the engine is running with the clutch disengaged, the pulley turns but its center hub remains stationary. When the clutch is energized, the center hub turns with the pulley.

If the compressor fails to operate, energize the clutch and make sure the center hub is turning. If it is not, or if it is slipping, check the voltage at the clutch and check its ground wire. A slipping clutch may also be the result of oil on the clutch. If there is a severe voltage drop or no voltage, test the clutch by jumping it out directly from the positive terminal on the battery. If the clutch still fails to operate, it needs replacing. Those on Tecumseh and York compressors are reasonably easy. Sankyo (Sanden) models require two special tools, which cruising sailors should buy. These are a front plate wrench (spanner) and a front plate puller (see Figure 12-4). A rotor puller and installer set and a clutch-plate installer are useful but not necessary.

To remove a York or Tecumseh clutch assembly, a special tool is normally used to lock the pulley hub so that the retaining nut can be undone. Some means of holding the hub will have to be devised. You can often do this by gripping the drive belt hard. Alternatively, a universal deck plate key works well (see Figure 12-3). Remove the clutch retaining bolt with the appropriate wrench. Do not ever tap or hammer on the clutch, wrench, or shaft. If you remove the compressor from your boat to work on it, you must never set it down such that its weight is resting on the clutch pulley, since this will stress the shaft seal. Keep the clutch overhanging the edge of your workbench.

Do not hit the pulley rim to break it loose from its tapered shaft. Find a $5/8$-inch NC (coarse thread) bolt to fit the threads tapped into the center of the pulley and wind in the bolt to back off the pulley. Unbolt the clutch retaining plate from the compressor block (four bolts). Replace the whole clutch and pulley assembly as one. The clutch retaining bolt has a Nyloc insert that is not reusable. If you cannot get a new bolt, be sure to clean the threads on the old one, and to smear them with Loctite or some other thread-sealing compound.

clutch coil
retaining bolt

Figure 12-3 continued. **(B)** *Using a universal deck plate key to hold the pulley stationary while undoing its bolt.* **(C)** *Screw off the pulley with a ⁵/₈-inch NC (coarse-thread) bolt.* **(D)** *The pulley has been removed to reveal the clutch coil, which is held by four bolts—one in each corner of its base plate.* **(E)** *The clutch has been removed to reveal the shaft seal assembly.*

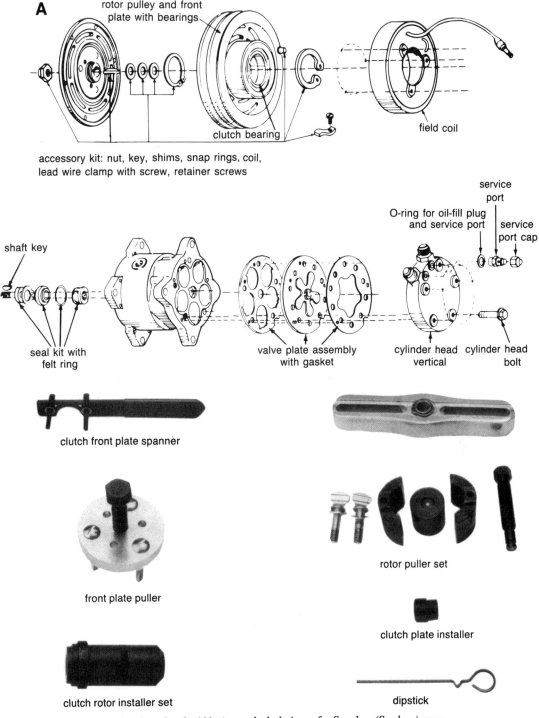

A

rotor pulley and front
plate with bearings

clutch bearing

field coil

accessory kit: nut, key, shims, snap rings, coil,
lead wire clamp with screw, retainer screws

service
port

O-ring for oil-fill plug
and service port

service
port cap

shaft key

seal kit with
felt ring

valve plate assembly
with gasket

cylinder head
vertical

cylinder head
bolt

clutch front plate spanner

front plate puller

rotor puller set

clutch plate installer

clutch rotor installer set

dipstick

Figure 12-4. *Renewing a Sanden clutch.* (**A**) *An exploded view of a Sanden (Sankyo) compressor. The pulley, clutch bearing, and field assembly (top) mount on the end of the shaft (bottom left). Note the special tools needed to service these compressors.*

Figure 12-4 continued.
(B) *To replace the clutch on this type of compressor, insert the two pins of the front plate spanner into any two threaded holes of the clutch front plate. Hold the clutch plate stationary. Remove hex nut with ³/4-inch (19mm) socket.* **(C)** *Remove clutch front plate using puller. Align puller center bolt to compressor shaft. Thumb tighten the three puller bolts into the threaded holes. Turn center bolt clockwise with ³/4-inch (19mm) socket until front plate is loosened. Note: Steps A and B must be performed before servicing either the shaft seal or clutch assembly.* **(D)** *For HD compressors, remove bearing dust cover as shown.* **(E)** *Remove shaft key by lightly tapping it loose with a screwdriver and hammer.* **(F)** *Remove the internal bearing snap ring using snap ring pliers (pinch type).* **(G)** *Note that on some later model clutches, the snap ring is below the bearing, and step F will not be necessary.*

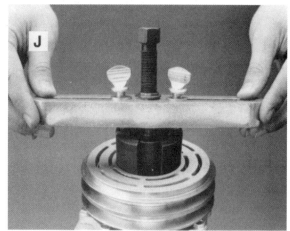

Figure 12-4 continued.
(H) *Remove the external front housing snap ring by using snap ring pliers (spread type).* **(I)** *Remove rotor pulley assembly. First insert the lip of the jaws into the snap ring groove (snap ring removed in step F). Then replace the rotor puller shaft protector (puller set) over the exposed shaft.* **(J)** *Align thumb-bolts with puller jaws and finger tighten.* **(K** and **L)** *Turn puller center bolt clockwise using ³/₄-inch socket until the rotor pulley is free.*

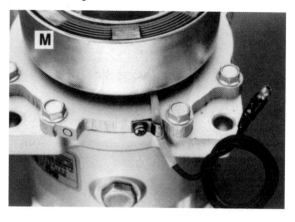

Figure 12-4 continued.

(M) *Remove field winding; loosen winding lead wire from its clip on top of compressor front housing. (Early models do not use this clip; 1979 and later models use a snap-ring retainer for the field coil; 1978 and prior model 508s are held with screws.)* **(N)** *Use spread-type snap ring pliers to remove snap ring and field coil.* **(O)** *Now for the clutch installation. First install field coil. Reverse the procedure outlined in step M. Coil flange protrusion must match hole in front housing to prevent coil movement and correctly locate lead wire. Next, replace rotor pulley. Support the compressor on the four mounting ears at the compressor rear. If using a vise, clamp only on the mounting ears—never on the compressor body. Then align rotor assembly squarely on the front housing hub.* **(P)** *Using rotor installer set, place the ring part of the set into the bearing cavity. Make certain the outer edge rests firmly on the outer race of the rotor bearing. Now place the tool set driver into the ring as shown.*

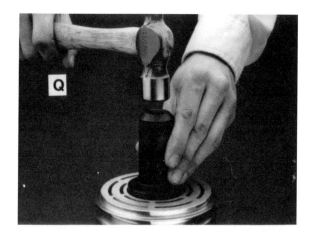

Figure 12-4 continued.

(Q) *Tap the end of the driver with a hammer while guiding the rotor to prevent binding. Tap until the rotor bottoms against the compressor's front housing hub (there will be a distinct change of sound during the tapping process). Reinstall internal bearing snap ring with pinch-type pliers. Reinstall external front housing snap ring with spread-type pliers. Replace front plate assembly. Check that the original clutch shims are in place on the compressor shaft. Next replace compressor shaft key. Then align front plate keyway with compressor shaft key.* **(R)** *Using shaft protector, tap front plate onto shaft until it bottoms on the clutch shims (there will be a distinct sound change). Replace shaft hex nut. Torque to 25 to 30 foot pounds. Note SD−505 torque is ± 26 in./lbs.; 180 ± 30 kg./cm.* **(S)** *Check air gap with feeler gauge to 0.016 to 0.031 inch. If air gap is not consistent around the circumference, lightly pry up at the minimum variations; lightly tap down at points of maximum variation. Note: The air gap is determined by the spacer shims. When reinstalling or installing a new clutch assembly, try the original shims first. When installing a new clutch onto a compressor that previously did not have a clutch, use 0.040, 0.020, and 0.005 shims from the clutch assembly kit. If the air gap does not meet the specifications, add or subtract shims by repeating the steps used in* **(Q)** *and* **(R)**.

Appendix 1

Summary of Unit Sizing Procedures

1. Determine the overall daily Btu requirement of the icebox in its chosen use (refrigerator or freezer—see Chapter 2).
2. Decide on what type of refrigeration unit to use: constant-cycling or cold-plate (see Chapter 3).
3. If you chose constant-cycling refrigeration, divide the daily Btu requirement (step one) by 24, then select a condensing unit with a minimum rating of three times this figure, plus 25 percent, at the anticipated operating temperatures and pressures in the system.
4. If you select cold-plate refrigeration, with either an engine-driven or high-capacity AC system, determine the minimum daily running time of the refrigeration unit in hours. If the cold plates are coupled to a DC system, determine the capacity of the compressor at the temperatures and pressures that will prevail in the system, and then downgrade this figure by 20 percent to allow for mechanical heat.
5. Enter Table 4-2 with the figure in step one and, in the case of engine-driven and high-capacity AC systems, the running time in hours (step four) to read off the minimum

plate eutectic volume, the overall plate volume, and the required rate of pull-down in Btus per hour. On a DC system, this last figure will be the compressor capacity as determined in step four, which on a $1/2$-h.p. unit will be approximately 2,250 Btus per hour in refrigerator use and 1,500 Btus per hour in freezer use. On an engine-driven system using an automotive compressor, the compressor becomes the limiting factor when the rate of pull-down reaches 8,000 Btus per hour in a refrigerator, and 5,000 Btus per hour in a freezer.

6. Now enter Table 4-3 with the rate of pull-down and read off the tubing size and lengths needed in the evaporator coil, in either refrigerator or freezer use, and to see how many plates must be mounted in parallel.
7. Engine-driven systems: Enter Table 5-2 with the rate of pull-down and read off the volume of refrigerant that must be circulated in either refrigerator or freezer use.
8. Engine-driven systems: Search in the body of Table 5-3 for the volume of refrigerant found in step seven, and then read off compressor sizes and speeds of rotation that will move

this volume of refrigerant. Check the compressor specifications to find a suitable compressor.

9. Condenser sizing procedures are summarized in Tables 6-2, 6-3, and 6-4 for any given Btu capacity, starting either from a known water pump volume of flow or a given condenser water tube size and length.

10. Expansion valve sizing is summarized in Chapter 7.

11. Line sizes are given in Table 8-1.

12. A receiver, filter/drier, sight glass, and accumulator or heat exchanger need to be built into the system (see Chapter 8).

Appendix 2

Useful Data

Useful Equivalences

1 gallon water (US gal.) = 8.3 pounds

1 cubic foot water = 7.5 gallons (US gals.)

1 gallon eutectic solution = approximately 1,000 Btus holdover capacity

Vapor volume of R-12 at 0°F = 1.6 cu. ft. lbs.

Vapor volume of R-12 at −20°F = 2.5 cu. ft. lbs.

Maximum temperature rise through a condenser is 10°F.

Temperature differential between average water temperature (AWT) in a water-cooled condenser and the condensing temperature (CT) is 15°F.

The water flow rate through a condenser is between 50 and 200 feet per minute.

Table 6-5. *Tubing Sizes*

Nominal size	Actual size (OD)		Wall thickness			
	Water	Refrigeration	Water K	Water L	Water M	Refrigeration L
1/8	0.250″	——	0.032″	0.025″	0.025″	——
1/4	0.375″	0.250″	0.035″	0.030″	0.025″	0.030″
3/8	0.500″	0.375″	0.049″	0.035″	0.025″	0.032″
1/2	0.625″	0.500″	0.049″	0.040″	0.028″	0.032″
5/8	0.750″	0.625″	0.049″	0.042″	0.030″	0.035″
3/4	0.875″	0.750″	0.065″	0.045″	0.032″	0.035″
7/8	1.000″	0.875″	0.065″	0.045″	0.032″	0.040″
1	1.250″	1.000″	0.065″	0.050″	0.035″	0.040″

Type-L Refrigeration Tubing

Size	Wall thickness	O.D.	Outside circumference	I.D.	Inside radius	Inside CSA (sq.in.)	Outside surface area per ft. of length sq.in.	sq.ft.	Inside volume per ft. of length (cu.in.)
1/4 "	0.030	0.250	0.785	0.190	0.095	0.028	9.42	0.065	0.340
3/8 "	0.032	0.375	1.178	0.311	0.156	0.076	14.13	0.098	0.917
1/2 "	0.032	0.500	1.570	0.436	0.218	0.149	18.84	0.131	1.791
5/8 "	0.035	0.625	1.963	0.555	0.277	0.241	23.55	0.164	2.891
3/4 "	0.035	0.750	2.355	0.680	0.340	0.363	28.26	0.196	4.356

OD = outside diameter
ID = inside diameter
CSA = cross-sectional area
CSA of a tube = πR^2
Surface area of a tube = $\pi D \times$ length
Volume of a tube = $\pi R^2 \times$ length

(All measurements in inches unless otherwise specified.)

Appendix 3

Useful Books

The Perfect Box: 39 Ways to Improve Your Boat's Ice Box. The Spa Creek Instrument Co., Annapolis, MD; 1982. *The* book on iceboxes—how to make them and how to correct faults in existing boxes.

The Box Book. Adler Barbour, IM Industries, Guilford, CT; (call 203-453-4374, extension 410). Packed with useful information on box construction and heat loss calculations. Dozens of different boxes well illustrated—there is sure to be one to fit any boat.

Living on 12 volts with Ample Power. David Smead and Ruth Ishihara. Rides Publishing Co., Seattle, WA; 1988. Much information on 12-volt electrical systems and refrigeration systems.

Modern Refrigeration and Air Conditioning. Althouse, Turnquist, and Bracciano. The Goodheart Willcox Co. Inc., Homewood, IL; 1988. A very complete textbook on all aspects of refrigeration.

Other Books by Nigel Calder

Marine Diesel Engines: Maintenance, Troubleshooting and Repair.

Repairs at Sea.

Boatowner's Mechanical and Electrical Manual.

All published by International Marine/Seven Seas, An imprint of TAB BOOKS, Blue Ridge Summit, PA 17294.

Appendix 4

Useful Addresses

Compressors

Sankyo/Sanden, Sanden International (USA) Inc., P.O. Box 1808, 601 S. Sanden Blvd., Wylie, TX 75098-1808. Tel: 214/442-8400.

York, Climate Control Inc., 2120 N. 22nd St., P.O. Box 2329, Decatur, IL 62526. Tel: 217/422-0055.

Tecumseh Products Co., 100 East Patterson, Tecumseh, MI 49286. Tel: 517/423-8411.

Danfoss, P.O. Box 606, 16 McKee Drive, Mahwah, NJ 07430. Tel: 201/529-4900.

Condensers

Packless Industries, P.O. Box 8799, Imperial Drive, Waco, TX 76710. Tel: 817/666-7700.

Standard Refrigeration Co., 2050 N. Ruby St., Melrose Park, IL 60160. Tel: 312/345-5400.

Cold Plates

Dole Refrigeration Co., 1420 Higgs Rd., Lewisburg, TN 37091. Tel: 1-800/251-8990.

Adler Barbour and Grunert, see "Marine Refrigeration Companies."

Expansion Valves

ALCO Controls Division, Emerson Electric, P.O. Box 12700, St. Louis, MO 63142. Tel: 314/569-4666

Marine Refrigeration Companies

Adler Barbour, IM Industries, P.O. Box 308, New Whitfield St., Guilford, CT 06437. Tel: 203/453-4374.

Grunert, 2000 N. Andrews Ave., Pompano Beach, FL 33069-1497. Tel: 1-800/327-3137.

Sea Frost, CF Horton and Co. Inc., P.O. Box 36, Dover, NH 03820. Tel: 603/868-5720.

Automotive Air-Conditioning Supplies

Four Seasons, 500 Industrial Park Ave., P.O. Box 789, Grapevine, TX 76051. Tel: 1-800/433-7508.

Deep-Cycle Batteries

Surrette America, Division of Atlantic Battery Co., P.O. Box 249, Tilton, NH 03276. Tel: 617/745-4444.

Rolls Battery Engineering, P.O. Box 671, Salem, MA 01970. Tel: 508/745-3333.

High-Output Alternators and Marine Voltage Regulators

Ample Power Co., 4300 11th Ave. NW., Seattle, WA 98107. Tel: 206/789-4743 or 1-800-541-7789.

Appendix 5

Abbreviated Glossary

Absolute pressure—see *pressure*.

Accumulator—a tank installed in a compressor suction line. An accumulator is designed to catch any liquid refrigerant emerging from the evaporator coil in order to prevent *liquid slugging* of the compressor.

Ambient temperature—the temperature of the surrounding environment.

Annealing—a process of heating and cooling metals in order to soften them.

Antifreeze solution—a solution that progressively freezes as the temperature lowers.

Atmospheric pressure—see *pressure*.

Average water temperature (AWT)—the average temperature of the cooling water in a water-cooled condenser—i.e., the entering water temperature added to the discharge water temperature and divided by two.

British Thermal Unit (Btu)—the quantity of heat required to raise one pound of water by one degree Fahrenheit.

Capillary tube—a small diameter tube made of soft copper, used either in place of an *expansion valve* to meter the flow of refrigerant in a system or to connect a *sensing bulb* to the diaphragm on an expansion valve.

Cold plate (holding plate)—a tank containing an evaporator coil set in a solution that has a freezing point below that of water. When the refrigeration unit is running the solution is pulled down and frozen, and it then holds down the temperature in the icebox after the unit is shut down.

Compressor—the pump that circulates refrigerant through a unit, and maintains the necessary operating pressures on the high and the low sides of the system. Compressors are hermetic, (compressor and drive motor placed in a sealed canister), or open (the motor mounted independently).

Condenser—a unit designed to remove heat from gaseous refrigerant at a rate that allows the refrigerant to liquefy at the desired head pressure. Condensers are air- or water-cooled.

Condensing temperature (CT)—the temperature below which vaporized refrigerant will liquefy at a given pressure.

Condensing unit—a compressor, condenser, and other associated components (but not the evaporator unit and expansion valve) mounted on a common skid.

Desiccant—a substance that absorbs moisture.

Drier—a tank filled with desiccant to remove moisture from the inside of a refrigeration system.

Entering water temperature (EWT)—the temperature of cooling water as it enters a condenser.

Eutectic solution—a solution with a freezing point below that of water and that freezes at a constant temperature.

Evaporator—the unit in which liquid refrigerant decompresses and boils off into a vapor, absorbing *latent heat* of evaporation and so cooling an icebox.

Evaporator coil—the length of tubing within an evaporator or cold plate in which the liquid refrigerant boils off.

Expansion valve—a device for metering the flow of liquid refrigerant into an evaporator coil.

Flash gas—the formation of pockets of gas in the liquid line before the refrigerant reaches the expansion valve, an undesirable situation cured by sub-cooling of the liquid.

Gauge manifold—a unit on which is mounted a set of refrigeration gauges, valves, and hoses.

Gauge pressure—see *pressure*.

Head pressure—the pressure on the discharge (high) side of a compressor.

Heat exchanger—a device for transferring heat from the liquid refrigerant emerging from a condenser to the vaporized refrigerant on the suction side of a compressor; also used to transfer heat from the freshwater side of an engine cooling circuit to the raw-water side.

Heat leak—the infiltration of heat into an icebox.

Heat load—the total amount of heat absorbed by an icebox and its contents in a specific set of conditions and over a specific period.

High-side pressure—the pressure between the discharge side of a compressor and the upstream side of the *expansion valve.*

Holdover plates—see *cold plates.*

Hygroscopic—the ability of a substance to absorb moisture.

Latent heat—the heat absorbed or given up by a substance during a change of state at a constant temperature and pressure. Latent heat causes no change in temperature and cannot be measured with a thermometer.

Liquid slugging—a situation in which unevaporated refrigerant or pockets of oil are drawn into a compressor still in a liquid state.

Low-side pressure—the pressure on the suction side of a system between the downstream side of the expansion valve and the compressor suction.

Mechanical heat—heat absorbed from extraneous sources by the refrigerant during the refrigeration cycle—i.e., not absorbed from the evaporator.

Pressure: Absolute pressure—gauge pressure plus atmospheric (14.7 psi).

   Atmospheric pressure—the pressure exerted by the atmosphere on the surface of the earth (taken to be 14.7 psi).

   Gauge pressure—pressure differences as measured with respect to atmospheric pressure.

   Vacuum pressure—a pressure below that of atmospheric.

Purging—a process of removing air from refrigeration hoses before making a connection to a refrigeration system.

Receiver—a tank that holds a reservoir of liquid refrigerant.

Saturated vapor—gaseous refrigerant at its condensing temperature for a given pressure. Any further fall in temperature at this pressure will result in the refrigerant's liquefying.

Sensible heat—heat that causes a change in temperature and therefore can be measured with a thermometer.

Service valve—a valve that allows a refrigeration hose to be connected to a refrigeration system. Schrader valves have a spring-loaded stem as in a car tire valve, whereas stem-type valves have to be manually opened and closed.

Specific heat—the amount of heat absorbed by one pound of a substance during a rise in temperature of 1°F.

Sub-cooling—the cooling of liquid refrigerant below its condensing temperature at a given pressure.

Superheat—the difference between the temperature of gaseous refrigerant and its saturation temperature at a given pressure—i.e., the amount by which its temperature has risen above its saturation temperature at its existing pressure.

Ton (of refrigeration)—the removal of heat at the rate of 12,000 Btus per hour.

Vacuum—see *pressure*.

Vacuum pump—a device designed to evacuate all the gases from a refrigeration system and pull it into a complete vacuum.

Index